FIELD MANUAL

Legal Guide for New York Farmers & Food Entrepreneurs

Cari B. Rincker, Esq. and

Patrick B. Dillon, Esq.

ISBN-10: 1484965191
ISBN-13: 978-1484965191

"This publication is designed to provide general information prepared by professionals in regard to the subject matter covered. It is sold with the understanding that the publisher is not engaged in rendering legal, accounting or other professional service. Although prepared by professionals, the publication should not be utilized as a substitute for a professional service in specific situations. If legal advice or other expert assistance is required, the service of a professional should be sought."

(From a Declaration of Principles jointly adopted by a Committee of the American Bar Association and a Committee of Publishers)

Original sources of authority should be consulted by attorneys or other professionals dealing with specific legal matters.

NO CLAIM TO U.S. GOVERNMENT WORKS

NO CLAIM TO STATE GOVERNMENT WORKS.

This book is designed for farmers, agri-businesses, food entrepreneurs and their advisors. This book is **not a substitute for individual legal advice** tailored to individual facts and circumstances. No attorney-client relationship is intended or established by reading this material between the reader and the authors. Always confer with an attorney and the appropriate state or federal agency, to ascertain the current status of the law. Every effort has been made to include up-to-date information; however, the law is not static. Food and agriculture law is constantly changing. Research and background materials were completed in 2012-2013.

If you believe there are any inaccuracies in the law printed in this book, please email Cari Rincker at cari@rinckerlaw.com noting the page number and paragraph. Every effort will be made to update this Field Manual in subsequent versions.

DEDICATION

To my parents, who have given me both roots and wings and instilled a passion for the people who grow our food.

And to my grandparents, who showed me the value of hard work and the simple pleasures of farm life.

- Cari B. Rincker, Esq.

INTRODUCTION

What is the only segment of the economy with a cabinet-level division of government devoted to it? The answer is agriculture. From the regulation of agriculture production to the use of food aid as a foreign policy tool, the laws surrounding food and agriculture impact every person, every business, every industry, every single day.

The terms "agricultural law" and "food law" may not be as common as other practice areas but make no mistake – agriculture, food and the law are forever intertwined. It naturally follows that wherever there is government action creating legal issues there will be lawyers advocating for their clients in the food and agriculture industry.

So what exactly is "agriculture law?" This is a common question with an uncommon response. Prof. Susan Schneider at the University of Arkansas, School of Law, did an outstanding job discussing the complicated *definition* of "agriculture law" in the January 2009 American Agriculture Law Association's ("AALA") Agriculture Law Update. In her general definition, Prof. Schneider defined "agriculture law" as "the study of the network of laws and policies that apply to the production, marketing, and sale of agriculture products, i.e., the food we eat, the natural fibers we wear, and increasingly, the bio-fuels that run our vehicles." See Susan Schneider, "What Is Agriculture Law?", Agriculture Law Update, Vol. 26, No. 1, Whole No. 302 (January 2009) at 1.

What makes agriculture law and food law difficult to succinctly define is that instead of being a *subject-based* law practice like criminal law, family law, or personal injury law, it is *industry-based* law practice. In other words, food and agriculture lawyers help clients involved in those industries. Challengingly, the food and agriculture industry is diverse, multi-faceted, and touches on nearly every area of law.

When evaluating agriculture's contribution to our *Gross Domestic Product* ("GDP"), the *U.S. Department of Agriculture's*

("USDA") *Economic Research Service* ("ERS") includes the following industries: "farms, forestry, fishing, hunting, processed food, beverage, and tobacco products, textile and leather apparel, restaurants and drinking establishments." Therefore, food and agriculture law is arguably *all the statutes, regulations, common law, judicial decisions, and international treaties* that affect each of these various sectors of the food and agriculture industry.

This book cannot possibly address all of the legal issues affecting agricultural production and food businesses; however, as you skim through the Table of Contents you'll notice that this book addresses several different areas ranging from farm leases, to environmental regulations, to estate planning, to the direct marketing of farm products. If you're a farmer or food entrepreneur in New York, you'll encounter legal issues in a wide variety of settings, from fertilizer storage to tax withholding for labor, and just about every situation in-between.

To prevent problems before they happen, it is paramount that farmers and food entrepreneurs have a keen awareness of legal issues affecting the New York food and agriculture industry are paramount. In other words, you need to know at *least a little bit* about a myriad of subject areas relating to agriculture and food businesses. However, the most important take-home point from this book is as follows: find a team of professionals, including a food and agriculture lawyer that you trust, to help guide your farm or food business through potential issues.

TABLE OF CONTENTS

ACKNOWLEDGMENTS

Legal Research: Life Schneider, Esq.
Legal Research: William Li, Esq.
Legal Research: Alexander Chasan, JD Candidate
Legal Research: Kymberly Robinson, Esq.
Proofreading: Jessica Kagansky, JD Candidate
Cover Picture Credits: iStockPhoto and Fotolia
Headshot Photographer for C. Rincker: Michael Meyer
Headshot Photographer for P. Dillon: Barb Grabil
Book Cover Design: Ranch House Designs, Inc.

CHAPTER 1

GOVERNMENT PLAYERS REGULATING NEW YORK FOOD AND AGRICULTURE

Knowing the number of government agencies regulating the food and agriculture industry can be daunting. The government players regulating the food and agriculture industry in New York at the state and federal level, which can oftentimes look like alphabet soup. Although this Chapter is not all encompassing, it does discuss several government players affecting our food and agriculture industry.

Thinking back to fourth grade social studies, our government is divided into three branches: *legislative, executive* and *judicial.* Put simply, our legislative branch makes the law. Our executive branch enforces the law established by our legislative branch while our judicial branch interprets the law. This Chapter focuses on the *executive* branch of government.

U.S. Department of Agriculture ("USDA")-- www.usda.gov

This is the mother of all the food and agriculture government agencies. There are several notable sub agencies under the USDA umbrella.

The USDA is divided into seven main sections, each with its own appointed Under Secretary: (1) *Natural Resources and Environment,* (2) *Farm and Foreign Agricultural Services,* (3) *Rural Development,* (4) *Food, Nutrition, and Consumer Services,* (5) *Food Safety,* (6) *Research, Education and Economics,* and (7) *Marketing and Regulatory Programs.* Each section governs relevant USDA sub agencies, as described below.

Natural Resources and Environment

Forest Service ("FS") - http://www.fs.fed.us

FS manages 193 million acres of national forests and grasslands and works with state and local agencies by helping to manage an additional 500 million acres of non-federal rural and urban forests. Federal forests and grasslands are located across 44 states, including New York, and comprise 9% of the total land in the U.S.

FS is divided into *nine* regions across the United States, with headquarters located at:

- **Region 1** -- Missoula, Montana (covering Montana, Northern Idaho, North Dakota, Northwestern South Dakota and Northeast Washington), overseeing twelve national forests and one national grassland;

- **Region 2**-- Golden, Colorado (covering Colorado, Nebraska, Kansas and most of Wyoming and South Dakota), overseeing sixteen national forests and seven national grasslands.

- **Region 3**-- Albuquerque, New Mexico (covering New Mexico and Arizona) overseeing eleven national forests.

- **Region** 4-- Ogden, Utah (covering Southern Idaho, Nevada, Utah and Western Wyoming), overseeing twelve national forests.

- **Region 5**-- Vallejo, California (covering California and Hawaii), overseeing eighteen national forests.

- **Region 6**-- Portland, Oregon (covering Washington and Oregon), overseeing 21 national forests and one national scenic area.

- **Region 8**-- Atlanta, Georgia (covering Alabama, Arkansas, Florida, Georgia, Kentucky, Louisiana, Mississippi, North and South Carolina, Tennessee, Texas, Oklahoma and Virginia; and Puerto Rico and the US Virgin Islands), overseeing thirty-four national forests.

- **Region 9**-- Milwaukee, Wisconsin (covering Maine, Illinois, Ohio, Michigan, Wisconsin, Minnesota, Iowa, Missouri, Indiana, Pennsylvania, West Virginia, Maryland, **New York**, Connecticut, Rhode Island, Massachusetts, Vermont, New Hampshire, Delaware, and New Jersey), overseeing seventeen national forests, one grassland and America's Outdoors Center for Conservation, Recreation, and Resources.

- **Region 10**-- Juneau, Alaska (covers Alaska) and oversees two national forests.

Region 7 was eliminated in 1965.

FS's *primary* statutory authorities are the following:

- *Forest Service Organic Administration Act* (1897) (16 U.S.C. §§ 473-478, 479-482 and 551);

- *Multiple-Use Sustained Yield Act* of 1960 (16 U.S.C. §§ 528-531);

- *National Forest Management Act* of 1976 (16 U.S.C. §§ 1600-1614);

- *Cooperative Forestry Assistance Act* of 1978 (16 U.S.C. §§ 2101-2111);

- *Forest and Rangeland Renewable Resources Research Act* of 1978 (as amended by the Food Agriculture, Conservation, and Trade Act of 1990 ("*Farm Bill*"), Title XII, Subtitle B) (16 U.S.C. §§ 1641-1648);

- *Food Conservation and Energy Act* of 2008 (the "*Farm Bill*") (P.L. 110-234) (specifically, Title VIII on Forestry and Title IX on Energy);

- *Foreign Operation Appropriations Act* of 1978 (16 §§ U.S.C. 4501 note, 4501, 4502, 4503, 4503a-4503d, 4504, 4505, 1641, 1643, 2101, 2109);

- *National Environmental Policy Act* (42 U.S.C. §§ 4321-4347) ("NEPA"); and

- *Endangered Species Act* (16 USC §§ 1531-36, 1538-40) ("ESA").

Livestock producers who wish to graze livestock on land managed by FS may apply for a grazing permit. There are essentially three types of permits.

- **Temporary Grazing Permit**--used for a short period of time, usually to allow livestock to remain on national forest land while the FS processes the application for a Term Grazing Permit.

- **Livestock Use Permit**—issued for incidental use and are not intended to authorize commercial livestock production on federal lands. These permits may be issued for up to one year (typically much shorter), and are more commonly used to authorize a Guide's stock animals during a short period when operating in a national forest.

- **Term Grazing Permit**—issued by the FS for up to ten years and are commonly used in the West.

To be eligible for a permit, the applicant must be (1) be a citizen of the U.S. or have demonstrated intent to become a U.S. citizen by filing a petition for naturalization) or if a corporation or partnership must be 80% owned by U.S. citizens and (2) of legal age. If applying for a Term Grazing Permit, the farmer or rancher must own a base farm/ranch property and livestock.

Natural Resources Conservation Service ("NRCS")--
http://www.nrcs.usda.gov/

NRCS was established in 1935 by President Franklin D. Roosevelt

("FDR"). It administers conservation programs to help preserve our natural resources and environment. It manages several national centers including but not limited to the (1) National Soil Survey Center, (2) National Water and Climate Center, (3) National Water Management Center, and (4) National Agroforestry Center. There is a NRCS office in each state and field offices in most New York counties.

The *Food, Conservation, and Energy Act of 2008* (the *"Farm Bill"*) established the following natural resource conservation programs to be managed by NRCS:

- Agricultural Management Assistance Program ("AMA"),
- Chesapeake Bay Watershed Initiative ("CBWI"),
- Cooperative Conservation Partnership Initiative ("CCPI"),
- Conservation of Private Grazing Land Program,
- Conservation Reserve Program ("CRP") (administered by the Farm Service Agency ("FSA")),
- Conservation Stewardship Program ("CSP"),
- Environmental Quality Incentives Program ("EQIP"),
- Agricultural Water Enhancement Program ("AWEP"),
- Conservation Innovation Grants ("CIG"),
- Farm and Ranch Lands Protection Program ("FRPP"),
- Grassland Reserve Program ("GRP"),
- Healthy Forest Reserve Program ("HFRP"),
- Small Watershed Rehabilitation Program,
- Wetlands Reserve Program ("WRP"), and
- Wildlife Habitat Incentive Program ("WHIP").

More specifically, *Agriculture Management Assistance* ("AMA") is available to producers in sixteen states, including New York, where participation in the Federal Crop Insurance Program (" is historically low. The program pays up to 75% of the cost of installing certain conservation practices (with a $50,000 max per year).

Furthermore, under the *Environmental Quality Incentives Program* ("EQIP"), the *Agricultural Water Enhancement Program* ("AWEP") enters into partnership agreements with agricultural producers to plan and implement conservation practices. NRCS also has easement programs affecting agriculture including the *Farm and Ranch Land Protection Program* ("FRPP") aimed at purchasing *development rights* to keep farmland in agricultural production.

Farm and Foreign Agricultural Services ("FFAS")

Farm Service Agency ("FSA") -- http://www.fsa.usda.gov

FSA oversees several agriculture programs including, but not limited to, credit and loan programs, conservation programs, and disaster and farm marketing programs. State and county field offices distribute FSA programs to agriculture producers at the local level. In New York, the FSA state office is located in Syracuse. A map of New York State Farm Loan Teams can be found at http://www.fsa.usda.gov/Internet/FSA_File/flp_teams_fy2013.pdf.
The heart and soul of the FSA is the management of farm loan programs. FSA is the *lender of last resort* for many farms. To be eligible for a federal farm loan, a farmer must be *unable to secure private lending* to purchase, sustain or expand the family farm. FSA loans are temporary in nature and its goal is to help the farm graduate to private commercial lending. FSA loans offer several different types of loan programs, including:

- **Guaranteed Loan Program** –FSA approves all eligible loans. The loans are serviced by commercial lenders, such as the Farm Credit System, and guaranteed by the FSA up to 95% of the lender's loan again.

- **Direct Loan Program**—Direct loans are serviced by FSA using government monies. FSA is charged with the responsibility of providing credit counseling and supervision to its borrowers by evaluating the adequacy of the farmer's real estate, machinery, equipment, management and production goals.

- **Land Contract Guarantee Program** – FSA provides land contract guarantees to the owner of a farm or ranch who wishes to sell his/her property to a beginning farmer or socially disadvantaged farmer (e.g., race or sex). In this case, the seller can request either a *Prompt Payment Guarantee* (up to the amount of three amortized annual installments plus cost of real estate taxes and insurance) or *Standard Guarantee*

(90% of the outstanding principal balance on a land contract with a private loan servicing agent).

Within these programs, FSA offers different types of loans including (1) farm ownership loans, (2) operating loans, (3) emergency loans, and (4) conservation loans.

To expand, FSA also oversees several natural resource *conservation programs* including:

- Conservation Reserve Program ("CRP"),
- Conservation Reserve Enhancement Program ("CREP"),
- Emergency Conservation Program ("ECP"),
- Farmable Wetlands Program ("FWP"),
- Grassland Reserve Program ("GRP"), and
- Source Water Protection Program ("SWPP").

CRP land is the most recognized program managed by FSA- this is where farmers voluntarily "rest" their farmland between 10 to 15 years to control soil erosion, develop wildlife, and make use of other environmental benefits. FSA is also the agency charged with the responsibility to manage farm payments including the *Direct and Counter-Cyclical Program* ("DCP") and *Average Crop Revenue Election* ("ACRE") payments.

Furthermore, FSA manages a myriad of disaster assistance loan programs, including:

- **Emergency Loan Program** ("ELP") (from physical losses due to drought, flooding and other natural disasters);

- **Disaster Set-Aside Program** ("DSAP") (to help producers with existing loans with FSA who are unable to make scheduled payments due to a disaster);

- **Emergency Conservation Program** ("ECP") (when a farmer's crop was damaged by a natural disaster and he/she needs to implement conservation practices);

- **Noninsured Disaster Assistance Program** ("NAP") (to help farmers with crop losses when federal crop insurance is not available);

- **Supplemental Revenue Assistance Payments** ("SURE") (to assist producers who suffered crop losses within counties declared a disaster by the USDA);

- **Tree Assistance Program** ("TAP") (providing payments to orchardists and nursery tree farms for qualified tree losses from a natural disaster within counties declared a disaster by the USDA);

- **Emergency Forest Restoration Program** ("EFRP") (giving payments to nonindustrial private forest ("NIPF") owners to carry out emergency measures to restore land damaged by a natural disaster);

- **Livestock Forage Disaster Assistance Program** ("LFP") (providing monies to livestock producers who suffered grazing losses due to drought on private lands or fire on federally grazed lands (e.g., Forest Service grazing permit));

- **Emergency Assistance for Livestock, Honeybees, and Farm-Raised Fish Program** ("ELAP") (providing payments for grazing and feed losses due to blizzards and wildfires);

- **Livestock Indemnity Program** ("LIP") (giving monies to livestock farmers for animal death losses in excess of normal mortality due to adverse weather conditions);

- **Haying and Grazing of Conservation Reserve Program** ("CRP") (allowing qualified livestock producers to hay or graze CRP land during an emergency); and,

- **Emergency Assistance for Livestock, Honeybees and Farm-Raised Fish Program** ("ELAP") (providing monies for death or feed losses of honey bees and farm-raised fish in counties declared a disaster by the USDA).

FSA also performs statistical analyses in Kansas City on the following:

- Dairy and Sweeteners Analysis ("DSA"),
- Farm Loan Analysis ("FLA"),
- Feed Grains and Oilseeds Analysis ("FGOA"),
- Fibers, Peanuts and Tobacco Analysis ("FPTA"),
- Food Grains Analysis ("FGA"),
- Natural Resources Analysis ("NRA") (including the Agricultural Foreign Investment Disclosure Act ("AFIDA")).

Foreign Agriculture Service ("FAS")--
http://www.fas.usda.gov

FAS works to improve market access for U.S. food and agriculture products around the world. In terms of organizational structure, FAS is divided into the following offices:

- Office of the Administrator ("OA"),
- Office of Agreements and Scientific Affairs ("OASA"),
- Office of Country and Regional Affairs ("OCRA"),
- Office of Global Analysis ("OGA"),
- Office of Trade Programs ("OTP"),
- Office of Capacity Building and Development ("OCBD"), and
- Office of Foreign Service Operations ("OFSO").

FAS has 98 offices around the globe in over 162 countries to advance food exports and imports of the following agricultural commodities: biofuels, coffee, cotton, dairy, fruit, grains, oilseeds, planting seeds, potatoes, raisins, meat, livestock, poultry, eggs, organic food, sugar, tree nuts, and wine.

FAS also administers two food assistance programs to help people in need of food security around the world: (1) *Food for Progress* and (2) *McGovern-Dole*. FAS also has non-emergency food aid programs available to help encourage long-term economic development to help these countries become a commercial buyer of U.S. food products.

Risk Management Agency ("RMA")

RMA helps farmers manage financial risks via the *Federal Crop Insurance Corporation* ("FCIC"). FCIC reinsures federal crop insurance offered to farmers for disaster assistance. RMA, FCIC and crop insurance are discussed in greater detail in the chapter on Insurance.

Rural Development ("RD")

Rural Development- http://www.rurdev.usda.gov/

RD is the USDA sub agency for the Under Secretary of Rural Development. It offers financial assistance to improve the quality of life in rural America. Structurally, RD has offices in every state and is divided into the following offices:

- **Rural Business-Cooperative Service**: It provides for business credit needs in rural areas oftentimes in partnership with private lenders through various *loan programs* (e.g., Business and Industry Guaranteed Loans, Intermediary Relending Program, Rural Energy for America Program Guaranteed Loan Program, Rural Economic Development Loan and Grant, Rural Business Investment Program) and *grant programs* (e.g., Repowering Assistance Program, Bioenergy Program for Advanced Biofuels Payments, Rural Business Enterprise Grant Program, Rural Energy for America Program Grants).

- **Rural Housing Service**: It provides loans and grants for *housing and community facilities* in rural communities (e.g., single family homes, apartments for low-income persons or elderly, housing for farm laborers, childcare centers, schools, nursing homes). Loan and grant programs include: Rural Housing Repair and Rehabilitation Grants, Housing Preservation Grants, Farm Labor Housing Loans and Grants, Individual Water and Waste Grants, Community Facilities Grants.

- **Rural Utilities Service**: It provides payments, grants and loans to build or improve the *infrastructure of utilities* in rural areas (e.g., High Energy Cost Grant Program, Distance

Learning and Telemedicine Loan and Grant Program, Community Connect Grant Program, Weather Radio Transmitter Grant Program, Water and Waste Disposal Direct Loans and Grants, Wastewater Revolving Fund Grants).

- **Office of Community and Economic Development**: It administers various *Community and Economic Development Programs* ("CEDP") supported by partnerships among private, public and nonprofit organizations.

New York's RD office is located in Syracuse and has local offices in the Western Region (Batavia, Bath, Canandaigua), Northern Region (Canton, Watertown and Cortland) and Eastern Region (Greenwich, Scholharie, Marcy, and Middletown).

Food, Nutrition and Consumer Services

Food and Nutrition Service ("FNS")--
http://www.fns.usda.gov

FNS works to *reduce food insecurity* and hunger by providing children and low-income persons access to healthy, nutritious food. Specifically, FNS administers fifteen federal nutrition programs. Organizationally, it is divided into the following units:

- **Special Nutrition Programs** (overseeing Child Nutrition Division, Food Distribution Division, and Supplemental Food Program Division);

- **Supplemental Nutrition Assistance Program** ("SNAP") (overseeing the Benefit Redemption Division, Program Accountability and Administration Division, and Program Development Division);

- **Office of Management, Technology and Finance** (and Chief Operating Officer) (overseeing Office of Civil Rights, Office of Management, Office of Information Technology, Office of Financial Management);

- **Office of Policy Support** (overseeing the Office of Research and Analysis and Office of Strategic Initiatives, Partnerships and Outreach); and,

- **Office of Regional Operations and Support** (managing seven regional offices, Office of State Systems and Office of Emergency Management).

New York is administered in the *Northeast Regional Office* located in *Boston, Massachusetts*.

Some of FNS's most recognized programs and services include the following:

- **Women, Infant and Children Program ("WIC")**: provides state grants for supplemental foods, health care referrals and food nutrition education for lower-income pregnant, breastfeeding, and non-breastfeeding postpartum women and children up to the age of five who are at a nutritional risk. Within this program are the *WIC Farmers' Market Nutrition Program* ("FMNP") and *WIC Senior Farmers' Market Nutrition Program* ("SFMNP"). New York is an authorized state under FMNP and SFMNP to authorize farmers to accept WIC Cash Value Vouchers at farmers' markets.

- **Supplemental Nutrition Assistance Program ("SNAP")**: provides assistance to lower-income individuals. FNS also works with state government agencies, nutritionists and neighborhood organizations to provide nutrition education.

- **School Meals:** These programs include the *National School Lunch Program* ("NSLP"), which provides federal support for public and private schools pursuant to the *National School Lunch Act* ("NSLA"), the *School Breakfast Program* ("SBP"), *Summer Food Service Program* ("SFSP"), and the *Fresh Fruit and Vegetable Program* ("FFVP").

Center for Nutrition Policy and Promotion ("CNPP")--
http://www.cnpp.usda.gov

CNPP was created in 1994 and sets forth dietary guidance linking scientific research to the nutrition needs of consumers. Structurally, CNPP has three divisions: (1) Nutrition Marketing and Communication Division, (2) Evidence Analysis Library Division, and (3) Nutrition Guidance and Analysis Division.

CNPP and *Department of Health and Human Services* work together to set forth the dietary guidelines. CNPP's most notable program is *MyPlate* – www.choosemyplate.gov. MyPlate took the place of the old *food pyramid* and is based on the 2010 Dietary Guidelines.

Food Safety

Food Safety and Inspection Service ("FSIS") --
http://www.fsis.usda.gov

FSIS aims to protect public health and well-being by protecting the public from foodborne illness and ensuring that the nation's meat, poultry and egg products are safe for human consumption. Its authorizing statutes include the *Federal Meat Inspection Act* ("FMIA"), *Poultry Products Inspection Act* ("PPIA"), *Egg Products Inspection Act* ("EPIA"), and *Humane Methods of Livestock Slaughter Act* ("HMLSA") of 1978.

FSIS inspects and monitors all meat, poultry and egg products sold in interstate and foreign commerce. It provides requirements for *Hazard Analysis and Critical Control Point* ("HACCP") and *Sanitation Standard Operating Procedures* ("SSOP's"). FSIS also conducts food recalls when a food safety issue arises.

Research, Education and Economics

Agriculture Research Service ("ARS")--
http://www.ars.usda.gov

This is the USDA's primary research agency in the areas of (1) Nutrition, Food Safety and Quality, (2) Animal Production and Protection, (3) Natural Resources and Sustainable Agricultural Systems, and (4) Crop Production and Protection. ARS is currently involved in over 800 research projects, some of which are conducted at Cornell University, New York's land grant university for agriculture research and education. ARS also conducts international research programs on food security, biosecurity and international partnerships.

National Institute of Food and Agriculture ("NIFA")-- http://nifa.usda.gov

NIFA aims to advance knowledge for agriculture, the environment, and human health by funding research, education, and cooperative extension. This sub agency was created by Congress in the *2008 Farm Bill* replacing the former Cooperative State Research, Education and Extension Service.

NIFA's research is in the area of:

- *agricultural systems* (e.g., farm safety, manure management, organic agriculture, sustainable agriculture),

- *livestock* (e.g., animal breeding, animal well-being, aquaculture, animal health),

- *biotechnology and genomics* (e.g., plant breeding, animal genomics),

- *economics and community development* (e.g., farm financial management, financial security),

- *education* (e.g., *1890 Land Grant Programs* including Cornell University, Higher Education Programs, Hispanic Serving Institutions);

- *families, youth and communities* (e.g., Youth Development and 4-H, Urban Protections, Child Care & After-School Programs, Family & Consumer Sciences);

- *food, nutrition and health* (e.g., food safety, health and wellness, obesity, food security);

- *international* (e.g., global engagement);

- *environment and natural resources* (e.g., air quality, ecosystems, forests, soils, water, wildlife and fish);

- *pest management* (e.g., pesticides, pest management);

- *plants* (e.g., horticulture, plant breeding); and

- *technology and engineering* (e.g., precision agriculture).

Economic Research Service ("ERS")--
http://www.ers.usda.gov

ERS is a social science research agency communicating findings via briefings, analyses and major reports for issues relating to agriculture, food, natural resources and rural America. Structurally, it has the following four divisions:

- **Food Economics Division** (with Branches on Diet, Safety and Health Economics, Food Assistance and Food Markets);

- **Information Services Division** (with Branches on Applications Development, Information Technology Services, Publishing Services, Research Support);

- **Market and Trade Economics Division** (with Branches on Agricultural Policy and Models, Animal Products and Cost of Production, Crops, Food Security and Development, International Demand and Trade); and,

- **Resource and Rural Economics Division** (with Branches on Agricultural Structure and Productivity, Farm and Rural Business, Farm and Rural Household Well-Being, Production Economics and Technology, and Resource, Environmental and Science Policy).

Specifically, ERS conducts research on *animal products* (e.g., marketing issues, aquaculture, dairy, eggs, etc.), *crops* (e.g., corn, cotton, sugar), *farm economy* (e.g., farm labor, federal tax, land use), *farm practices and management* (e.g., biotechnology, irrigation), *food and nutrition assistance* (e.g., SNAP, WIC, food security, child nutrition), *food choices and health* (e.g., obesity, access to food, food labeling), *food markets and prices* (e.g., local food movement, food

15

consumption), *international markets* (e.g., trade policy, global food security), *natural resources and environment* (e.g., climate change, conservation programs, organic agriculture), and *rural economics* (e.g., migration, rural poverty).

National Agriculture Library ("NAL")--
http://www.nal.usda.gov

NAL provides technical information about agriculture research to scientists, educators and farmers. It is one of the four national libraries in the United States. NAL has the following specialized information centers:

- Alternative Farming Systems Information Center ("AFSIC"),
- Animal Welfare Information Center ("AWIC"),
- Food and Nutrition Information Center ("NIC"),
- Food Safety Information Center ("FSIC"),
- National Invasive Species Information Center ("NISIC"),
- Rural Information Center ("RIC"), and
- Water Quality Information Center ("WQIC").

Books and reference materials can be reserved upon request.

National Agriculture Statistics Service ("NASS")--
http://www.nass.usda.gov

NASS offers statistical data to farmers, ranchers, agribusinesses and public officials. It conducts monthly and annual surveys on agricultural production, supply, prices, etc. NASS also conducts the *Census of Agriculture*, which is conducted every 5 years. Historical results from the Census of Agriculture are available at NAL. New York's NASS Field Office is located in Albany, New York.

Marketing and Regulatory Programs

Agriculture Marketing Service ("AMS") – www.ams.usda.gov

AMS works with the marketing of agriculture products at the domestic and international level. It too works to ensure there exists fair trading practices with respect to the food, fiber and specialty crop industries.

AMS promulgates regulations for the following federal programs:

- **Perishable Agricultural Commodities Act of 1930** ("PACA"): requiring buyers and sellers of fresh and frozen fruit and vegetables to comply with contractual requirements and establishes for Alternative Dispute Resolution ("ADR");

- **Federal Seed Act** ("FSA"): protecting buyers of seed by prohibiting false labeling and advertising of seed in interstate commerce;

- **Plant Variety Protection** ("PVP"): providing for intellectual property rights protection to developers of seed-reproduced and tuber-propagated plants, including farm crops and flowers;

- **Shell Egg Surveillance Program** ("SESP"): requiring AMS to oversee shell egg surveillance inspections pursuant to the *Egg Products Inspection Act* ("EPIA"); and

- **Country of Origin Labeling Program** ("COOL" or "mCOOL"): requiring retailers to label food products with the country of origin.

AMS is the government agency responsible for establishing the yield and quality grade marks for beef, pork and lamb. It has also established standards for grading, certification and verification of chicken, turkeys, ducks, geese, guineas, pigeons, shell eggs, and dairy products. Furthermore, AMS has established quality grades for *wholesale* purchasers of fresh and processed fruits and vegetables.

Organizationally, AMS has the following programs:

- Cotton and Tobacco Program ("CT"),
- Dairy Program ("DP"),
- Fruit and Vegetable program ("FV"),
- National Organic Program ("NO"),
- Transportation and Marketing Program ("TM"),
- Compliance and Analysis Program ("CA"),
- Livestock and Seed Program ("LS"),

- Poultry Program ("PP"), and
- Science and Technology Program ("ST").

AMS is also greatly involved with farmers' markets and other forms of direct marketing for livestock producers. Specifically, AMS facilitates the *Farmers Market Promotion Program* ("FMPP") and *Federal State Marketing Improvement Program* ("FSMIP") grant programs. A list of farmers' markets around the country can be found at http://search.ams.usda.gov/farmersmarkets/.

Additionally, AMS administers commodity research and promotion programs funding through *Checkoff programs* (e.g., Beef Checkoff). It is also involved in the *Specialty Crop Block Grant Program* and *Organic Cost Share Program*.

Animal and Plant Health Inspection Service ("APHIS")- http://www.aphis.usda.gov/

This sub agency regulates the health and care of animals and plants. Specifically, it is charged with the responsibility to monitor animal diseases, veterinarian accreditation, promulgate regulations under the *Animal Welfare Act* ("AWA"), *Horse Protection Act* ("HPA"), and *Animal Disease Traceability* ("ADT").

Furthermore, AMS regulates the import and export of animals, animal products, veterinary biologics, plans, plant products, pests, soil, *genetically modified organisms* ("GMO's"), semen, embryos, and other materials derived from animals (e.g., hormones, bacteria, meat products). It too works with the *U.S. Department of Homeland Security's* ("DHS") *Federal Emergency Management Agency* ("FEMA") to provide assistance during emergencies including natural disasters (e.g., Hurricanes Irene and Sandy).

Organizationally, APHIS administers the following programs:

- Animal Care ("AC"),
- Biotechnology and Regulatory Services ("BRS"),
- International Services and Trade Support Team ("IS"),
- Plant Protection & Quarantine ("PPQ"),
- Veterinary Services ("VS"), and
- Wildlife Services ("WS").

Grain Inspection, Packers and Stockyards Administration ("GIPSA")- http://www.gipsa.usda.gov/

GIPSA regulates the marketing of livestock, poultry, meat, cereals, oilseeds and related agricultural products by promoting fair and competitive trading practices for the overall benefit of consumers. It administers two main programs:

- **Agency Packers and Stockyards Program** ("P&SP"): This program regulates fair trading practices for meat animals and its products under the *Packers and Stockyards Act* ("PSA"). The PSA regulates stockyard owners, market agencies, dealers, packers, swine contractor, and live poultry dealers.

- **Federal Grain Inspection Service** ("FGIS"): This program regulates the marketing of grain and related agriculture products under the *Agriculture Marketing Act* ("AMA") and *United States Grain Standards Act* ("USGSA").

Its *Business and Economic Analysis Division* ("BEAD") is headquartered in Washington D.C. It has several roles, among them conducting industry economic and risk assessment analysis; examining competitive implications of concentration, integration in the meat animal industries; and, providing technical support for meat animal industry surveillance. Additionally, GIPSA has regional field offices in Atlanta, Denver, and Des Moines.

U.S. Department of Health and Human Services-- http://www.hhs.gov/

The U.S. Department of Health and Human Services administers several government agencies regulating our food system including but not limited to the *Food and Drug Administration* ("FDA"), *Center for Disease Control and Prevention* ("CDC"), and the *National Institute of Health* ("NIH").

Principally, the FDA consists of nine centers and offices regulating food, dietary supplements, tobacco, and medicines. It enforces the *Food, Drug, & Cosmetic Act* ("FDCA"), the *Food Safety Modernization Act* ("FSMA"), and *Dietary Supplement Health and Education Act* ("DSHEA").

U.S. Department of Interior- http://www.doi.gov/

The U.S. Department of the Interior is a Cabinet-level agency, like the USDA, that also regulates the food and agriculture industry. Organizationally, there are five assistant secretaries managing the following bureaus:

- **Fish, Wildlife and Parks**: National Park Service and U.S. Fish and Wildlife Service

- **Indian Affairs**: Bureau of Indian Affairs

- **Land and Minerals Management**--Bureau of Land Management, Office of Surface, Mining, Reclamation and Enforcement, Bureau of Safety and Environmental Enforcement

- **Water & Science**: U.S. Geological Survey and Bureau of Reclamation

Notably, the *Branch of Agriculture and Rangeland Development* within the Bureau of Indian Affairs assists with farm and range planning, rangeland improvements and protection, collection of inventory information on pasture leases and grazing permits, and manages agriculture extension on our Indian reservations.

The *Bureau of Land Management* ("BLM") plays its most recognized role in the livestock industry with its issuance of livestock grazing permits on approximately 155 million acres of public lands in our western rangelands. In way of history, Congress passed the *Taylor Grazing Act* ("TGA") of 1934 during the era of homesteading in the West. TGA created grazing districts for ranchers and regulated its use to prevent damage to the natural resources. The federal grazing program is available in 16 Western states and fees are calculated on an *animal unit month* ("AUM"). Qualified ranchers must apply for a grazing permit to the BLM.

Environmental Protection Agency ("EPA") - www.epa.gov

The EPA is the principal agency regulating environmental laws. Environmental law touches upon many aspects of the food, fiber and agriculture industry. Organizationally, the EPA contains some of the following offices:

- **Office of Air and Radiation** ("OAR") – OAR administers the *Clean Air Act* ("CAA"), *Atomic Energy Act* ("AEA"), and other environmental laws affecting our air.

- **Office of Chemical Safety and Pollution Prevention** ("OCSPP") – OCSPP implements the *Federal Insecticide, Fungicide, and Rodenticide Act* ("FIFRA"), *Federal Food, Drug and Cosmetic Act* ("FDCA"), *Toxic Substances Control Act* ("TSCA"), *Pollution Prevention Act* ("PPA"), and other environmental statutes regarding chemical safety and pollution.

- **Office of Enforcement and Compliance Assurance** ("OECA") – OECA works with EPA regional offices, state governments and tribal nations to enforce environmental laws. It too is involved in civil and criminal enforcement actions. OECA is also involved in environmental justice issues in underserved communities.

- **Office of General Counsel** ("OGC") – OGC is the chief legal adviser to EPA, assisting the EPA with agency rules and decisions regarding permits and response actions. OGC works with the *U.S. Department of Justice* ("USDOJ" or "DOJ") with court actions.

- **Office of International and Tribal Affairs** ("OITA") – OITA works with EPA regional offices, other federal government agencies, and international organizations to help identify international environmental issues (e.g., climate change, sea- level rise).

- **Office of Research and Development** ("ORD") – ORD supports research programs on environmental health issues.

- **Office of Solid Waste and Emergency Response** ("OSWER") – OSWER regulates *brownfields*, Superfund sites (responding to abandoned and active hazardous waste sites and accidental oil and chemical releases), *reduction in GHG emissions* through land and materials management, emergency management and response procedures, federal facilities cleanup programs, waste management, and *underground storage tanks* ("UST").

- **Office of Water** ("OW") – OW administers the *Clean Water Act* ("CWA"), *Safe Drinking Water Act* **("SDWA")**, and portions of several other environmental statutes affecting the ocean and marine biology.

Furthermore, the EPA has 10 regional offices. New York is served by *EPA Region 2*, headquartered in *Manhattan*. Region 2 also serves New Jersey, Puerto Rico and the Virgin Islands. Regions are able to offer decisions in certain areas that are binding in that region. This may be especially important for certain areas affecting the food and agriculture industry, such as *Concentrated Animal Feeding Operations* ("CAFOs").

Other Federal Agencies

There are a number of other federal players that affect our food and agriculture system including the *U.S. Department of Commerce, U.S. Department of Energy* ("DOE"), Internal Revenue Service ("IRS"), *U.S. Department of Homeland Security* ("DHS"), *U.S. Department of Labor* ("DOL"), and *U.S. Department of Transportation* ("DOT"). Furthermore, the *U.S. Department of Justice* ("DOJ") is involved in litigation regarding federal decisions and enforcement. Nearly every federal agency is associated with the U.S. food, fiber and agriculture system in some way.

New York Agencies

New York State Department of Agriculture & Markets ("NYSDAM")-- http://www.agriculture.ny.gov/

NYSDAM is the principal government agency in New York regulating food and agriculture. Organizationally, it has the following divisions:

- **Agriculture Development**: Generally, this division works with market development, consumer education, access to healthy food, and agri-business development. Its specific programs include the *Agri-Business Child Development* ("ACD"), *Agriculture Producers Security* ("APS") (working with Farm Products Dealer Licensing), *Commodity Procurement* ("CP"), *Crop Insurance and Risk Management* ("CIRM"), *Farm/Cuisine Trails* ("F/CT"), *Farmers' Markets* (including the Farmers' Market Nutrition Program ("FMNP"), *Senior Farmers' Market Nutrition Program* ("SFMNP"), and *Fresh Connect* ("FC"), *Farm to College/School* ("FtC/S"), *International Trade* ("IT"), *Marked Order Administration* ("MOA") (apples, sour cherries, onions and cabbage), *Organic Certification Reimbursement* ("OCR"), *Organic Farming Development/Assistance* ("OFD/A"), *Pride of New York* ("PNY"), *Specialty Crop Block Grants* ("SCBG"), *Trade Shows & Consumer Events* ("TRCE"), and *WIC Vegetables and Fruit Checks* ("WICVFC").

- **Animal Industry**: This division has several specific programs for beef and dairy cattle, equine, poultry, sheep & goats, swine, cats & dogs, and deer. For example, it administers the *New York State Cattle Health Assurance Program* ("NYSCHAP") and *New York Ram Project* ("NYRP"). It also works with animal disease control, biosecurity and import/export of animals. It too awards licenses for slaughterhouses.

- **Counsel's Office** ("CO"): This is NYSDAM's legal office used when NYSDAM is bringing a civil or criminal complaint or defending a lawsuit. It also provides legal support to NYSDAM internally.

- **Food Laboratory** ("FL"): This division tests food, dairy products, and beverages for health hazards and accurate labeling.

- **Food Safety & Inspection** ("FSI"): FSI works to enforce regulations to help maintain food safety. This is the largest division of NYSDAM with over 200 full-time employees.

- **Kosher Law Enforcement** ("KLE"): This division enforces the New York Kosher Law Protection Act of 2004 regarding packaging, advertising, disclosure and record keeping.

- **Land and Water Resources** ("LWR"): This division works with agriculture districts, farmland protection/conservation, and soil/water conservation. It has a myriad of helpful guidance documents on local laws affecting the control of farm animals, use of wetlands, composting, direct-farm marketing, land use & zoning regulations, wind/solar energy development, nurseries, farm distilleries, breweries and wineries, and on-farm open burning.

- **Milk Control and Dairy Services** ("MCDS"): This division works with sanitation, inspection, and economic control of the New York dairy industry. It also works with the *Milk Price Gouging Law* and reviews milk labeling and advertising.

- **Plant Industry** ("PI"): This government division works with plant health by preventing the spread of disease and harmful invasive species. Among other programs, it administers the *Apiary Inspection Program/Honey Bee Health Program* ("AIP/HBHP") and the *Cooperative Agriculture Pest Survey* ("CAPS").

- **State Fair**: Who doesn't love going to the *New York State Fair* ("NYSF")? This division plans the NYSF and other events held at the fairgrounds throughout the year.

- **Weights & Measures Bureau** ("WMB"): Importantly, this division inspects scales, gas pumps and other types of measuring devices used in the New York food and agriculture system to ensure its accuracy.

NYSDAM also works with permits and licenses related to commercial feed, farm product dealers, food establishments, milk dealers, nursery dealers, and pet dealers.

New York State Department of Environmental Conservation ("DEC") – www.dec.ny.gov

Headquartered in Albany, DEC enforces New York environmental statutes and regulations pursuant to Title 6 of *New York Codes, Rules and Regulations* ("NYCRR"). DEC regulates New York's forests, open space, watersheds, lakes, rivers, oceans, wetlands, groundwater, dams, mining industry, marine life, livestock production, wildlife, and animals. It administers water pollution, air pollution, waste management, environmental cleanup, pest management, chemical and pollution control programs. It also issues permits for fishing, hunting, and trapping. For *concentrated animal feeding operations* ("CAFO's"), the DEC issues *State Pollution Discharge Elimination System* ("SPDES") permits.

The DEC is divided into 9 regions throughout New York including:

- **Region 1 (Long Island)**: Nassau and Suffolk counties

- **Region 2 (New York City)**: Kings (Brooklyn), Bronx, New York, Queens, and Richmond (Staten Island) counties

- **Region 3 (Lower Hudson Valley)**: Dutchess, Orange, Putnam, Rockland, Sullivan, Ulster, and Westchester counties

- **Region 4 (Capital Region/ Northern Catskills)**: Albany, Columbia, Delaware, Green, Montgomery, Otsego, Rensselaer, Schenectady, and Schoharie counties

- **Region 5 (Eastern Adirondacks/ Lake Champlain)**: Clinton, Essex, Franklin, Fulton, Hamilton, Saratoga, Warren and Washington counties

- **Region 6 (Western Adirondacks/ Eastern Lake Ontario)**: Herkimer, Jefferson, Lewis, Oneida, and St. Lawrence counties

- **Region 7 (Central New York)**: Broome, Cayuga, Chenango, Cortland, Madison, Onondaga, Oswego, Tioga and Tompkins counties

- **Region 8 (Western Finger Lakes)**: Chemung, Genesee, Livingston, Monroe, Ontario, Orleans, Schuyler, Seneca, Steuben, Wayne and Yates counties

- **Region 9 (Western New York)**: Allegany, Chautaqua, Cattaraugus, Erie, Niagara, and Wyoming counties

Other New York State Players

As at the federal level, there are a myriad state and local government agencies not discussed in this chapter that affect the New York food and agricultural system, including but not limited to, your local *zoning board* ("ZB"), *NYS Department of Health* ("NYSDOH"), *NYS Department of Labor* ("NYSDOL"), *NYS Department of Motor Vehicles* ("NYSDMV"), *NYS Division of Taxation and Finance* ("NYSDOTF"), *Workers Compensation Board* ("WCB"), *Port Authority of New York and New Jersey* (PANYNJ"), *NYS Division of Alcoholic Beverage Control* ("NYSDOABC"), *NYS Division of Consumer Protection* ("NYSDOCP"), and the *New York Office of the Attorney General* ("OAG").

Final Thoughts

The number of government agencies and legislative bodies affecting the New York food and agriculture system can be a bit overwhelming. It is easy to see how complex the regulatory system for our food and fiber system really is. This book only gives a cursory overview of the laws that affect the New York food and agriculture industry.

New York farmers, agribusiness owners and food entrepreneurs should get involved in the legal process and have positive relationships with state and federal officials. Many New York agriculture organizations offer the opportunity to visit with elected officials and government officials at the state and local level.

Additional Resources

American Agriculture Law Association, "Ag Law News" at http://aglaw-assn.org/ag-law-news (last visited August 16, 2013).

Cari Rincker, "How Can You Help Change the Law?" (August 24, 2010), at http://rinckerlaw.com/blog/food-ag-orgs/2010/08/24/how-can-you-help-change-the-law/ (last visited August 16, 2013).

Cari Rincker, "Part One: How to Find the Right Attorney for You" (September 15, 2010) and "Part Two: How to Find the Right Attorney for You (October 12, 2010), at http://rinckerlaw.com/blog/food-ag-orgs/2010/09/15/part-one-how-to-find-the-right-attorney-for-you/ and http://rinckerlaw.com/blog/attorney-client-relationship/2010/10/12/part-two-how-to-find-the-right-attorney-for-you/, respectively (last visited August 16, 2013).

Cari Rincker, "Some Thoughts on Contacting an Attorney for a Consultation," (July 25, 2011), at http://rinckerlaw.com/blog/attorney-client-relationship/2011/07/25/some-thoughts-on-contacting-an-attorney-for-a-consultation/ (last visited August 16, 2013).

Monika Roth, "Guide to Farming in NY" available at http://nebeginningfarmers.org/publications/farming-guide/ (last visited May 19, 2013).

National Agriculture Law Center's Reading Rooms available http://nationalaglawcenter.org/readingrooms/ (last visited May 19, 2013).

National Agriculture Law Center's "Ag and Food Blog" at

http://www.agandfoodlaw.com (last visited August 16, 2013).

New York State Assembly, "Assembly Members" available at http://assembly.state.ny.us/mem (last visited July 13, 2013).

New York State Government Agency Directory, at http://www.nysegov.com/citguide.cfm?superCat=102&cat=449 (last visited August 16, 2013).

New York State Governor's website, at http://www.governor.ny.gov (last visited July 13, 2013).

New York State Legislature, "Laws of New York," available at http://public.leginfo.state.ny.us/MENUGETF.cgi?COMMONQUE RY=LAWS+&TARGET=VIEW (last visited July 13, 2013).

New York State Senate, "Senators" available at http://www.nysenate.gov/senators (last visited July 13, 2013).

New York State Unified Court System, "NYCourts.Gov", at www.courts.state.ny.us (last visited July 13, 2013).

Senator Charles E. Schumer's website, at http://www.schumer.senate.gov/Issues/agriculture.htm (last visited July 13, 2013).

Senator's Kirsten Gillibrand's website, at http://www.gillibrand.senate.gov (last visited July 13, 2013).

U.S. Department of Agriculture, "Laws and Regulations," available at http://www.usda.gov/wps/portal/usda/usdahome?navtype=SU&nav id=LAWS_REGS (last visited July 13, 2013).

U.S. House of Representatives, "Directory of Representatives" [for New York] available at http://www.house.gov/representatives/#state_ne (last visited July 13, 2013).

CHAPTER 2

NEW YORK BUSINESS ENTITIES

Whether you are a food and agriculture entrepreneur starting a new operation or you are a part of a well-established sixth generation farm family, it is prudent to look at your current business structure and evaluate whether it should be changed to better fit your business needs, long-term goals, and risk appetite.

Each type of business entity has its own characteristics, offering different strengths and weaknesses depending on the type of operation. Furthermore, establishing certain business entities helps in the succession planning process by helping to facilitate the transfer of partial interests in farm operations.

One main purpose of some types of business entities is to protect the business owners from personal liability from the business's debts; however, if business formation is done incorrectly, it may cause a significant tax issue or other problems which the "Do-it-Yourself" LLC or "Form your own corporation" kits sold on the Internet likely will not accurately identify. To explain, corporations and limited liability companies in New York have specific corporate formalities to adhere to. If you disregard these corporate formalities, then the court may disregard your corporate shield.

A wise food or agriculture business person will consult certain professionals before deciding on the proper business structure: a food and agriculture lawyer, a financial advisor, and an accountant. There is no "one size fits all" solution to business structure. In fact, the proper choice of entity *may evolve along with the business.*

Business Plans

When deciding as to the best business structure for your food or agriculture business, it is always useful to reference a business plan that memorializes your operations short and long-term plans. For start-ups and agri-businesses that hope to expand quickly, business plans are a useful way to *"reality test"* your business model. NY FarmNet has some helpful publications available on its website about business plans, including "Starting an Agricultural Business?", available at http://www.nyfarmnet.org/index.php/useful-resources/guides-workbooks. Don't forget that business plans are a *"working document"* that can (and should) change over time; therefore, it should revisited and updated on a periodic basis.

Sole Proprietorships

Sole proprietorships are the simplest and most informal business structure as they do not require a separate business structure or filing documents with the NYS Department of State. You are the *alter ego* of your business (think Clark Kent and Superman). You reap all of the rewards but you also pay all of the taxes and expose yourself to 100% of the risk. Stated differently, sole proprietors have less administrative overhead than other business types but they also have unlimited personal liability for business debt.

As discussed in later chapters in this book, this "unlimited personal liability" is a *big deal* for certain types of enterprises. To illustrate, if you are a farm or food business selling food products directly to consumers via farmers' markets, roadside stands or Community Supported Agriculture ("CSA's"), it is highly recommended to form a business entity that will shield personal assets in case there is a food safety issue. Furthermore, if you are participating in agri-tourism (e.g., corn mazes, hay rides, petting zoos, pick-your-own berries) and inviting members of the public to your farm, you should strongly consider another entity in case there is an accident on your property (e.g., slip-and-fall).

As far as taxes are concerned, a sole proprietor will be subject to *self-employment tax*. Sole proprietors do not need to transfer assets to the business name; however, it is advisable to have a separate bank account for your business.

A sole proprietorship is not a perpetual business entity; to the contrary, when you die your business dies with you. If you have a business you wish to smoothly pass on to your heirs, you are strongly suggested to form another business entity.

Even though it is not required to do so, sole proprietorships should obtain a *Federal Employer Identification Number* ("FEIN") from the *Internal Revenue Service* ("IRS"). Obtaining a FEIN helps protect your personal information – i.e., you won't have to use your personal *social security number* ("SSN") on tax documents relating to the business (e.g., W-9's), vendor applications, or payroll documentation. Your accountant or banker can help you obtain one or you can apply for online at http://www.irs.gov/Businesses/Small-Businesses-&-Self-Employed/Apply-for-an-Employer-Identification-Number-(EIN)-Online. As noted above, sole proprietorships should open a business account and keep personal finances separate to help ease business accounting. Your bank will likely require a FEIN to open up a business account.

"Doing Business As" (D/B/A's)

Many sole proprietorships (and other types of business entities) operate under an "assumed name." Many food and agriculture businesses in the state of New York that operate under an assumed name are not properly registered. Pursuant to Section 130 of the *NY General Business Law* ("GBL"), no person or entity can "(i) carry on or conduct or transact business in this state under any name or designation other than his or its real name, or (ii) carry on or conduct or transact business in this state as a member of a partnership" unless a *Certificate of Assumed Name* is properly filed.

If the person or entity is not a corporation, limited partnership or a limited liability company, then this person or entity is required to file a Certificate of Assumed Name with the county clerk of each county in which such business is conducted or transacted. In this instance, the Certificate of Assumed Name must set forth the: (i) name or designation in which business is being conducted (e.g., Rincker Cattle Co.), (ii) address within the county in which business is being transacted, and (iii) full name(s) of the people conducting or transacting business.

If the entity is a general partnership, the Certificate of Assumed Name must also contain the names and residences of all partners. The age of any person less than eighteen (18) years of age involved in the business must be included. This certificate must be signed and duly acknowledged by all persons conducting the business before a notary public.

If the entity is a corporation, limited partnership or limited liability company, then the entity is still required to file the Certificate of Assumed Name with the NYS Secretary of State that must set forth: (i) its real name, (ii) its assumed name, (iii) business structure, (iv) its principal place of business within the state of New York, (v) names of every county in which it does business or intends to carry out a business, and (vi) the street addresses for each place where it carries on or transacts businesses in the state. This Certificate of Assumed Name shall be signed by the corporation's officer, limited partnership's general partner, or a limited liability company's member/manager. See GBL § 130(1)(b).

An example of this scenario would be if Farmer Joe, Inc. was doing business under the name Redacre Farm. The "real name" would be Farmer Joe, Inc. Since it is doing business under a different name, a Certificate of Assumed Name should be filed.

There is a $100 filing fee for each county in which the corporation, limited partnership or limited liability company transacts or intends to transact business if a Certificate of Assumed Name is necessary.

Please note that corporations, limited partnerships and limited liability companies, require filing documents with the NYS Department of State upon formation. If a partnership has not filed limited partnership papers, then it is a **general partnership**.

The Certificate of Assumed Name *does not need to be renewed*; however, pursuant to Section 130(3), farms and agri-businesses are required to *file an amendment within thirty (30) days* if there are any change to the name and contact information of the partners. A *Certificate of Discontinuance* should also be filed once the business is no longer active. A certified copy of the original certificate, or if it has been amended then the amended certificate, must be **conspicuously displayed on the premises at each place in which business is conducted.**

If you have a farmstand on your property where consumers come and buy produce, place the copy of the Certificate of Assumed name there in the farmstand. If you have a horse stable, put the Certificate of Assumed Name conspicuously in the horse stable so that horse boarders may see it.

Importantly, it is a misdemeanor to "knowingly make a false statement" in a Certificate of Assumed Name or make a fraudulent omission (e.g., failure to disclose the name/address of a partner). Please note that any person or entity that fails to comply with this law will be prohibited from maintaining any action or proceeding in any court in the State of New York on any contract, account or transaction made in a name other than its real name until the entity has complied with this statute. This can have dire consequences for the farm or agri-business.

It is easy to overlook details like this when starting a business from the ground up. It is even easier to push aside details once a food or agri-business has been operating for several years without properly filing a Certificate of Assumed Name. *It hasn't caused any issues so far, so why do it?*" (or "If it ain't broke- don't fix it.") However, that is the wrong attitude to have. It might not have been an issue yet but it may create serious issues in the future.

Partnerships

At one point or another, most food and agriculture operations form a partnership with another person or entity. Perhaps it is a partnership on a single head of livestock (e.g., stallion, bull, boar, show heifer) or perhaps it is a more long-term partnership where profits and losses will be shared among family members or multiple people and entities.

Partnerships can happen when two or more people conduct business and share profits. Traditionally, the partnership's profits or losses pass through to the partners on either a predetermined percentage or in accordance with their contributions to the partnership. There is no taxation on gain at the partnership level; instead, each individual pays tax on the amount of gain that passes through to him or her individually, avoiding the double taxation of the C-Corp. However, each partner is personally liable for the partnership's debts and each one is fully responsible for the actions of the other partners.

> For example, Joe and Sue begin milking together. Sue orders feed in the partnership name that Joe didn't want delivered. Nevertheless, Joe is just as responsible as Sue for paying the feed bill, and the debt can be collected against Joe's personal assets, such as real estate, bank accounts, and other holdings.

There are two types of partnerships: *general partnerships* and *limited partnerships*. This section will breakdown the major differences in these two types of business partnerships. If your business only has one owner then a partnership is not for you – partnerships require two or more owners.

General Partnerships

A general partnership is formed when two or more people go into business to share *profits* – not necessarily losses, but to share *profits*. If you are currently sharing profits with another person or entity then you might be in a general partnership. You don't have to *intend* to form the partnership- if you are sharing profits and you did not create a formal business entity then the law forms it for you.

> Partnerships are sometimes formed inadvertently. For example, if Farmer Joe asked Farmer Jane to take his Simmental –Angus heifers out on the New York show circuit and in return she got to keep 90% of the show premiums for her efforts in caring for his cattle and promoting them while Farmer Joe paid for all the expenses, then they likely formed a general partnership.

As the name infers, there must be at least two members of a general partnership. Please note that the "partners" do not have to be individuals– they could be other business entities such as corporations, limited liability companies, trusts, partnerships, or DBA's.

An *advanced estate planning strategy* might be to create multiple layers of business entities to help with succession planning and tie up the land for *estate tax purposes*. For example, the real property might be owned by one LLC while the operating farm might be owned by another LLC. Next, the two LLC's form a family limited partnership. These layers of business entities create more bookkeeping and more administrative overhead; however, it might be the right ticket for certain operations. Trusts can also be useful in many cases.

Among every type of business organization, the general partnership also offers agriculture producers the greatest flexibility. As a caveat, the general partners are jointly and severally liable for the debts of the partnership whereas other types of formal business entities may shield owners from personal liability (i.e., the "corporate shield"). Furthermore, each partner has the ability to bind the partnership without the express written consent of all partners.

In the above example, Farmer Jane agreed to sell Farmer Joe's best show heifer for half (50%) of her fair market value. Absent an agreement otherwise, it is possible that a court could hold that Farmer Jane can do this as an agent of the partnership.

Farmer Joe should have had an independent contractor agreement with Farmer Jane stating the terms of the agreement. The independent contractor agreement would specifically prohibit her to act as Farmer Joe's agent and it would specify that they are not in a partnership.

Alternatively, a simple partnership agreement could have been drafted by an ag lawyer saying that Farmer Jane does not have the ability to sell or lease Farmer Joe's animals and the partnership is narrowly tailored to show premiums.

Here's another example: Farmer Dan and Wall Street Businessman Larry decide to go into the llama business together out on Long Island. Larry doesn't know a whole lot about the llama business but enjoys spending his weekends out in Suffolk County near the farm (and beach); besides, he thought it was a profitable investment. Farmer Dan manages the llama farm each day. Without a written agreement, Larry could bind the partnership in a contract to sell some of the prized llamas.

Another drawback of a general partnership is the lack of flexibility with ownership transfers. By default, general partnerships require unanimous consent before that interest is transferred.

Section 130 of NY General Business Law requires partnerships to file a certificate with their county clerk in each county in which they are doing business. This step is oftentimes overlooked by general partnerships.

Limited Partnerships

Pursuant to NY Partnership Law, a *limited partnership* or a *family limited partnership* ("FLP") includes at least one *general partner* and at least one *limited partner*. The general partners are really the ones "running the show" by *controlling most business operations* including day-to-day responsibilities; however, that control comes at a price. General partners have *unlimited personal liability* for all debts, liabilities and obligations of the limited partnership. Please note that a general partner need not have the largest ownership share -- even with a small share (e.g., 1-2%), a general partner has most of the control.

Conversely, limited partners have a *liability shield* for the debts, liabilities and obligations of the limited partnership. Here again, this comes at a price. When receiving this liability shield, the limited partners give up their control in the business operations and receive limited voting rights on certain activities such as the admission of new partners or on the dissolution and liquidation of the limited partnership. If any of the limited partners become involved with the day-to-day operations then they may lose their liability shield.

Leaving the general partner at risk for debts and liabilities of the limited partnership isn't a perfect scenario; however, it's a solid improvement from a general partnership in which all partners are liable for the debts of the partnership. This choice of entity may be appropriate for an agri-business participating in activities with lower risk. Limited partnerships also work well with family farms and agri-

> If Farmer Judy started a livestock photography business and her parents, brother and a few friends decided they wanted to help out with start-up expenses, Farmer Judy could be the general partner while her family and friends were limited partners. In this scenario, if Farmer Judy lacked the money for start-up expenses, Farmer Judy might only have 10% equity in the limited partnership while her family and friends (the limited partners) held 90% of the equity. However, Farmer Judy would still have sole control over all aspects of her business.
> On the flip side, if Farmer Judy started a direct farm marketing business selling food products directly to consumers, Farmer Judy would not want to bear all the financial responsibility for potential liability arising from a food safety issue. Farmer Judy would probably prefer a limited liability company in that scenario where all members would have a liability shield.

businesses where the elder generation wants most of the management control while the heirs enjoy limited liability before the farm transfers to their control.

Additionally, keep in mind that start-up expenses for forming a limited partnership are cheaper than a limited liability company or a corporation. This should be a factor when determining the choice of entity to best meet your needs. The publication requirement for limited liability companies, depending on county it is situated in, can be expensive.

Partnership Agreements

Farmers, agri-businesses and food entrepreneurs are highly encouraged to put the terms of an agreement in writing. Simple partnership agreements are also recommended for agreements to share ownership in one livestock animal, such as a bull, ram, boar, or show animal.

Partnership agreements serve several purposes. First, absent a partnership agreement, the New York *"default rules"* will apply. Second, when there is an oral agreement among partners, it is easy for a "misunderstanding" to arise on key issues. Memorializing a partnership agreement ensures that everyone is on the *same page.* Third, drafting a partnership agreement may bring up potential issues that the partners had not discussed. Not only is it legally prudent to put a partnership agreement in writing but it is also a helpful exercise forcing everyone to think about the "what if's."

Additionally, partnership agreements may salvage long-term relationships with people when a dispute arises. Unexpected things happen outside of the control of all parties that may create a disagreement (e.g., eminent domain or a major flood). The agriculture industry needs to have a change in mindset—**putting agreements in writing does not indicate lack of trust, rather it's just a sound business practice that everyone in the food and agriculture industry should engage in**.

Some provisions that should be considered in the partnership agreement include the following:

1. **Names and Addresses of the Partners**. This section in the partnership agreement should include the names of any formal business organizations (e.g., Curt Rincker d/b/a Rincker Simmentals and Blackacre Ranch, LLC). If this is a limited partnership agreement, then the general and limited partners should be identified.

> If one of the partners is a corporation, limited liability company or limited partnership, it might be appropriate to ask ask for a copy of the Certificate of Good Standing from the NYS Department of State.

2. **Name of the Partnership**. A name of a partnership is always encouraged. Before deciding on a partnership name, make sure you are not infringing any trademarks. Run a quick Google and trademark search to see if anyone else is using that name. Any restrictions for use of the name for any other activities should be noted. For example, a farm family may decide to draft a formal partnership agreement under the name of Rincker Cattle Co. for raising seedstock agriculture but prohibit the use of the name for agri-tourism efforts (e.g., hay rides).

3. **Purpose of the Partnership**. It is important to include the purpose and scope of the partnership agreement and enumerate authorized business activities. For example, the purpose of the partnership may be to produce show pigs out of thirty designated sows while authorized business activities may include advertising and marketing.

4. **Term of the Partnership**. The term of the partnership should be narrowly defined. For example, will the partnership agreement last for certain number of years, until a certain stallion dies or is sold, or until one of the partners dies? The partnership could also end when one party is in default for a certain period of time (e.g., failure to pay maintenance or operating expenses for 90 days).

5. **Initial Contribution From Each of the Partners**. The partnership agreement should clearly define the amount of capital each partner should contribute initially and list instructions on *how* and *when* that payment should be delivered. The initial contribution could be in the form of cash, property or services.

CBR Farm was formed. "C" gave the partnership $2 million worth of land and equipment while "B" contributed $300,000 worth of livestock for the partnership's use. "R" was hired as the herdsman to run the ranch, work on salary and keep a small portion of the profits. Additionally, a graphics design company was a **silent partner** who developed the partnership's website for a percentage of the profits. Each of these four partners had very different initial contributions.

6. **Additional Contribution Requirement**. After the initial contribution, any other required maintenance or required payments or services should be provided in the partnership agreement.

For example, each partner may be obligated to pay $2,000 per month for operating expenses for a certain number of years until the partnership gets financial traction. Alternatively, in the above example, perhaps the graphics design company is required to develop monthly magazine ads and coordinate daily social media efforts of the partnership for its share of the profits.

The partnership agreement should also discuss any interest owed for outstanding payments or services promised, give directions for the timing and delivery of payment, and note any *notice requirement* for unanticipated expenses.

7. **Assets of the Partnerships**. Understandably, enumerating a complete list of partnership assets may be onerous for some large food and agriculture operations but it is important to itemize and accurately describe the assets of the partnership in the agreement itself. This not only assists in the valuation of a partner's contribution but also mitigates future disputes during the winding up stage.

8. **Liability of the Partnership**. The agreement should include the liability that the other partners have to one another. For example, will partners indemnify each other for their own negligent acts that have harmed the partnership's property and/or third parties?

9. **Allocation of Profits and Losses**. Unless agreed upon differently, under the *"default rules"* profits and losses will be shared evenly among the partners. If there is a salaried partner who does not share in losses, this should be specifically addressed in this section. Perhaps a partner who fronts all maintenance and marketing expenses on a show bull will want to keep 60% of the profits from semen sales and 100% of *show winnings*. Whatever the agreement is, allocation of profits and losses should be clearly memorialized to avoid a possible dispute.

10. **Distribution of Profits**. *Distribution* and *allocation* of profits are different concepts. Typically, some profits may go back into the partnership to help with operating expenses or growth.

"Distribution" is identified as the *actual payout* of the profits. The agreement should memorialize procedures for making the distribution, ability to receive advance payments or draws from anticipated earnings, identification of person(s) that will declare the distributions, and timing of distributions. Furthermore, any limitation on distributions should be noted.

11. **Duties of the Partners**. The partnership agreement should not only specifically address the *responsibilities* of each partner but also *prohibition of activities*. For example, one partner may be in charge of the care and maintenance of a flush cow while the other partner makes all management decisions in regard to artificial insemination and marketing. Alternatively, one partner may be in charge of customer development, relations and marketing with a CSA while two other partners may be farmers charged with the day-to-day responsibility of growing and harvesting food.

12. **Confidentiality**. If a *Non-Disclosure Agreement* ("NDA") was not entered into separately, confidentiality should be addressed in the partnership agreement. For example, Livestock Producer A might not want Livestock Producer B to disclose to third parties his/her feed rations, business relationships, or actual sale price of embryos made known through the partnership. Alternatively, a food entrepreneur may wish to keep his/her *family recipes* confidential. The partnership agreement may also prohibit all partners from discussing finances with third parties.

13. **Salaries and Other Benefits of the Partners**. Not only should the salaries be properly memorialized, but *vacations*, holidays, retirement, *health insurance* and other benefits should also be discussed in the partnership agreement. If a farmer goes on a family vacation for a week after the All East Livestock Exposition, is it okay for the neighbor kid to feed and care for the livestock owned by the partnership? Should one partner owe another partner any type of notice before such taking time off? These types of issues should be explicitly discussed and memorialized.

14. **Expenses of Partnership**. It is important to enumerate all the anticipated expenses of the partnership. To illustrate, perhaps an expensive show heifer was purchased by the partnership to be flushed for embryo transplants. Even though each partner initially

contributed 50% of her sale price, there are other potential expenses in maintaining this female including feed, veterinary care, shelter, embryo flush expenses, semen, travel and advertising costs. Even though each partner may informally decide to pay 50% of all these expenses, these costs should be enumerated in the partnership agreement in case one partner later decides that he/she cannot afford his/her share of the fees.

15. **Management of the Business**. If a particular partnership is to be managed by less than all the partners, the agreement should identify the managing partners. For example, perhaps ten businessmen in Oklahoma decide they want to invest monies in the a pig operation based around Binghamton, New York but know very little about the industry. These businessman find Rockin' R Livestock, Inc. to invest $200,000 pig operation. It would likely be appropriate for Rockin' R Livestock, Inc. to be identified as the managing partner while the Oklahoma businessmen are the limited partners with little control over the management of the business.

16. **Effect of a Default**. The partnership agreement should discuss what would happen if one or more partners is in *default after a certain period of time* (e.g., 30 days, 60 days). If one partner fails to pay his/her half of the rent to a horse stable, will that partner then forfeit his right to make management decisions? Should the partner(s) give the defaulting partner some kind of notice and time to cure a default before management rights are affected? Is there a penalty?

17. **Amendments to Partnership Agreement**. For both long and short-term business ventures, it is unrealistic to think that partnership agreements will not need to be amended. *Family operations grow*, life has *unexpected twists*, and business plans change. The partnership agreement should allow for amendments to be made in writing agreed by a certain percentage of the votes from the partners.

18. **Partner Changes**. The partnership agreement should discuss the process for voting on any additional or substitute partners and any redistribution of assets in such an occurrence. The partnership agreement should include procedures for the *removal of a partner* and any *limitations on a voluntarily withdraw* of a partner. Buy-out prices should be noted in the partnership agreement in addition to the consequences of a partner's death.

19. **Assignability**. The agreement should enumerate any limitations on the ability to sell his/her ownership interest to another. For example, the partnership agreement could give the other partner(s) first right of refusal or limit the pool of buyers in some way (e.g., restrict the sale to a competitor).

20. **Alternative Dispute Resolution** ("ADR"). Arbitration and mediation can be less costly and faster than the traditional court system. For example, the partnership agreement can have a mediation clause requiring the parties to participate in non-binding mediation with a qualified private agriculture mediator. If futile, then the partnership could still require binding arbitration.

> However, the partnership agreement should always allow the parties to seek court intervention in an emergency. For example, one party may need to obtain a **Temporary Restraining Order** ("TRO") on cash in a bank or assets in a safe deposit box.

21. **Forum Selection**. The partnership agreement may identify a particular court in which disputes must be tried. For example, it could state that disputes will be resolved in the New York Supreme Court of Orange County, a court mutually convenient for all partners.

22. **Choice of Law**. Partnership law is a *state law* issue. If a partnership is created among partners of more than one state then the agreement should identify whose state law applies to enforce the partnership agreement and "fill in the gaps" where the agreement is silent.

> A choice of law provision is particularly helpful when doing business internationally or across state lines. For example, a partnership is formed among three horse breeders – one in New York, one in the District of Columbia, and one in Canada. However, the thoroughbred horse is being kept at a horse stable in Germany by a French horse trainer. When a partnership dispute arises, what law applies?

23. **Attorneys' Fees**. Should a dispute arise between partners, it is recommended that the losing partner be obligated to pay the other partner(s) for *reasonable* attorneys' fees. However, some people prefer not to award a partner for litigation and want each partner to take the financial risk of litigation.

24. **Dissolution and Winding Up**. The partnership agreement should enumerate facts and circumstances that may lead to the dissolution of the partnership (e.g., death of a partner, death/sale of livestock, withdrawal of a partner, insolvency) and procedures for winding up the business including distribution of assets.

On a final note, it is very important to tailor your partnership agreement to your particular needs. Although you can take partnership agreements off the Internet or Legal Zoom, it's best to think through the legal issues for your situation with an agriculture lawyer.

When thinking through the pertinent issues for your partnership agreement, it may be useful to identify agreed upon attorneys, accountants, veterinarians, embryologists, chefs, financial institutions for partnership loans, feeding programs, herdsmen and hired help, food/agriculture shows or conferences to regularly participate in, magazines to place monthly ads in, approved photographers, approved sires for artificial insemination, payment of registration papers a breed association or membership to a food or agriculture organization, farmers' markets that the partnership will participate in, or responsibility to develop an employee handbook and/or train employees in proper animal handling. Tweak your partnership agreement for each specific business venture.

When in doubt, err on the side of detail in your partnership agreement. Think through all the *worst case scenarios* and make sure the agreement covers these situations.

Bull Partnership Agreements

The devil is in the details – as the saying goes. As noted above, partnership agreements can also be applied for *shared ownership in one animal*. For you cattle producers, think about the following issues in a bull partnership agreement:

• Who are the original business partners and ownership shares?

- Will unanimous or majority consent be required if a partner decides to sell his/her management interest?

- If management interest is sold, will the original partners retain right to semen?

- How much can partnership units be sold for?

- How will expenses be divided among the partners?

- How will profits from semen sales or any other income be divided among the partners?

- Who is charged with the duty of accounting for the bull partnership?

- Will cloning rights be reserved for certain partners?

- Will each of the partners be given a certain number of semen units?

- Will the producer of the bull be allowed to sell full siblings to the bull or will the partnership own any full siblings and/or progeny from the same cow?

- Is the partnership contingent on DNA marker tests or show ring success?

- How will management decisions be decided?

- Who will be taking on what responsibilities? For example, will one partner be in charge of advertising and marketing?

- Where will the bull be kept? (e.g., partner's farm, bull stud)

- Where will semen be sold? Will a certain farm in another country have exclusive semen rights for X number of years?

- Are there specific feed concerns that should be addressed?

Corporations

Under *NY Business Corporation Law* ("BCL"), a corporation is formed in New York by filing a *Certificate of Incorporation* with the NYS Department of State. Individual shareholders will not be held personally liable for the debt of the corporation unless the *"corporate shield"* can be pierced. The corporate shield can be pierced in New York if a court finds that the corporation was an *alter ego* of the shareholders, it was *grossly undercapitalized*, if personal and corporate funds were *intermingled*, or if there was a disregard of corporate formalities (e.g., shareholder minutes, setting forth Bylaws, annual Board of Directors meetings).

It is not uncommon for lenders to require shareholders to make personal guarantees for the repayment of corporation loans. Among all of the different types of business entities, corporations are the most expensive to start-up and maintain. Please note that unless provided otherwise, corporations have perpetual existence surviving the death or withdrawal of a shareholder.

Who's Who in a Corporation

The owners of a corporation are called *"shareholders*, who own *"stock"*. The corporation should memorialize *Bylaws* setting forth the procedure for shareholder to elect the *Board of Directors*. The Board of Directors will then elect *officers* (e.g., President, Vice-President, Secretary, and Treasurer). The Board of Directors is charged with management responsibilities of the business.

C-Corp, S-Corp, and B-Corp – Picking the Right One

There are three main types of corporations for tax purposes: *C-corporations* ("C-corp"), *S-corporations* ("S-corp") and *B-corporations*. C-corps and S-corps are the most common types of corporation for New York farms and agri-businesses. Each have its own inherent advantages and disadvantages.

C-corps are taxed twice: (1) the corporation will be taxed on its earnings for the tax year and (2) the corporation's shareholders will be taxed on their distributions from the corporation. Reasonable employee salaries can be paid to help reduce corporation taxes. A company must be a C-corp to be a publically traded company.

C-Corporations ("C-Corps") were once favored by the estate and business-planning community. The advantages to C-Corps include limited liability to share-owners, tax deductions not available for other types of entities, and a low tax rate on the first $75,000 of income made. However, the C-Corp has some built-in disadvantages, particularly if it has highly-appreciated land in it. Check out the below example:

> A C-Corp owns farmland with a low $1,000 per acre basis. When it goes to sell the ground at $4,000 an acre, not only will it have to pay capital gains tax on the transaction, but then also when that profit is distributed to the shareholders via dividend, that dividend is subject to tax again. Conversely, if the land was owned outright by the individuals, only the capital gains tax would be paid. Also, C corps cannot pass losses on to the owners.

S-Corporations ("S-Corps") are a meld of partnership principles and the limited liability of corporations. Like partnerships, the S-Corp *passes through* the losses and gains to the shareholders, so it is *not subject to the double tax problem* that C-Corps face. So what exactly is a "pass through" tax? If the S-Corp makes $100K in profit, then the shareholders will pay taxes on that $100K even if the monies are kept in the business.

> With limited exceptions, under 26 USC § 1361, a food or agriculture business can file for an S-corp election if (1) there are **100 or fewer** shareholders (2) shareholders are **natural persons** (i.e., not a corporation or trust), (3) shareholders are **not non-resident aliens**, and (4) there is only 1 class of stock.

S-Corps are limited to a certain number of shareholders, and they do not offer all the tax advantages available with a traditional C-Corp. This election is only available to *small business corporations*.

B-corps ("Benefit Corporations") must have an underlying purpose of a *general public benefit* as defined in Article 17 of the NY Business Corporation Law. This is a fairly new type of business structure and has been available in New York since February 2012. Under Section 1708, a B-corp must give its shareholders an *Annual Benefit Report*.

Bylaws

Bylaws are an *internal governing document* and need not be filed with the NYS Department of State; however, like other corporate records, the Bylaws should be maintained at the *principle place of business*. Bylaws set forth procedures to elect the Board of Directors. More generally, bylaws outline the *operating procedures* for the corporation and provide guidelines and rules for *resolving any disputes* that may arise. Bylaws also define the organization and structure of the corporation.

A corporation's bylaws should include, but not be limited to, the following provisions:

- **Corporation**: the corporation's name and purpose; office locations; organization of the corporation; and the definition of its fiscal year

- **Board of Directors**: the Board of Directors' duties; the number of Directors; how they are appointed/elected; their qualifications; and what constitutes a quorum

- **Stockholders**: shareholder meeting protocols; notice of meetings and waiver of notice; definition of a quorum for voting purposes; the voting of stocks; the transfer of stocks; and shareholder liability

- **Committees**: who is in the committee and what are the different roles; meeting protocols; indemnification

- **Amendments**: procedures for amending bylaws and articles of incorporation

- **Seal**: corporate seal

Shareholder Agreements

In addition to Bylaws, some corporations choose to also set forth shareholder agreements that may discuss share transfer provisions transferability and voting control among shareholders. These agreements set forth more specific and more inclusive rights and responsibilities of shareholders other than what are inherent in their shares. New York recognizes the rights of two or more shareholders to form an agreement on how their shares will be voted on together. To illustrate, shareholder agreements may note the composition of the Board of Directors and *corporate governance*, while memorializing protocols for resolving disputes. For closely-held corporations, the limitation on transferability of shares is arguably the most important provision in a shareholders agreement.

> For example, you would not be happy if you are in small business with your brother and one day he decides to transfer all of his shares to your arch enemy down the street.

In a shareholders agreement, two people could incorporate a provision limiting the transfer of stock in various ways. Commonly, shareholders elect to include a "right of first refusal" in the agreement. This gives the corporation and other shareholders the right to buy the other shareholder's stocks before he/she could transfer his/her shares to a third party. Similarly, the agreement could set forth a different purchase price for shares being bought by the corporation or other shareholders, versus by an outsider.

Shareholder agreements could also provide for termination of ownership of shares upon termination of employment. Without a shareholder agreement, the New York Business Corporation Laws and New York common law govern shareholder's rights and obligations. By having a shareholders agreement, shareholders can better control the shares.

Additionally, absent a shareholder agreement to the contrary, shareholders do not have a continuing duty to make capital contributions beyond their initial contribution. This is another reason for having a shareholder agreement, especially in a small corporation.

Drafting shareholder agreements can be challenging since they are very specifically tailored to individual shareholder's intents and needs.

Corporate Formalities

It is important to abide by corporate formalities for multiple reasons. Corporate formalities are designed to protect individuals, personally, from liability arising out of the corporation and are focused on clearly delineating the individual from the corporation. Corporate formalities include:

- Having corporate Bylaws;
- Having a Board of Directors and shareholders meetings that occur regularly and in which minutes are recorded;
- Keeping a stock ledger that is up to date;
- Setting up a bank account in the name of the corporation and keeping accurate and up to date records;
- Consistently using the corporation's name, rather than the individual(s) name(s);
- Filing corporate taxes;
- Having assets and capital in the corporation's name (separate from personal assets); and,
- Ensuring shareholders never personally guarantee debt on behalf of the corporation.

As a caveat, a corporation *should not* do the following:

- Commingling corporate funds with personal assets;
- Using their personal name and the corporation's name interchangeably;
- Signing their name on corporate documents instead of the corporation's name; and,
- Using other shareholders or directors for corporate transactions such as loans, leases, etc.

There is an important legal doctrine called *"piercing the corporate veil."* Shareholders can be personally liable for corporation debt if the court finds that the corporation is the *alter ego* of the owners or a *dummy corporation.* Adherence to corporate formalities is one of the factors that the court looks when deciding whether to pierce the corporate veil. If you disregard corporate formalities, so may the court disregard the liability shield. An agriculture lawyer can help your food or agri-business with a *corporate formality* review to make sure you're up-to-date.

Limited Liability Companies

A *limited liability company* ("LLC") is the newest (and arguably the most popular) choice of business entity in New York. A *family limited liability company* ("FLLC") is a type of LLC owned by a family business.

Pursuant to *NY Limited Liability Company Law, Articles of Organization* must be filed with the NYS Department of State. The owners of a limited liability company are called *"members."* Limited liability companies can elect to be taxed as a *C-corp* (for corporation tax) or *S-corp* (for pass-through tax-treatment). Unless otherwise provided, LLC's have perpetual duration (so it outlives the members).

Please note that the members of a LLC can be kept *private* in New York. In other words, the Articles of Organization does not need to list the members. In some cases, this privacy can be helpful.

When forming a limited liability company, it is important to remember that New York has a *publication requirement*. Publication requirements can vary significantly depending on what county in New York the business is located. The publication requirement can be *particularly expensive* in New York City and surrounding counties (Westchester, Nassau, and Suffolk). This is one disadvantage in filing a LLC vs. a corporation; however, LLC's have less administrative overhead over the long haul.

New York requires publication of the Notice of Formation in two publications for six successive weeks in the county in which the LLC is located (one daily paper and one weekly paper). Contrary to popular belief, you cannot just pick any publication that you want. You must work with your county clerk's office (and your attorney) to ensure you comply with the strict publication requirement. Once you have completed the publication requirement, a *Certification of Publication* must then be filed.

Professional Service Limited Liability Companies

Pursuant to Article 12 of the NY Limited Liability Company Law, a *professional service limited liability company* ("PLLC") may be formed by one or more "professional" licensed within the State of New York as defined in Title 8 of the *NY Education Law*. This is a special type of limited liability company in New York. The list of professionals includes, but is not limited to, attorneys, veterinarians and physicians. New York requires members of certain professions to be licensed in the state of New York.

After formation, the PLLC is required to file a copy of the Articles of Organization and each amendment thereof, with the licensing authority within 30 days after the filing of such articles or amendment with the NYS Department of State.

Operating Agreement

All types of limited liability companies must have an operating agreement within ninety (90) days of formation. This step is oftentimes overlooked by start-up businesses. Forgetting this step could potentially have deleterious effects on the business.

An operating agreement does not need to be filed with the county or state to become public record--it is an internal document governing the procedures of the limited liability company. The members of the LLC need not be disclosed publically in the Articles of Organization but they should be listed in the Operating Agreement.

Operating Agreements should discuss some of the following information:

- Formation, name and registered agent of the company;
- Purpose of the LLC;
- Any initial capital contributions or additional contributions made by the members;
- How profits, losses and distributions will be distributed;
- How the LLC will be managed (member-managed or manager-managed);
- How interest will be transferred (e.g., requiring unanimous consent or right of first refusal);
- Whether the members or manager(s) will be paid a salary or other forms of compensation (including "in kind" compensation such as housing and/or food);
- Bookkeeping, records, and accounting methods (cash basis or accrual basis); and,

- How the LLC will be dissolved and liquidated.

Many of the issues in an Operating Agreement overlap with Partnership Agreement; please review this section in this chapter for more information on the types issues that should be addressed.

Cooperatives

A *cooperative* ("co-op") is an association of multiple people organized to carry on business on a cooperative basis for the benefit of its members. For examples, a co-op might be formed in order to produce and market food products on a collective basis. Pursuant to Section 11 of *NY Cooperative Corporations Law* ("CCL"), there needs to be five or more organizers in order to form a cooperative. Owners of a cooperative are called *"members."* The members of a cooperative will be given the same limited liability protection as a corporation or limited liability company.

Under Section 15 of the CCL, agriculture cooperatives may be formed for the purposes of "marketing, processing, manufacture, sale or other dispositions of agricultural products, agricultural waste product, or agricultural compost, ... or the purchase of supplies for producers of agricultural products." An example of a non-agricultural cooperative commonly found in New York is a cooperative condominium association.

A cooperative is more akin to a corporation as opposed to a partnership. For example, the members elect a Board of Directors to manage the corporation. The Board of Director may in turn appoint officers. However, a co-op is more democratic than corporations with each member receiving one vote. Furthermore, members of a cooperative are primarily looking for access to collective markets or services.

Finding the Right Formula

Now consider how to use the foregoing forms to the greatest advantage when planning a *business transition*. The business form you select can be used in conjunction with *estate planning* tools to produce favorable results for both the elder generation and its heirs. Here's an example:

The elder owners of a farm could form an LLC, which would both rent the ground from the owners and also operate the farm. An on-farm heir could work as an employee of the LLC for a few years, ensuring that the heir both operates well with the parents and also acquires the necessary skills to successfully continue business into the future. The parents can choose to either gift or sell an interest in the LLC to the heir, using buy-sell agreements to control who could buy out whom, for how much, and when. The elder generation would have some income, from rents and from the proceeds of any sale of an interest to the next generation. The estate plan could include off-farm heirs receiving non-farm assets and allowing the on-farm heir to inherit the farm. If no non-farm assets exist, valuation mechanisms can be put into place to ensure that the on-farm heir can buy the farm ground from the estate at a reasonable price. This funds the off-farm heirs' estate bequests and avoids the on-farm heir simply inheriting new landlords (the siblings) when the parents die.

Sound complex? It certainly can be, and unless you are truly familiar with the rules and confident that you know what you're doing, you should *consult a lawyer and/or an accountant* before making decisions about the business form you select and how to use it. *Failing to follow the rules can be dangerous.* Here's a real-life example:

The IRS was recently successful in challenging the tax return of a farm couple during the year they transferred the farm operation to a corporation. While the couple set up a corporation, they failed to deed their business property over to the corporation or make the farm program payments payable to the corporation. After they received the payments in their own name, they transferred the funds to the corporate account. On their taxes, they claimed the income under their own operation and then claimed an expense for transferring it to the corporation, reducing the self-employment tax to under $500 for $250,000 of gross income. They followed that with a corporate income tax filing showing the income and offsetting it with the following year's expenses. Instead, the IRS established that the farm couple really owed self-employment tax on the funds, and was able to raise their tax liability to over $28,000, plus penalties.

Had the couple established the corporation and correctly followed the rules for transferring the land and the government payments to the corporation *prior* to receiving the funds, a different result may have been achieved. The key, like with most things in life, is to know the rules and follow them.

A word on liability: No matter what corporate structure you choose to use, *you cannot protect yourself from yourself*. If you choose to tell an employee to climb on a grain bin in a lightning storm, and he gets hurt and sues you personally, you are personally responsible for your act, no matter whether you did it in your LLC, corporation, or limited partnership. Alternatively, if you were in the right corporate structure, you might be able to avoid personal liability for accidents caused by others.

As an addendum, if you have more than one business entity under your control, it is equally important that your two companies deal with one another *"at arm's length,"* keeping business funds separate with formal contractual agreements.

> Smith Revocable Living Trust owns the real property on a farm while Smith Farms, Inc. owns the livestock and farm equipment. Smith Farms, Inc., the farm operator, is the tenant to the Smith Revocable Living Trust, the landlord. There should be a formal farm lease between these two entities with a fair lease payment according to the current market conditions.

Hobby Farm Rules

Those who are just beginning a farm operation or food business, those who work off-farm or those who are slowly withdrawing from farming would do well to familiarize themselves with the *Internal Revenue Code § 183, "Activities Not Engaged in for Profit,"* occasionally referred to as *"The Horse Shelter"* or *"Hobby Loss Rules."*

IRC § 183 is designed to *prevent taxpayers from claiming business losses* (and thereby reducing income available for taxation) on activities the taxpayer primarily engages in for *recreation, entertainment and personal enjoyment*, rather than a legitimate business purpose. Specifically, *horse farms* and *cattle operations* of small sizes are eyed with greater scrutiny.

The IRS trains its *Section 183 examiners* (who may have no prior knowledge of farm operations), to use manuals and policies to familiarize its agents with everything from the world of competitive show animals, to the distinction between registered and commercial herds of cattle. Several factors are considered by these examiners, and knowing what agents look at can help you make important decisions about your farm's business activity and record-keeping.

The IRS agent-training manual advises Section 183 examiners to consider calculating the volume of feed purchased versus animals sold, to ensure no under-reporting of income, such as cash sales.

Several factors are reviewed by the IRS, each briefly examined below:

1. **Books and Activities Maintained**: The examiner will review the *level of sophistication* of the records, namely if the enterprise has a separate checkbook from the personal living expense checkbook of the taxpayer. The mere presence of records is not enough; the taxpayer must show that he or she is relying on the records to make decisions and changes to the operation to make it profitable, not just to satisfy, for example, a breed association records-keeping requirement.

2. **Business Plan**: The examiners want to review a formal, *written business plan*, demonstrating *realistic growth* and an *economic forecast* for the enterprise, which, if successful, would result in a viable operation. Relying on occasional profits or windfall activities, such as only being profitable in the event of twin colts, for example, fails to meet the concept of a solid business plan.

3. **Methods and Efficiency of the Operation**: The IRS will review the use of experts or specialists by the taxpayer in order to *achieve profitability*. A good example of this is

56

documentation of Cornell Cooperative Extension programs, publications consulted, and demonstrable selection criteria for genotype of seed or breeding stock selected and retained. If the taxpayer has failed to heed advice to change operations without a justification (such as lack of funds to change), this will cause concern on the part of the examiner. Likewise, if the taxpayer devotes little time to an activity but generates a large loss, it will attract scrutiny.

4. **Disguised Expenses**: An example of this might include overzealous advertising via *"vanity ads."* This will attract an examiner's attention. Consider the true purpose of any advertising spent by the operation. For example, an ad with a picture of a child and horse, wishing luck to the taxpayer's children in the upcoming horse show is not usually viewed as a legitimate business expense. On the other hand, advertising an upcoming cattle sale be an legitimate advertising expense.

5. **Potential for Increase in the Value of Assets**: If a business is showing a loss, but can demonstrate that its assets (e.g., land) will increase due to the business activity over time, it may help appease an examiner's concerns of hobby loss. The intent to capture the increase in value must be demonstrated as well.

6. **Taxpayer's Success in Other Activities**: A taxpayer with a high profit margin in a sideline restaurant, who annually loses large amounts on cattle production because of high expenses, will be scrutinized to determine whether his best efforts are also being applied to the cattle operation. Additionally, taxpayers with substantial sources of income have generally not fared well in tax court.

7. **Pleasure Element**: IRS training manuals warn examiners not to be lulled by the argument that farming is a drudgery, though case law supports the concept that devoting hours upon hours to crop input, attending to calving and foaling at all times of the night, and enduring the elements is not normally undertaken without a profit motive. And the IRS does not mandate that taxpayers cannot enjoy their income production. However, passion without profit paints the picture of an enterprise not undertaken for purposes of profit.

Showing a profit can help you avoid much of this kind of searching IRS analysis of your business deductions. A presumption in the law indicates that a profit once every few years, depending on the enterprise, shows the activity is engaged in for-profit enterprise. Consider this example:

A person who worked as an accountant for 20 years also operated a thoroughbred horse racing and breeding enterprise. After examination and a subsequent court case, it was determined that no business losses could be gleaned from the enterprise. The court looked at (1) a lack of businesslike manner of activity, to include a separate checking account or records to determine profitability; (2) a lack of changes designed to increase profitability; (3) failure to obtain personal expertise advice of experts in an attempt to make a profit; (4) a failure to sell a horse for more than $750; (5) the accountant had no experience in operation of any type of business; (6) losses spanned for over 20 years; and (7) the losses shielded income from the accounting business.

The lesson to take home for part-time farmers is to:

- Make sure you have a separate checking account;
- Visit a Cornell Cooperative Extension seminar or a field day (and make a record of attending);
- Make a record of your consultations with herd improvement, crop consultants or area managers of service providers regarding your enterprise;
- Have a written business plan on how you intend to make profit at your endeavor; and
- Consider how you can manage your taxes to show a profit approximately once every five years.

Additional Resources

Bruce L. Anderson, Brian M. Henehan, and Charles J. Sullivan, "Doing Business in New York State: Structures and Strategies," available at http://cooperatives.dyson.cornell.edu/pdf/resources/eb04-07.pdf (last visited December 28, 2012).

Cari Rincker, "Partnership Agreements" 32nd Annual Agriculture Law Symposium, slides available at http://www.slideshare.net/rinckerlaw/partnership-agreements-for-the-agriculture-community (last visited July 3, 2013).

Cornell Cooperative Extension, "Starting an Ag Business? A Pre-Planning Guide" (EB-2004-08) available at http://www.nyfarmnet.org/index.php/useful-resources/guides-workbooks (last visited December 28, 2012).

Internal Revenue Service, "Business Structures," available at http://www.irs.gov/Businesses/Small-Businesses-&-Self-Employed/Business-Structures (last visited July 13, 2013).

Jeffrey Perry and Richard Overton, "Business Planning for the Agriculture Sector: A Guide to Business Plan Development for Start-Up to Mid-Size Operations" available at http://www.nyfarmnet.org/index.php/useful-resources/guides-workbooks (last visited December 28, 2012).

National Agriculture Law Center, Reading Room for "Business Organizations" available at http://nationalaglawcenter.org/readingrooms/businessorganizations (last visited January 9, 2013).

New York State Department of State, Division of Corporations, State Records & UCC, available at http://www.dos.ny.gov/corps/index.html (last visited July 13, 2013).

CHAPTER 3

ESTATE AND SUCCESSION PLANNING

In the words of Winston Churchill, "[f]ailing to plan is planning to fail." About 90% of farming operations do not survive the transition to the next generation. There are many possible reasons why a family farm does not succeed to the next generation; however, poor estate and succession planning are prominent roadblocks.

The *complex dance* of passing a family farm from one generation to the next while balancing taxation concerns, estate planning, emotional connection to the land, off-farm heirs' expectations, long-term care planning, and family communication can be *overwhelming to almost anyone*; it can be especially overwhelming for farm families. Most farm operations have invested dearly in land, farm equipment and livestock. While some families have access to retirement accounts, oftentimes farmland is the only significant source of wealth for the elder generations who have spent their lives working on the farm. This is especially problematic if a younger generation wants to take over the family farm.

Estate and succession planning is *emotional*. "Giving up the farm" is more than a transfer of wealth or a dollars-and-cents cash-out; it is a change in lifestyle, status, and profession. It is a change of identity that affects the sense of heritage and right to control the farming operation. This challenge is derived when a farmer toils through years of blood, sweat, and tears to create something unique and personal.

> For clarification, the term **"estate planning"** involves how the farm assets will be distributed to the heirs while **"succession planning"** delves into how the farm or agri-business will continue to the next generation.

It's important to understand that estate planning isn't just for the *elderly* or the *ultra rich* – to the contrary, younger families with smaller estates may have a greater need for estate planning. Estate planning involves more than just drafting a Last Will and Testament – it requires a thorough understanding of the farm family's goals in order to develop the most effective strategy possible

Let's face it. Estate planning is easy to push off. What's another week... another month... another year... another five years... "After all, I'm healthy. My spouse is healthy. We don't have kids. We don't have a lot of assets. I can't afford to pay an attorney. Estate planning is for the elderly or for the rich farmer-- it's not for me (or at least not right now)."

But this is incorrect. Even though someone who is over the age of retirement may be in a better financial position to hire an estate planning attorney, a much younger person/couple with a significantly smaller estate may have a greater need for an estate plan. In the words of Neil Harl in his book titled Farm Estate & Business Planning (16ed):

> [a] young couple with minor children is generally least able to afford a breakup of property interests among heirs, the complications of property ownership by minors and erosion of family capital to pay debts and estate settlement costs in addition to ownership interests in a family business that are likely to pass to their off-farm brothers and sisters.

Estate and succession planning is a *life-long journey* that will morph along with the changes that life brings both to you and your family members.

Farm Estate Planning

Definitions

Knowing these *basic estate-planning definitions* may be helpful in any conversation you may have with an estate planning professional:

- A *Last Will and Testament* (usually just called a *"will"* for short), is a document that gives your directions on what to do with your property when you die. It takes effect only after you have actually died, and it must be signed by you before a notary public in the presence of two **disinterested** witnesses (i.e., not someone who is related to you by blood or marriage and not an heir to your estate). Your Last Will and Testament should not include instructions for a funeral or burial – this should be in a separate document (i.e., *Burial and Funeral Directive*). Please beware of the Internet Do-It-Yourself programs for Last Will and Testaments.

- A *trust* is a legal entity, created by the terms of a document drafted on behalf of a person, the *grantor* or *settlor*, who transfers assets into the trust to be held or used for the benefit of named people – i.e., the *beneficiary(ies)*. A *trustee(s)*, selected by the grantor, is placed in charge of the trust. A big advantage to trusts is that they pass by *"operation of law"* and avoid probate. This is helpful for farms that participate in federal farm programs. Trusts also help family maintain privacy avoiding probate, which is public record.

> There are many different types of trusts. Trusts can be **revocable** or **irrevocable**. In most cases, revocable trusts are recommended (e.g., Revocable Living Trust). Revocable trusts can be amended at any time. Irrevocable trusts can be a useful mechanism for Medicaid planning in New York.
>
> Trusts can be a type of business entity with its own accounting records and **Federal Employer Identification Number** ("FEIN"). Putting farm assets into a trust can have several advantages. For example, trusts pass by **operation of law** and avoid probate. This expedites the transfer to the beneficiaries and protects the farm family's privacy.
>
> **Testamentary trusts** can also be created within the Last Will and Testament, which can be especially useful if minors are involved.

- A *Power of Attorney* is a document that designates another person to act in your stead for business and financial decisions when you are unable to do so -- a "pinch hitter" of sorts. It gives the *agent* the ability to care for the principal's property (e.g., real estate, bank accounts, bonds, stocks, safety deposit boxes, taxes, retirement plans, social security, insurance, pets and service animals) and conduct business transactions on behalf of the *principal*. Typically, power of attorneys are drafted so that they are only effective upon the incapacitation of the principal; however, they can be utilized in any circumstance. In New York, a power of attorney for medical decisions is called a *Health Care Proxy*. A Power of Attorney can be revoked by you at any time, and it has no further effect after you die. If the principal lacks capacity to sign a Power of Attorney then an expensive guardianship proceeding may be required. In the words of Veronica Escobar, Esq., a New York City elder lawyer, with estate planning **"it can never be too early but it can always be too late."**

> There are three types of **Power of Attorneys**: 1) Durable, 2) Limited, and 3) Springing. A durable power of attorney is effective immediately whereas a limited power of attorney (as the name suggests) is only effective for a certain period of time (e.g., real estate transaction, when the principal is backpacking Europe). A springing power of attorney is effective only after some stated event (e.g., disability).

- A *Living Will* (a.k.a. *Advance Directive for Health Care* or *Health Care Declaration* complements the *Health Care Proxy* allowing you to memorialize religious and/or moral beliefs as it applies to medical care (e.g., artificial nutrition, hydration, cardiac resuscitation, mechanical respiration, antibiotics, pain medicine).

Estate Planning is a Lifelong Journey

Many people think that estate planning involves only the creation of a Last Will and Testament; however, it is just one puzzle piece in a *comprehensive estate plan.* A good estate plan that involves a food or agriculture business will address tax planning, business succession, financial considerations, off-farm heirs, and the person's individual desires (or goals). These are all fairly heady topics that cannot be handled by filling out a standardized form from the Internet or inputting a little basic information into a do-it-yourself kit. Proper estate planning can often help increase the size of the estate that you're able to pass on to your heirs.

A good estate-planning attorney will have you complete an *Estate Planning Questionnaire* giving him/her information on your family tree, assets and liabilities in order to help see the bigger picture. Not only will the estate planning lawyer look at *what property is held* but at *how the property is held* (e.g., individual name, business/corporation/partnership/trust name, joint tenants with rights of survivorship, tenancy in common). Furthermore, an estate planning attorney will also look at whether the client lived or obtained property in a *community property state* (e.g., Texas, California) and the client's insurance program (e.g., life insurance, disability insurance, long-term care insurance). Keeping in mind the client's objectives, the estate planning lawyer will help guide the client through the myriad options available to decide the best strategy at that particular juncture. Because tax laws, assets and families change overtime, so should your estate plan.

Determining Your Goals For the Estate Planning Process

Your objectives will drive the entire estate-planning process, so it is important to clearly articulate your goals. These goals should serve as a guidepost to your estate-planning attorney in helping to formulate the correct game plan. It might not be possible to fully meet all of your goals; therefore, when you meet with your estate-planning lawyer, make sure to emphasize your priorities (which may change overtime).

It's important to stress that the estate planning process is a very individual process. *No two farm families are the same -- nor are their objectives.* Generally speaking, the following are common priorities among farm families that *may be of concern*:

(1) **To have enough income through the retirement years.** Keep in mind that it is impossible to accurately predict future medical expenses and how long a person will live, so liberally plan to have ample cash. Statistically, women live longer than men

thus should consequently save more for retirement.

(2) **To avoid/reduce the estate tax (i.e., the "death tax") and/or mitigate probate expenses to help pass on as much wealth as possible to the heir(s)**. Although not taxable income, keep in mind that life insurance is *federal estate taxable*. Business planning is one strategy that could be helpful in this area. Tying up the farm property with *multiple layers of business entities* reduces its *fair market value* ("FMV") (but creating more administrative overhead – and headache).

(3) **To pass the family farm down to a future generation -- whether it be to the children, grandchildren or extended family**. It's paramount for these families to think about transferring the *management responsibility* of the farm to the future generation (e.g., phasing-out period) to ensure that they are properly trained.

(4) **To treat children equally** keeping in mind gifts made during the life of the children (including help with advanced professional degrees, the purchase of a home or other major assets, or starting a business).

(5) **To give the spouse ownership**. Many farm women are especially concerned about their ability to manage the finances and/or the labor of the farm or agri-business if their husbands predecease them.

Good Estate Planning is a Lifelong Endeavor

It is prudent to revisit your estate plan every *3-5 years* or when there is a major life event (e.g., marriage, divorce, purchase/sale of major assets, bankruptcy, children). *Estate planning* leads to *business planning*, which leads to *tax planning*, which leads to *business succession*, which should lead to *disaster planning*, which may lead to *federal farm program planning*, which should lead right back to *estate planning*; hence, estate and succession planning is a lifelong circle.

Estate planning can be a bit of a balancing act. In fact, you could look at each estate-planning element as being like a ball in a juggler's performance. At any given moment in time, not every one of the balls can be at the highest point (meaning only one or two of these areas will likely have the benefits currently realized or maximized), and some balls will be on the down-swing (meaning the goal may not be fully implemented at that time). To demonstrate, the business structure most beneficial for federal farm programs may not the same as the one for succession planning. However, the entire performance only works if each ball is in its appropriate place at the *right time*.

Good Estate Planning Requires Professional Advice

Historically, farmers have been accused of being nearly religious about not wanting to pay income tax; however, simply avoiding income tax may not help you achieve all of your goals. Sometimes, depending on the circumstances, paying a little tax now to avoid a big tax later is worth the hit.

For example, owning a lot of machinery that is fully depreciated out to avoid income tax saves an immediate tax, but this method may trigger recapture tax when sold. If an item is sold to a family member, the tax is payable in the first year, even if a contract sale is contemplated for the item. That information may be critical to the 70-year-old mother who is contemplating buying a new tractor with which to feed hay, in a joint operation with her 40-year-old daughter. Effective planning might call for the daughter to buy that piece of equipment rather than the mother.

The problem with planning is that it takes time, energy, money, and knowledge about how laws in several areas interplay to produce a final result. You don't learn to juggle these interests overnight; your estate planning should involve advice from an estate-planning professional.

Consider the following case of family members who did not take the time to plan, or even to communicate with one another, and the disastrous results that followed:

A son resigned his non-farm job in 1974 and moved to

Wyoming to manage his father's ranch with the understanding he would inherit the ranch upon the last of his parents to die. In 1992, the father (the surviving parent) asked the son to leave the ranch. Upon the son's refusal to leave, the father filed an action against the son. The son counterclaimed for breach of contract, alleging that he and his father had an oral contract which provided that the son would receive the ranch upon the death of his parents in exchange for his running the ranch. The trial court determined that an oral contract existed and awarded the land, livestock and machinery to the son, subject to the father's life estate. The father appealed and also amended his estate plan to disinherit the son, making a daughter the sole beneficiary of the father's estate. After the father died, the Wyoming Supreme Court reversed the trial court and said no contract existed. So, the son, after nearly 20 years of work, ended up with no job, no inheritance, strained (at best) family connections, and presumably plenty of legal bills.

If the family above had considered a formal transition from father to son, and had made plans to either include the daughter or provide her with another source of income, the result could have been much different.

While a guide like this one can help equip you with an introduction to some general principles at play in estate planning, it should not substitute for appropriate advice, specific to your situation, from personal consultation with experienced estate-planning professionals.

Estate Planning for Companion Animals

Farms and pets go hand-in-hand. There are three vehicles that can be used to protect your pets (including horses) after you die: 1) Last Will and Testament, 2) Pet Trusts, and 3) Pet Protection Agreement.

- **Last Will and Testament:** In New York, pets are considered personal property like a car or a diamond ring. It should be noted that wills are not enforced immediately; sometimes it can take years to go through the probate process. Unlike vehicles, jewelry, or monies, pets are living creatures that need to be cared for during the period before a will goes into effect. A will does not distribute funds over a lifetime of a pet like a Pet Trust or Pet Protection Agreement.

- **Pet Trusts:** The great thing about pet trusts is that they can be enforceable during the pet owner's life, after his/her death, or help fill in the "gap" while a will is going through the probate process. Both pet trusts and pet disbursement agreements control funds used for the pet's care and can ensure that the pet is properly cared for if the owner become incapacitated.

- **Pet Protection Agreements:** This is a simple legal document where the pet owner and pet guardian open a small joint bank account. The pet owner would be able to draw from this joint account during his/her life to care for the pet.

Farm Succession Planning

Succession planning is oftentimes confused with estate planning – it has to do with a business being passed down from one generation to the next. Farm succession planning usually begins in one of the following scenarios:

- A farm that is not planned for survival past the current generation;
- A farm that is making plans to have the farm survive; or
- A farm that has refused to pick one of the first two.

Oftentimes certain common specific concerns of the elder generation must be addressed before any plan is approved. These concerns can be diverse; however, the most common succession-planning goals of the elder generation include:

- Preventing a heavy *management burden* upon the surviving spouse;
- Preventing *harm to children from* the possible *remarriage* of one's surviving spouse;
- Providing for *off-farm heirs*;

- Retaining *lifetime income flow* for the elder generation; and
- Limiting *estate taxes*.

Succession planning is not something that is usually resolved after Thanksgiving dinner before the dessert is served. On the other hand, it often requires multiple discussions and planning by multiple generations of a family.

Competing Interests

The goals and desires of each generation are typically not in line with one another. What should be kept in mind is that maximization of all aspects of the farm succession plan is highly unlikely. No model has been achieved that simultaneously satisfies all of these *competing interests of multiple generations*:

- An elder generation that wants plenty of income and retained ownership and control of the farm, while not providing labor;
- Off-farm heirs who are entirely satisfied, with no desire to interfere with on-farm heirs' ability to run the farm;
- On-farm heirs who are secure and able to grow the business; and
- Tax-free consequences for everyone involved.

Professionals can provide objective input to a succession plan, to help all of the parties come to a reasonable compromise of their objectives and goals. There are usually issues involving the *"golden rule" of estate planning* --in estate planning, *those who have the gold usually make the rules*. While frequently money is the gold, in some family dynamics, however, labor, expertise or reputation can be the gold. In any event, it is necessary to have an open and frank discussion regarding who is going to wield the power of decision-making and who will receive which benefits.

Using a Mediator

In some instances, it can be useful to have a neutral third-party with farm family experience enter the discussion. The trained agriculture mediator (with knowledge on estate and succession planning) may give useful insight and can help facilitate a conversation in which there is an impasse among family members.

Mediators are also trained to help *reality test* estate and succession plans to make sure that the suggest plan "on the table" is workable. Furthermore, mediators are trained to help defuse disputes by facilitating a conversation among the family members on what they really need. Oftentimes, built up anger and resentment can create unnecessary roadblocks in the estate and succession planning process. Sometimes a neutral third party can help the participants work through those emotions and focus on what is really important in a family operation.

Planning Tools

Business Entities

Intrinsically, business planning and succession & estate planning are intertwined. In fact, business entities can be a useful (and oftentimes forgotten) tool succession planning tool with farms and agri-businesses.

The majority of farm operations are still held by sole proprietorships (meaning no formalized business filing), which means that technically, when the farmer dies, so does the legal existence of the business. This causes upheaval and unnecessary costs to the next generation, if it has any desire to keep farming.

Some multi-generational farms, such as limited partnerships, limited liability companies and S-Corporations, can benefit from more advanced forms of business enterprises – or even multiple layers of business entities. As discussed in greater detail in the chapter on New York Business Entities, each type of business structure offers both advantages and disadvantages, some of which affect estate and succession planning.

Now, consider the following example demonstrating that a *choice of business form* can be made to produce the greatest advantage, addressing the *competing succession-planning interests* discussed above, when planning a business transition from one generation to the next:

The elder generation could form an LLC to operate their farm and the LLC could rent the ground from the elders, producing maximum tax advantages and offering limited liability for the LLC's owners. The on-farm heir could work as an employee for the LLC for a short period of time to ensure that operating with the parents is going to work and to acquire the necessary skills to ensure successful continuation of the business. Then, the on-farm heir can be gifted or buy in to the LLC. Buy-and-sell agreements between the members would outline who could buy out whom, for how much, and when.

Meanwhile, the elders' estate plan could provide for the off-farm heirs to receive non-farm assets, while allowing the on-farm heir to inherit the farm. If no off-farm assets exist, valuation mechanisms can be put into place to ensure that the on-farm heir can buy the farmland from the estate at a reasonable price. This funds the off-farm heirs' estate bequests and prevents the on-farm heir from simply inheriting new landlords (the siblings) when the parents die.

The elder generation in this arrangement still retains an income stream to provide for its own needs during life, as it sells the membership interest to the next generation and receives rent from the LLC. It has provided itself some assurance that the farm's management will be passing into the competent hands of the on-farm heir, whose performance has been tested. Finally, it has provided an inheritance adequate to satisfy off-farm heirs' needs, making it less likely that later arguments among the siblings would lead to legal troubles with the estate, thus ensuring the greatest likelihood of successfully achieving the transfer of the farm operation to the on-farm heir.

Property Ownership

Planning *how a farm holds assets* is as important as acquiring the assets in the first place. When starting any business, an exit plan should also be developed. Asset ownership is a component of that plan. Failure to plan can result in unnecessary exposure of assets to

72

claims of creditors.

Most farm families purchase **land** jointly between husband and wife. There are different *forms of joint ownership* that they can choose, and the selection of a particular form of joint ownership can affect the issue of who will be in a *decision-making* position when ownership passes on, after one of them dies. As explained in greater detail in the chapter on Real Estate, joint property ownership between spouses usually takes one of *two common forms*:

- **Joint Tenancy with Rights of Survivorship** ("JTWROS" or "JT") – This is a form of ownership in which each spouse has an undivided one-half interest in the entire property (the property is not physically divided in half). When the first "joint tenant" dies, the survivor takes title to the entire property through operation of the law of property ownership, with no need for probate (i.e., ownership rights need not pass through a probate estate action).

- **Tenancy in Common** ("TIC") – Alternatively, this form of ownership is where two parties again own an *undivided one-half interest* in the property, but when one of the "tenants in common" dies, that person's half interest passes via *probate* to the dead tenant's heirs. This allows for a *"step up"* in the tax basis of the property for capital gains purposes, and can be used to bring in the next generation as a co-owner with the surviving spouse.

A *"step-up in basis"* is a tax concept that allows a person who receives property from an estate to only pay *capital gains tax* on the *difference between date of death value and the date of sale*. If the property is gifted to the person while the donor is alive, the cost that the donor paid for the property *transfers* to the new person and becomes that person's tax basis, with resulting higher capital gains tax to be paid if the property is eventually sold.

> Consider the difference in capital gains tax between a farm bought in 1950 for $300 an acre and given to the next generation during the owner's lifetime. If the next generation turned around to sell it at market price in 2011 at $10,000 per acre, capital gains would be paid on $9,700 per acre. Conversely, if the next generation inherited the property in 2011, and sold it for $12,000 an acre in 2014, only $2,000 per acre would be subject to capital gain tax.

On occasion, the elder generation has one farm-operating spouse and one non-operating spouse. Depending on how things are set up, death of the operating spouse could leave the non-operating spouse in a sudden position of total ownership. Having both spouses involved in the process of estate planning and business transition is important, both to the spouses and to those in the next generation who expect a certain outcome. Promises made by a dead parent are rarely enforceable against another parent who decides not to honor them, unless some prior action is taken to set up legal rights that will fulfill those promises.

Transfer of Power

The concept of *power transfer* needs to be addressed. Some elderly landowners believe that unless they hold the ground, the younger generation will ignore them, fail to take care of them, or place them in managed care, never to see the light of day again. Addressing this concern is an important facet of transition planning.

A method that works with some success is the *transfer with lease-back*. This is where the *elder generation* transfers the land to the next generation but *retains a lease-back* to the elder generation for a reasonable number of years. The lease provides some security for the elder generation and allows them to be on the farm for as long as they like. The downside is as follows: unless the land is already paid for, it is a hard thing to acquire an asset and then lease it back to the elder generation if a mortgage has to be paid from the asset. In addition, with a transfer like this, the next generation misses out on the step-up in tax basis, opening up the possibility of higher capital gains taxes down the road.

For many years, a *life estate to the surviving spouse with a remainder interest to the children* was a cheap, effective way to pass on real estate without a lot of complex will-drafting. Further, it ensured that a second spouse and that spouse's children didn't "get their hands on" family assets (usually farmland). The elder generation essentially got to behave as if the ground was still entirely theirs (i.e., rent collected, taxes paid, military and homestead exemptions applied) until their death.

Property is like a bundle of sticks. Each aspect of property (e.g., right to use, development rights, responsibility to pay taxes, mineral rights, wind farm rights, water rights) is one of the sticks in the bundle. Under a life estate, one person (the *life estate holder)* holds onto the right to occupy and use the property along with the responsibility to pay the taxes. Another person or people (the *remaindermen*) hold the rest; when the life estate holder dies, then those "sticks" transfer to the remaindermen.

Modern legal realities have weakened the value of the life estate as an estate-planning tool. First, while the transfer of full ownership occurs upon the life estate holder's death, the remaindermen cannot take those sticks without clearing a *Medicaid lien* on the property. The value of the life estate holder's interest is figured just prior to his death. This can mean that, despite transfer of substantial interest in the farm prior to death, a life estate holder on Medicaid assistance can be made to pay back part of the money advanced for their care in a long-term care facility.

Second, the *tax basis* for a life estate property is established at the *time of creation of the life estate* -- not at death. If it was not a sale with a retained life estate, then the remaindermen get the transferor's presumably low basis in the property, *not the higher "stepped up" basis* that they would have received had the property been transferred via *probate* proceedings.

Matters become even more tangled and snarled when folks create life estates that span multiple generations, restraining the future ability of interested parties to sell the property. For example, a person might retain a life estate to their spouse, then a life estate to their children, and then make the grandchildren the remaindermen. This can *run afoul of federal gift tax law* because the gift to the grandchildren is a gift of a *future interest.* No gift tax exclusion is available for such a gift. While the life estate may still have some applicability in estate planning, its use as a quick and easy way to altogether avoid the need for real succession planning should be fading.

Gifts

An individual can give *up to $5.25 million during his or her lifetime without paying a federal gift tax.* For *couples* that threshold is multiplied by two -- *$10.50 million.* New York has a much lower individual threshold with a $1 million estate tax exemption. This amount is indexed for inflation and tied to the amount your estate can have before it is subject to tax. Additionally, you can give an annual gift that is indexed for inflation that doesn't count against the lifetime total. As land prices continue to rise, a smart estate plan could utilize the gift tax exclusion to pass on highly-valued farm ground to the next generation. If a gift recipient decides to sell, the land's presumably *low basis also transfers* with the title, creating a capital gains tax issue.

The *capital gains event* can be wiped out by holding on to the property until death. However, the land is then subject to creditors' claims, and if the value rises, the estate is put in the position of having to pay estate tax, which is usually higher than capital gains tax.

Deciding the best course of action requires a delicate balancing of interests, and no single course of action fits all parties. The question is what the next generation intends to do with the property that it is slated to receive. The best answer may determine when and how the next generation receives it.

Open Family Dialogue about Estate and Succession Planning

Don't be afraid to have open and honest conversations with your family about estate and succession planning. **"The only things certain in life are death and taxes,"** Ben Franklin famously said; so, let us not make the topic taboo. In order for a farm or agri-business to successfully pass on to the next generation (if that is what you want), clear communication is paramount to devising a successful estate and succession plan.

Here are some conversation starters:

- **Does everyone have legally operative estate planning documents** such as a Last Will and Testament, Power of

Attorney, Health Care Proxy, Living Will, and (if appropriate) a Revocable Living Trust?

- **Are there any changes that need made to the estate-planning documents?** When is the last time that everyone has had a formal estate-planning review?

- **Where does your family keep their signed original copies of these documents?** Family members should exchange scanned versions of these documents and keep them either in a binder that is easily accessible or a jump drive on a keychain. It is important that family members have the contact information for the attorney(s) who drafted the documents.

- **Are there any surprises in the Last Will and Testament that need discussed?** For example, is the farm or family business going to be left solely to the children who are actively working on the farm?

- **Is your family prepared for the unexpected?** Play out scenarios over the dinner table. What if Grandpa died? What if Father and Mother died tomorrow in a car accident? Who would manage the farm? Do those people know where the farm records are kept? More importantly, do the heirs know how to manage the farm operation?

- **Are there any issues that need to be discussed regarding retirement?** Who has a retirement account and will it be enough for retirement?

- **Do the family members have ample life insurance?**

Important Information

What Should be Kept in a Fire-Proof Safe Deposit Box?

Your safe deposit box should have a *photocopy* of your Last Will and Testament and the *original copy* should be kept at your home;

however, original copies of other documents, including birth certificates, marriage certificates, death certificates, divorce decrees, deeds, titles to automobiles, citizenship papers, adoption papers, veteran's papers, and contracts (e.g., partnership agreements) should be kept in a fire-proof box while photocopies should be kept at home. I recommend getting an "Estate-Planning Binder" so that all the estate planning papers are easily accessible.

Confidential Information Sheet

In an emergency, your family should be able to easily access your important information, including your social security number, driver's license number, passport number, passwords to get into your computer, passwords to online accounts (including banking), passwords for other electronic devices (e.g., smartphone), insurance, banking account information, location of a safe deposit box, and contact information for advisors (e.g., attorneys, accountants, financial planners).

Think about this: if something were to happen to you and a family member needed to step into your shoes to manage the food or agri-business, what information would he/she need and where is it located? Should spare keys be given to certain family members?

In the words of Big Brother on CBS -- with estate and succession planning, "**expect the unexpected**." Even better: "be *prepared* for the unexpected."

Additional Resources

Agriculture.com, "Business Planning" at http://www.agriculture.com/family/estate-planning/business-planning and "Family Succession" at http://www.agriculture.com/family/estate-planning/family-succession (last visited August 17, 2013).

AgTransitions, at https://www.agtransitions.umn.edu (last visited July 14, 2013).

eLegacyConnect, at http://elegacyconnect.com (last visited August 17, 2013) (Cari Rincker is a participating advisor).

Farmers' Legal Action Group, Inc., "Glossary of Estate Planning

Terms" (2006) available at http://www.flaginc.org/wp-content/uploads/2013/03/GlossaryEstate.pdf (last visited May 19, 2013).

Farm Journal Legacy Project, at http://www.agweb.com/legacyproject/ (last visited July 14, 2013).

Jessica Shoemaker, "Managing Debt to Prepare for a Farm Transfer" (2006) available at http://www.flaginc.org/wp-content/uploads/2013/03/EstatePlanningBooklet2006.pdf (last visited May 19, 2013).

Kevin Spafford, "Buy/Sell Review" (March 5, 2010), available at http://www.agweb.com/legacyproject/article/BuySell_Review_193890/ (last visited July 14, 2013).

Kevin Spafford, "Goals Clarification Worksheet" (April 10, 2010), available at http://www.agweb.com/legacyproject/article/Goals_Clarification_Worksheet/ (last visited July 14, 2013).

Kevin Spafford, "Succession Planning Self Assessment," (March 5, 2010), available at http://www.agweb.com/legacyproject/article/Succession_Planning_Self_Assessment_193906/ (last visited July 14, 2013).

Kevin Spafford, "Trust-Will Review" (March 5, 2010), available at http://www.agweb.com/legacyproject/article/Trust__Will_Review/ (last visited July 14, 2013).

National Agriculture Law Center Reading Room on Estate Planning available http://nationalaglawcenter.org/readingrooms/estateplanning/ (last visited May 19, 2013).

NEIL E. HARL, FARM ESTATE & BUSINESS PLANNING (16ed) (2011).

CHAPTER 4

CONTRACTS

Contracts are made all the time, and no one really stops to think about them – that is, until something goes *wrong*. That's when you need to peel apart the equation to determine:

- Was an enforceable contract formed?
- If so, what damages or compensation may be available to the aggrieved parties?

The food and agriculture industry is a trusting community – one that oftentimes ends up in a "handshake" agreement. A contract is essentially an agreement between two or more parties. Although some types of *oral* contracts can be enforceable – *most are not*. Not only does it make *sound business sense* to put contracts in writing but it also helps *prevent future disputes* that may arise from a *misunderstanding* of the terms of the agreement.

Contract Formation

Whether a contract is written or oral (verbal), a contract is formed according to the following simple math equation:

> **Offer + Acceptance + Consideration + Meeting of the Minds = Contract.**

However, parties may assert various *defenses* that could make the contract void. Let's break down each piece of the *contract equation*.

The Offer

In dissecting the offer, the offer must be made with clear

communication to the other party. It must be seen as a *reasonable offer* and made with a *serious* intention. Furthermore, the subject-matter of the contract must *not be illegal.*

> For example, offering to sell your children is generally taken as neither serious or reasonable. However, even if it was taken seriously, it is illegal. Illegal contracts are voidable.

The terms of an offer should be both *certain* and *definite*, such as price per part with delivery on a specific day. If the contract is for performance of a service, it should state the nature of the work involved and the time when the work will be done. The offer must be clearly *communicated* to the other party, whether by words or conduct. In other words, the other party must know the full extent of the offer before he/she can accept it.

As a caveat, *advertisements* are generally too vague to be considered offers; instead, the law sees advertisements as an invitation to deal (unless you say "first come, first served").

> An advertisement selling your homemade jams and jellies for $5.00 would not be seen as an offer because it doesn't state a quantity term and who can accept it. You might only have 5 boxes of jams to sell. However, if you said "100 jars of jams and jellies selling for $5.00 each – **first come, first served**" in the advertisement, then this would be considered an **offer**.

Can you terminate an offer before the other party accepts? Usually. A contract expires when it is **TIRED**:

- **T**- After a reasonable period of **time** or after a **specific time** (i.e., the contract "lapsed") ("My bull is for sale for $5,000.00, but only until next Tuesday);

- **I**- **Incapacity** or death of either party (e.g., writing an offer while drunk at a salon on a bar napkin);

- **R**- **Revocation** ("I revoke this offer. I no longer want to sell my champion bull.");

- **E- Express rejection** or counteroffer ("I won't buy your bull for $5,000. But would you take $4,200?");

- **D- Destruction** of the subject matter of the contract itself or intervening illegality (e.g., gilt or barrow died).

> Farmer Joe tells Farmer Jane that he will sell her his Holstein bull for $5,000.00. Farmer Jane thinks about it while asking more questions about the bull's pedigree and evaluating his structural correctness. She decides to go home and sleep on it. Disappointed he didn't make the sale, Farmer Joe says "Okay, but I need to know by next week." In the meantime, Farmer Joe gets sentimental about the bull. Two weeks later, Farmer Jane calls up Joe and accepts his offer but he refuses to sell her the bull. Farmer Jane gets wildly upset. However, Farmer Joe's offer lapsed before Farmer Jane accepted. He revoked his offer to Jane to sell his bull.

An offer can usually be revoked anytime before acceptance. However, there are a few exceptions:

- *Option contacts* are considered irrevocable offers.

- If it is *reasonably foreseeable* that the other party *detrimentally relied* on the offer (i.e., the *doctrine of promissory estoppel*).

- The *other party started to perform* (Example: Farmer Joe says, "I will pay you $1,000 to paint my barn." The next day, you start painting his barn. Farmer Joe cannot revoke his offer to pay you $1,000).

Rewards are offers that lapse after a rational amount of time. For example, finding a lost kitten or puppy two years after a "reward" flyer was posted does not get you the $100 reward.

Acceptance

Acceptance is fairly straightforward (usually). If you indicate that you *agree* to the terms of a contract (either oral or written), then you have accepted. Folks can accept offers by *words or conduct* but must be clear about their intentions. An acceptance is effective *in the mail* when it goes *into the mailbox* unless the offer provided otherwise. Similarly, with electronic mail ("e-mail"), the offer is accepted once you press "send" and the email leaves your outbox to cyberspace.

Silence is not acceptance. However, if someone offers to combine your corn for $1,000 and you watch them do it without stopping them, your silence in that situation may be considered *non-verbal acceptance*. You knowingly allowed the performance to take place knowing the price tag.

A *conditional acceptance* isn't an acceptance at all. For example, you offer to sell your bull to Farmer Jane for $5,000. She responds, "I will buy your bull for $5,000 so long as you come help me show him at the New York State Fair and the All-East Livestock Exposition." This is a conditional acceptance. This is really a *counter offer* putting the burden on the other party to accept.

Consideration

Consideration (or the "*Quid Pro Quo*", which is Latin for "something for something", or "tit for tat") is *anything of legal value* that is exchanged. In real estate, it is referred to as "*earnest money*" when you enter into the contract.

Consideration can be in the form of a *promise* ("I will pay you $5,000 for your bull once you deliver him to my farm"), *performance* ("I will bale your hay this summer if you feed my pigs while I'm on vacation with my family"), or some type of *detriment* ("I will pay you $1,000 if you don't smoke or chew tobacco for a week"). An interesting concept in contracts is that the actual money does not have to be in hand, in order for there to be consideration. The mere promise to pay is held to have value; therefore, the promise to pay can create an enforceable obligation to pay. In fact, most contracts are formed when mutual promises are made before anything else actually changes hands.

Defenses

A court may view a contract as void if one party has a valid *defense*. There are several different kinds of defenses to contacts, namely:

- Lack of capacity (such as infancy, insanity or intoxication),
- Fraud,
- Unconscionability,
- Undue influence,
- Mistake (if the mistake went to a material term),
- Duress,
- "Unclean hands" (i.e., the other party is misbehaving),
- Impossibility, and,
- Statute of Frauds (for some oral contacts)

Let's break a few of these defenses down:

1. <u>Capacity</u>

As noted above, there are three main capacity defenses: infancy, insanity, and intoxication. First, with a few limited exceptions, people *under the age of 18* cannot enter into contracts. Second, *an intoxicated person* cannot enter into a contact if he/she cannot understand what he/she is agreeing to. Third, persons *lack mental capacity* or are *adjudicated to be incompetent or insane* cannot enter into a legal agreement without a guardian or agent (e.g., Power of Attorney, Health Care Proxy).

To illustrate, Doogie Howser, MD, might save lives, but he couldn't contract to order the toilet seat covers at his hospital. Why? Because he was *under age*. If you make a contract with a minor, the kid can revoke your contract at any time. As long as the minor who revokes a contract leaves the other party in the same position as they were before the contract, no damages can be sought.

> If you're thinking about selling your 756 IHC to that 16-year-old kid from the FFA, get a parent to sign the purchase contract; otherwise, you will risk having the tractor show back up after planting time.

Legally insane or *drunk persons* also lack capacity to enter valid contracts. A *person without authority to bind another* lacks capacity to enter into a contract on behalf of that other.

> For example, your neighbor can't decide to sell your tractor to either the 16-yr-old FFA kid or to his parents, unless you have given your neighbor **authority** (like a Power of Attorney) to enter that contract on your behalf.

Authority can also come through the terms of *employment contracts*. For example, an international buyer for a huge department store may have authority to purchase goods, but a store clerk may not (otherwise, the world's least favorite corporations might be stuck buying lots of goods they didn't want). A *lack of authority* to bind someone else to purchase something is also the reason why, despite high-school pranks, like filling out dozens of magazine subscription cards in the principal's name, the school administrator will not be stuck paying for a five-year Cosmo subscription.

2. Fraud

Fraud is when a party makes a misrepresentation to a *material* (or important) term of the agreement. It also requires *guilty knowledge* (or scienter) of the falsity. For example, if Farmer Jane sells Farmer Joe a bred heifer for $2500 but knows that the female is "open" (i.e., not pregnant), then Farmer Joe could later argue that Farmer Jane committed fraud and demand his money back. Prevailing on a fraud claim could lead to *punitive damages*, aimed to punish the offender. Importantly, fraud is *difficult* and *expensive* to prove; therefore, don't hang your hat on this contract defense.

3. Unconscionability, Undue Influence & Duress

These defenses are rare and are easily confused. An *unconscionable* contract has oppressive terms at the time of the agreement. For example, if you sold your cowherd to Farmer Jim for $200,000 and accepted a payment plan at 30% interest, a court may view this interest rate unconscionable.

Someone is under *undue influence* if there is a special trusting relationship between parties resulting in an unfair persuasion of the other party. You might see this with a *pre-nuptial or post-nuptial* agreement when one party has more power (usually financial power). Because of this, courts require each side to be represented by a separate attorney.

Duress occurs when one party enters a contract over fear or induced by a threat. Duress can be physical, economic or emotional. Prenuptial agreements, for example, should be signed 3-6 months before the wedding, or before the wedding invitations are sent out. A prenuptial agreement signed the day before a wedding ceremony may be entered into under duress ("If you don't sign this I will leave you at the alter and embarrass you in front of your family and friends").

4. Mistakes

If one side makes a *mistake* and it is *material* (important) to the contract, that side is out of luck. On the other hand, if there is a *mutual mistake* (i.e., if both sides have made a mistake), the contract is *voidable* (i.e., the parties can decide not to perform the contract).

> If you hire someone to drill in soybeans, and you wanted them in 20-inch rows, not 30-inch rows, but you didn't mention that to the custom operator, then you are likely stuck with the 30-inch rows that resulted from the **unilateral mistake**. You get a different result, when you order a 25 horsepower tractor, the dealer sells you a 25 horsepower tractor, but a 45 horsepower tractor is delivered. You do not get to keep the more expensive tractor because it was a **mutual mistake** of the parties.

5. Impossibility

Due to changed circumstances arising after the contract was signed, the contract may be *impossible* to perform. In these circumstances, a party's nonperformance will not constitute a breach of contract. For example, you enter into an employment contract with a horse trainer to work with your thoroughbred racehorse for a year with an excellent signing bonus; however, the horse trainer died of a heart attack. Death caused the impossibility for the horse trainer to fulfill his end of the bargain.

6. Statute of Frauds

Even though oral contracts are quite common in the food and agriculture industry, it's important to understand that the Statute of Frauds requires certain contracts to be in writing to be enforceable. Here is a memory trick: **"MY LEGS"**

- **M-** Promises made in consideration of **marriage** (e.g., prenuptial agreements);

- **Y-** Service contracts that cannot be performed within one **year**;

- **L-** Contracts involving **land** (e.g., leases, easements);

- **E-** Promise by an **executer** of an **estate** to use his/her own funds to pay estate expenses;

- **G-** The sale or lease of **goods** for more than $500 (e.g., livestock, crops, farm equipment, pick-up trucks, eggs); and,

- **S-** A **suretyship** (i.e., back-up promise to pay the debt of another person).

Land and the sale of goods over $500 are the big ones – think about how often contracts in the food and agriculture industry fall into one of these two.

Even if you are dealing with a transaction that does not fall into one of these categories, it is always prudent to put the terms of the agreement in writing. It helps crystalize the terms of the agreement for everyone involved to help make sure there are no misunderstandings. Remember – valid contracts require a **"meeting of the minds."** Contracts are not about trust or distrust- they are about clarity and enforceability of the terms of the agreement.

Miscellaneous

Substantial performance is a legal doctrine in contract law which essentially means that "close enough" counts. If the majority of the contract performance has already been completed by one party to the contract, then the other party may be stuck having to perform its side.

For example, consider a situation in which you ordered a new Case tractor in white to match your fleet of white Case Agri Kings. When the Case IH tractor shows up, but it is red, you may likely be "stuck" with paying for it anyway.

A few words about auction sales: an *auctioneer* works for the seller, as the *seller's agent*. The seller picks the auctioneer, pays the auctioneer, and the auctioneer will not sell, if that's what the seller wants done. If the auctioneer, as an agent for the seller, exceeds the *authority* given to him by the seller, the buyer cannot bind the seller to perform.

For example, if a seller hires an auctioneer for the limited purpose of auctioning household items located inside the home of the seller's dearly-departed grandparents, but the auctioneer also auctions off family-heirloom items that were previously moved to a storage building way out back, the winning bidders on the heirloom items cannot force the seller to sell them under those terms.

Put simply, a bid is an offer to buy. If an auction is conducted *with reserve*, the auctioneer can reject all bids. In a *non-reserve* auction, the highest bidder wins, regardless. A winning bidder may not be bound to follow through with the purchase, if either the seller or the auctioneer has made *material, fraudulent representations* about the property being sold. *Puffing* by the auctioneer is acceptable, but fraud is not.

Warranties

For the *purchase of trade animals*, a *warranty of fitness* is often either expressed or implied. An *express warranty* is one that is *stated or promised*. Examples of statements creating an express warranty, which *passes with title* to the animal, include promises made about the condition of an animal, such as the following:

- "This heifer is open."

- "This bull is fertile."

- "These sheep are wormed."

If it turns out that the animal in question is not open, fertile, or wormed, then a *breach of warranty* may be found. If the defect is discovered before delivery, you can reject the shipment, but after accepting the delivery, the burden falls to the receiving party to *establish a breach* of warranty and to *seek damages* for it.

An *implied warranty* is one that is reasonably *assumed, under the existing circumstances*. For example, one would assume that the seller of a tractor actually owns the tractor that he or she is selling. If a buyer purchases the tractor, with no knowledge of a *title defect* (i.e., no reason to think that the seller may not actually own the tractor), then the buyer may prevail and receive damages, if some third party (the true tractor owner) shows up and claims to have good title to the tractor.

"Puffing" does not create a warranty. For example, "This boer goat will make you the top dog at your county fair," is not a warranty, but rather a puffing statement.

Specific Contracts

Production Contracts

A *production contract* can be defined as an agreement under which a *producer agrees* to *raise* a *commodity* in a manner established by the contractor and to *deliver* the commodity to the contractor; while the *contractor agrees to pay* the producer, in return.

- A *"commodity"* can include livestock, raw milk, and crops.

- *"Livestock"* may include beef cattle, dairy cattle, sheep, and swine.

- *"Crops"* typically include plants used for food, animal feed, fiber, or oil, if the plant is classified as a forage or cereal plant. This includes, but is not limited to, alfalfa, barley, buckwheat, corn, flax, forage, millet, oats, popcorn, rye, sorghum, soybeans, sunflowers, wheat, and grasses used for forage or silage, but not plants produced to create seed for sale.

What if the contractor refuses to pay, after the commodity has been grown and delivered? One inexpensive way that producers can reduce their risk is by filing a *commodity production contract lien*. If you are contracted to produce a commodity, then you can file a lien. The amount of the lien is equal to the amount owed to you, pursuant to the terms of the production contract. The lien applies to the actual product produced or the proceeds from sale of the product.

Custom Feeding Arrangements

Any custom feeding contract should make provisions for *(1) handling and feeding, (2) division of profit or loss*, and *(3) marketing of the livestock*. The contract should state the approximate *delivery date* and *deadline for delivery*. *Shrink* needs to be addressed, especially if rate of gain is used to determine any type of payment. *General management practices* and expectations should be written and agreed upon and provisions should be made for *repossession* of livestock that is not cared for properly.

Generally speaking, the feeder is responsible for the proper manure handling, storage, and liability. The agreement should include the type and weight of animal to be fed. The owner and feeder both know the approximate time of marketing and the desired state at marketing and how shipping is paid for. A clause should be included for *low-performing animals* and allow for their early departure.

Some feedlots will *finance* the *feed bill* for customers, and some will finance the *cattle*. However, it is not uncommon for the feedlot operator to require a *deposit upon delivery*. The deposit will be applied to overall expenses. Interest rates vary and are usually based off of the prime rate.

When cattle are fed under contract, the owner retains *title* to the cattle. The *risk of loss* due to *death* is usually borne by the *owner*, except for those death losses caused by *negligence of the feeder*. Death losses will usually be borne by the owner. The parties also have the option of agreeing to *share losses*, above a certain percentage of dead livestock. This is problematic as only one party will be around to verify the death loss. Both parties need to determine whose insurance company will cover losses due to *catastrophe,* such as fire, wind and lighting.

Feeding is central to the operation. Don't forget to consider the following aspects of any contract feed arrangement:

- **Ration composition**. The feedlot should provide cattle owners with a report of the ration composition. This report should include not only the amounts of each feedstuff but also note the total ration's energy, protein and major vitamins and minerals. A list of feed additives should also be included. Knowing where the feedlot gets its feeding program and whether they pay timely is often a key to understanding the nature of the operation you are dealing with.

- **Cost of feed charged by the feedlot**. Feed may be marked up to cover overhead costs. Some agreements mark up the feed a little and do not charge "*yardage.*" Others may charge a little more for yardage and not mark up the feed. Find out how both parties think this is going to work. The yardage fee will *vary from lot to lot.* Some charge a yardage fee and some don't. The important thing is to ask.

The two most common ways of charging for services are (1) *yardage* or (2) *yardage plus feed* markup. *Yardage* is usually charged on a *dollar/head/day basis.* In yards that have a higher yardage charge, the feed markup is generally less. *Cost of arrival* treatments usually includes cost of vaccination, dewormer, implants, etc. *Labor* cost may or may not be included in the yardage charge. The feedlot operator should send a complete record of the delivered feed and its cost.

Billings should reflect changes in *ration ingredient cost.* The bill should contain an itemized list of any other costs billed to the cattle owner. The first bill should state the cost of processing. If the feed is financed through the feedlot, look for a statement of interest on the bill. It is a good idea to specify with the feedlot the exact time when interest charges for feed begin to accrue.

Because feed prices can change, some feedlots allow customers to *prepay* for some or all of the feed. The key point to keep in mind is that *IRS regulations* do not allow one to pay a *true feed bill* in advance of its purchase and take a deduction, but the IRS allows the purchase of commodities such as grain, silage, or hay for future use to be deducted. Check with your tax preparer about *prepaying commodities* if you are feeding cattle into the next year.

Stocker Cattle Contracts

There are several issues to consider when a cattle producer hires a stocker feeder after the progeny are weaned. Besides the payment terms and term, example issues include the following:

- *Feed and nutrition* (including pasture quality and supplemental vitamins and nutrients);
- *Animal health* (including vaccinations, veterinary care, deworming for internal parasites); and,
- *Control of pests* (e.g., insecticides, fly control).

In some cases, stocker cattle contracts include promises for *average daily gain* ("ADG"). Like any contract, the parties have to look at the individual situation and discern what is most important.

Embryo Transfer Contracts

Each party in an embryo transfer transaction has specific interests to protect. Below are some suggested terms for the livestock industry that should be included in contracts dealing with embryo transfers.

Recipient Agreement

Livestock producers who are selling embryo transfer recipients should make sure that the following terms are included in the written contract:

- sale/rental price of recipient;
- payment terms including penalties for late payments;
- instructions for receipt of embryos;
- embryo transfer fees;
- dates/procedures/costs associated with pregnancy checks (e.g., palpation, ultrasound);

- duration that recipient will stay under the care of owner and any daily boarding/maintenance fees (e.g., feed, pasture);
- if necessary, reimbursement for routine veterinary care and transportation;
- limitation of liability for congenital birth defects or reasonable birthing difficulties; and,
- if appropriate, security on the embryo transfer progeny and the assignment of necessary registration papers.

Furthermore, the recipient owner may request additional fees for genetic DNA testing or marketing services.

Breeder Agreement

On the other hand, breeders should make sure that the recipient owner agrees to bear the burden that the recipient is:
- in *good health* and obtains necessary vaccinations;
- within the appropriate *age range*;
- has an acceptable *body condition score*;
- if appropriate, a *certain breed or color pattern* (e.g., solid black/red hided); and,
- is *structurally sound*.

The breeder may want to hold the recipient owner liable for gross negligence or intentional misconduct relating to the care of the recipient and the progeny including birthing complications and require that the recipient owner use best management practices. If the recipient owner will be raising the progeny until weaning and retaining ownership of the recipient, the breeder may want to list special management terms (e.g., early weaning, creep feeding, DNA testing).

Flush Agreement

If a livestock breeder is purchasing a flush from another owner, the breeder may want to memorialize a minimum number of transferable embryos from the flush (e.g., five embryos) and the date/procedures for the receipt of the flush. Additionally, this breeder would also want to make sure that that flush is guaranteed to be what was ordered (e.g., free of certain genetic defects, use of sexed semen) and note liquidated damages in case of an error. Conversely, the owner who will be flushing the embryos will want to enumerate the payment terms including shipping expenses and ensure that he/she is not responsible for the transfer of the embryos to the recipient or birthing problems that may occur.

Using Those "Suggested Sale Terms" from Livestock Breed Associations

There are many livestock breed associations that are developing *"suggested sale terms"* (e.g., American Simmental Association's ("ASA") Suggested Sale Terms and Conditions). It's great that livestock breed associations are giving members some *suggested guidelines* that memorialize important terms such as choice of law, health requirements, registration, identification, pedigree, guarantees for fertility/breeding, embryo transfer history, disclosure of genetic defects and other material information, genetic testing, return of animal, and other guarantees such as the development of scurs. However, it is important to note that **these terms are simply "suggested" and are not necessarily legally binding**. Both parties have to agree to the terms in order for them to be legally binding in a contract. As discussed above, agreements for the sale of cattle over $500 must be in writing in order to be enforceable.

If you are a seller and would like to abide by the suggested terms of your breed association, you are advised to have a copy of the breed association's suggested sale terms available for all potential buyers. You should also print very clearly in the sale catalog that the sale abides by the suggested terms and conditions set forth by your breed association. Finally, when a potential buyer registers at a sale, it is recommended to have the potential buyer agree in writing to the suggested terms of the breed association. Doing so will prevent an argument later that the buyer was not aware of such terms and that there was no meeting of the minds.

Additionally, I want to note that these terms are only suggested and parties can adopt all or part of the suggested terms and create additional terms. For example, the ASA Suggested Sale Terms and Conditions are silent about a guarantee for the *bull's semen's ability to freeze*. To illustrate, Cattle Farmer Jane wants to sell Cattle Farmer Joe a Simmental bull. Joe comes to see the sire and asks Jane her price. Jane makes her offer at $3,000. Jane also notes that she abides by the suggested sale terms and conditions provided by the ASA. Joe agrees but then counters by saying that he wants to ship semen to Brazil so it is important that the bull semen freeze. Jane accepts these terms so there is a "meeting of the minds." Assuming both Jane and Joe entered the agreement under their own free will then they will likely be considered competent parties. The contractual agreement should then be memorialized in writing.

Take Home Points

Here are a few important take home points from this Chapter on Contracts:

- Written contracts are appropriate with most transactions.

- If you don't put the agreement in writing, your oral agreement might not be enforceable.

- A contract does not need to be long and complicated; to the contrary, many great contacts are simple and to the point. The important thing here is to make sure that it covers all the material terms for that transaction.

- Getting a written contract doesn't mean that you don't trust the other party; instead, it helps ensure all parties have thought through the important issues and have reached an understanding on all points. It makes sound business sense.

- When drafting contracts, consider adding an Alternative Dispute Resolution clause, such as non-binding mediation and/or binding arbitration. Litigation can be expensive.

- Work with a food and agriculture lawyer for your contracts. Generic forms on the Internet may not fit your particular needs. Contracts should be tailored to your situation. Additionally, contract forms on the Internet may have terminology that you don't understand that may hurt your operation if included.

- Depending on the situation, a lawyer can help a farmer or

food entrepreneur draft form contracts that can be used in multiple situations (reviewed by the lawyer when needed).

- The larger the business, the more contracts that business has to manage. A food and agriculture lawyer can help manage those contracts for you keeping records of termination dates, instructions to cancel or amend the agreement, whether there is a confidentiality provision, what duties/responsibilities each party has, dispute resolution, and suggestions for improving the contract when opportunity arises.

- To save money in legal fees, some lawyers will simply review and edit contracts written by the client. Take the suggested changes by the lawyer seriously. In some cases, it is best for the lawyer to draft the contract themselves.

- Contracts are always negotiable. If someone hands you a contract in small print and it looks very official and boilerplate, it can still be negotiated.

- "I didn't understand what I signed" is rarely an excuse in court. Courts even uphold Terms of Use contracts that you find on websites that are rarely read by the participating parties. When in doubt, have an attorney review an agreement.

Additional Resources

Ag MRC Agriculture Marketing Resource Center, "Grower Contracts", at http://www.agmrc.org/business_development/operating_a_business/production/grower-contracts/ (last visited July 14, 2013).

Cari Rincker, "Drafting Embryo Transfer Contracts for Livestock Producers," Texas Bar CLE Agriculture Law Conference (recording available for purchase), slides available at http://www.slideshare.net/rinckerlaw/drafting-embryo-transfer-contracts-for-livestock-producers (last visited July 3, 2013).

Cari Rincker, "Need an Embryo Transfer Contract? Questionnaire for Recipient Agreements," (June 10, 2013) available at www.rinckerlaw.com/blog/uncategorized/2013/06/10/need-an-embryo-transfer-contract-questionnaire-for-recipient-agreements/ (last visited August 17, 2013).

Cari Rincker, "Protecting the Agri-Business: Managing Contracts, Trademarks and Non-Disclosure Agreements" (June 24, 2013) Fifth Annual Ohio Agriculture Law Symposium, slides available at http://www.slideshare.net/rinckerlaw/protecting-the-agribusiness-managing-contracts-trademarks-and-nondisclosure-agreements (last visited July 3, 2013).

Carrie Leslie, "Livestock Production Contracts: Information for Pennsylvania Farmers", Pennsylvania State University Extension Education (December 2001), available at http://law.psu.edu/_file/aglaw/Livestock_Production_Contracts.pdf (last visited July 14, 2013).

David Moeller, "Livestock Production Contracts: Risks for Family Members" (March 22, 2003) available at http://www.flaginc.org/wp-content/uploads/2013/03/artcf005.pdf (last visited May 19, 2013).

Farmers' Legal Action Group, "Farmers' Guide to Organic Contracts" (August 2012) available at http://www.flaginc.org/wp-content/uploads/2013/03/FGOC2012.pdf (last visited May 19, 2013).

Frayne Olson, "Production Contracts" North Dakota State University Extension available at http://www.ag.ndsu.edu/pubs/plantsci/rowcrops/a1133d.pdf (last visited July 14, 2013).

JULIE I. FERSHTMAN, EQUINE LAW & HORSE SENSE (1996) and MORE EQUINE LAW AND HORSE SENSE (2000).

Laura Klauke and Jill Krueger, "Questions to Ask Before Signing a Poultry Contract" available at http://www.flaginc.org/wp-content/uploads/2013/03/PoultryQuestionsRAFIFLAG_2005.pdf (last visited May 19, 2013).

Michigan Farm Bureau, "Checklist for Grain Production Contracts," available at http://www2.michfb.com/commodities (last visited July 14, 2013).

National Agriculture Law Center's Reading Room on Production Contracts available http://nationalaglawcenter.org/readingrooms/productioncontracts/ (last visited May 19, 2013).

Neil D. Hamilton, "Farmer's Legal Guide to Production Contracts" (January 1995) available at http://www.nationalaglawcenter.org/assets/articles/hamilton_produc tioncontracts.pdf (last visited July 14, 2013).

Phillip L. Kunkel, Jeffrey A. Peterson, and Jessica A. Mitchel, "Agricultural Production Contracts" available http://www.extension.umn.edu/distribution/businessmanagement/D F7302.html (last visited May 19, 2013).

Rachael E. Goodhue and Leo K. Simon, "Agricultural Contracts and Risk Management," University of California- Davis Extension available at http://agecon.ucdavis.edu/people/faculty/shermain-hardesty/docs/reducing_market_risk_for_specialty_crops/goodhue_a gricultural_contracts_and_risk_management.pdf (last visited July 14, 2013).

Rusty Rumley, "Agricultural Contracting" available at http://nationalaglawcenter.org/assets/articles/rrumley_agcontracting. pdf (last visited May 19, 2013).

CHAPTER 5

CONFIDENTIALITY

No matter the size of your farm or food business, there might come a time when a *Non-Disclosure Agreement* (a/k/a *"NDA"* or *Confidentiality Agreement*) will be appropriate. It is important for farms and food entrepreneurs to know when an NDA should be used, what it should protect and for how long. A misappropriation of confidential information could be devastating for a farm or food business. This chapter on confidentiality follows the chapter on contracts because a NDA is a special type of contract.

Background

When Are NDA's Used?

There are two common instances when confidentiality agreements are utilized:

- When a farm or agri-business is *entering into business discussions* with another party; and,

- When a farm or agri-business wants to *bind its employees* or independent contractors to keep certain information confidential.

For example, if a farmer approached a website developer about his or her proposed online agri-business, that farmer may wish to have a NDA with the website developer to keep the business plan confidential. Alternatively, a farm may wish for a bookkeeper to maintain secrecy on the operation's finances or for employees to stay hush-hush on secret food recipes. Or perhaps two food entrepreneurs are considering a joint venture. There are an infinite number of examples when a NDA may be used in the food and agriculture industry.

Is it a One-Way or Two-Way Street?

There are two basic types of NDA's: (1) *mutual* or bilateral and (2) *one-sided* or unilateral. Most NDA's with outside parties are bilateral putting responsibilities on all parties to maintain secrecy; however, if a farm or agri-business is presented with an unilateral NDA, it should be changed to a mutual NDA. Business discussions are almost always a two-way street --- so too should be the promise of confidentiality.

What Should an NDA Address?

Generally speaking, a well-drafted NDA should address the following issues:

- *Who* will be exchanging confidential information?

- What is the *purpose* of the exchange of confidential information?

- What *type of information* is to be considered "confidential" for protection under the NDA?

- How can this confidential information be *used and by whom*?

- *How will the secrecy* of the confidential information be maintained?

- *How long* will the confidentiality of the information be maintained?

- What are the *consequences of a breach* or misuse of the confidential information?

Though it is common for companies to use a generic form for their NDA's, special attention should be given to ensure it properly fits the needs of the parties in that particular situation. Don't just mindlessly sign something because you "trust" the other party; make sure the NDA properly protects you in the specific circumstances.

Common Provisions in Mutual NDA's

In most instances, bilateral NDA's should cover the following issues:

(1) **Legal Name of the Parties and Location**. The NDA should use the parties' legal name, address, and state of incorporation (if appropriate). It may be prudent to ask for a Certificate of Good Standing from the Department of State.

(2) **Purpose of the NDA**. The purpose of the NDA should be properly identified to help narrow down *what information* is to be considered confidential. Furthermore, the NDA should state that usage of confidential information should be limited to this purpose.

(3) **Permitted Parties**. *Who may or may not be privy* to any disclosed confidential information should be clearly identified. This may include employees and independent contractors on a "need to know" basis so long as they are bound by written agreement to maintain confidentiality.

(4) **Identification of Confidential Information**. Special attention should be made to how "Confidential Information" is defined in the NDA to ensure it properly includes every possible disclosure. This may include *ideas, concepts, know-how, trade secrets, intellectual property, business plans and financial information*. Keep in mind that disclosures may be either written or oral; thus, the NDA should state

how the Confidential Information will be identified.

> For example, the NDA could state that oral disclosures must be identified orally at the time of the disclosure and then followed up in writing within thirty (30) days.

(5) **Exceptions (or "Carve Outs")**. Typical exceptions to confidentiality include: (a) is *known prior* to the date of disclosure, (b) is in the *public domain*, (c) was *lawfully communicated* to the recipient by a third-party, (d) was *independently developed* by employees, (e) was part of the *written release* by the disclosing party, and (f) when the *law requires disclosure* (e.g., court order or subpoena) allowing the disclosing party reasonable notice to obtain a protective order.

(6) **Security**. The parties to a NDA should take *reasonable safety measures* to protect the Confidential Information. The other party should be promptly notified in writing if there has been a breach of confidentiality.

(7) **Term**. It is always better for the disclosing party to *have the longest term* possible; however, with mutual NDA's it is best to pick a reasonable term length that isn't *overly burdensome* for either party. A typical term for NDA's in the business community is three to five years. As a caveat, some NDA's measure this term from the date of disclosure vs. the effective date of the agreement (which should be avoided, if possible).

(8) **Procedures Upon Termination**. The NDA should discuss how confidential information should be treated at the end of the term. For example, should the recipient *return copies or destroy all written materials*? May the recipient *maintain a copy* of all written materials?

> Generally speaking, it's usually best to maintain a copy or written records (if allowed) in case a dispute will arise later. It can serve as proof of what you were given and what you gave the other party.

(9) **Ownership**. It is paramount that the NDA state that the disclosing party retains ownership to the Confidential Information. As a caveat, some NDA's include a *"feedback exception"* identifying ownership of all suggestions made during business negotiations; however, this may hinder open dialogue.

(10) **Relationship of the Parties**. The NDA should note the *relationship between the parties*. For example, if a farm or agri-business is entering into an NDA with an ag-technology company for preliminary business discussions, it should state that the parties are not in a joint venture, agency or partnership.

(11) **How Disputes Will be Settled**. The NDA should address how a *dispute will be settled*, under what state's law, and whether attorneys' fees and costs can be recovered for a prevailing party. The NDA should memorialize any preferences towards *Alternative Dispute Resolution* ("ADR") including mediation or arbitration. If the parties wish to litigate a dispute or emergency, the NDA should identify which state's courts may be used.

Maintaining Records

Farms and food businesses should maintain hard copies of NDA's in a separate *"NDA File"* that is readily accessible and keep an electronic spreadsheet of all NDA's that the farm or agri-business is a party to along with the following information: (1) parties and contact information, (2) date the NDA was effective, (3) term of NDA and/or expiration date, (4) any duty after the termination of the NDA, (5) any farm or agri-business employees or independent contractors who have been privy to some part of the confidential information which the business was under the obligation to keep confidential, and (6) any special notes concerning the NDA (e.g., requirement to put oral disclosures in writing within thirty days).

Final Thoughts

Don't get lost in the legalese -- confidentiality agreements can have grave importance for a farm or agri-business. Although the food and agriculture community has a trusting culture, maintenance of confidential information should not be taken lightly. It is highly suggested that farms and agri-businesses should speak to a licensed attorney before entering into a confidentiality agreement.

Additional Resources

Cari Rincker, "Protecting the Agri-Business: Managing Contracts, Trademarks and Non-Disclosure Agreements" (June 24, 2013) Fifth Annual Ohio Agriculture Law Symposium, slides available at http://www.slideshare.net/rinckerlaw/protecting-the-agribusiness-managing-contracts-trademarks-and-nondisclosure-agreements (last visited July 3, 2013).

Catherine Daniels, "Should your Agricultural Business Consider a Non-Disclosure Agreement?", Ohio Agricultural Law Blog (July 9, 2013), available at http://ohioaglaw.wordpress.com/2013/07/09/should-your-agricultural-business-consider-a-non-disclosure-agreement/ (last visited July 14, 2013).

Jere M. Webb, "A Practitioner's Guide to Confidentiality Agreements," available at http://www.stoel.com/files/ConfidentialityAgreementGuide.pdf (last visited August 17, 2013).

CHAPTER 6

LEASES FOR REAL ESTATE, ANIMALS AND FARM EQUIPMENT

Put simply, a *lease* is a contract granting permission to use another's real estate or personal property for a set period of time, in exchange for money or other consideration. All leases have basic legal similarities to one another, so some of the issues that you need to focus on will be similar with any lease. On the other hand, there are also major differences between leases of farm acreage, leases that involve a farmhouse and buildings, and leases of personal property, such as farm equipment or livestock. In dealing with these differences, you will encounter issues unique to each type of lease. Because of this, it is best to work with an agriculture lawyer to help ascertain what issues need to be addressed in the contract.

Farm Acreage Leases

Farm acreage leases to tenant farmers are vital to many farm operations. Whether you are the landowner or the tenant, some simple rules should be kept in mind with farmland leases.

Get it in Writing

While it is still not uncommon for people to base farmland leases on verbal agreements, modern farm operators in today's business environment are always well-advised to *put the terms of a real estate lease into writing*. Written leases prevent misunderstandings between the parties. Make sure *both* parties *sign the lease*.

Do your best to make sure **successors in interest** (heirs upon death) on both sides understand the terms of the agreement, as well, to avoid the kinds of quarrels that can arise when one party to a lease dies.

Three Common Types of Farm Acreage Leases

When deciding on the terms of your farm lease, consider the following three types of farm acreage leases:

- **Cash-Rent Lease**: This is where the tenant usually pays a *fixed dollar amount* in rent (either on a per acre or whole farm basis). These types of leases may be modified depending on *crop yield* (i.e., increase in good years and decrease in bad years). In this scenario, the landlord is not as involved in crop production giving the tenant more autonomy. As a caveat, because the landlord not *"actively engaged in farming"* he/she may not be able to participate in some federal programs. Furthermore, the income is not subject to *self employment tax* and is not considered to be earned income for the purposes of determining how social security may be modified if the farmer has previously retired.

- **Crop-Share Lease**: Typically, in these arrangements, *the landlord will share input costs* (including but not limited to seed, fertilizer, fuel) while the tenant provides all of the labor and remaining input costs. Once harvested, proceeds will be divided according to the agreement (normally ranging from 25/75 to 50/50). In this scenario, the farmers both share the risk with the other person and the landlord will typically satisfy the "actively engaged in farming" requirement of federal programs. The downside (or upside - depending on your view) for the tenant is that he/she loses autonomy because the landlord is involved in the decisions of the operation. Rental income will be subject to *self-employment taxes*.

- **Hybrid Leases**: In this type of lease, *the landlord will receive a minimum fixed rent payment* while sharing in some of the profits, losses, and decision-making. It's important to memorialize the rights and responsibilities of each party in this agreement.

Important Lease Terms

A good written farm property lease can contain a wide variety of very specific terms regulating the relationship between the parties and the manner in which the land may be used, but there are some basic terms that are crucial to every farm property lease:

- **Parties**: Ensure that all intended parties to the lease are named and adequately identified by the inclusion of their addresses or other unique identifying information.

- **Purpose**: It is recommended that farm leases note the purpose of the lease (e.g., corn production).

- **Property Description**: Ensure an accurate description of the leased ground is included. This should include a list of buildings and structures the tenant has access to.

- **Lease Term**: The length of the lease term should be clearly stated.

> Under New York law, a real estate lease can be for as long as the parties wish; however, if the terms are longer than three (3) years then the lease must be recorded, just like a deed or a mortgage would in the property records office.

- **Renewal Terms**: Include provisions allowing for any renewal of the lease and for notice of intent to renew (or not renew). A good farm property lease should also establish agreed-upon compensation for any fall fieldwork completion, in the event of nonrenewal of the lease.

- **Lease Price & Payment Terms**: Whether your agreement involves crop sharing, fixed-cash, flex-cash, or some other arrangement, your lease price should be spelled out in writing.

Additionally, payment terms should be memorialized (including when payment is due, where it should be sent, and how rent can be paid). Furthermore, the lease should clearly state who is responsible for property taxes, farm insurance, and utilities.

- **Duties and Prohibitions**: The lease should clearly state the duties and prohibitions of both the landlord and the tenant in the farm lease. For example, it might be the landlord's duty to perform all repairs and maintenance for the property.

- **Rights to Natural Resources**: The lease should state whether the tenant or landlord will retain rights to natural resources on the property including, but not limited to: wind rights, solar rights, mineral rights, timber rights, fishing rights and/or hunting rights. It might be appropriate to also describe recreational rights such as camping.

- **Reporting Requirements**: You should also discuss and include any reporting requirements, such as what must be reported, along with when and how the tenant must make those reports. For example, does the tenant have to provide *grid sampling, yield monitor data, weigh wagon* results or *test plot* results to the landowner? Can the landowner ask the cooperative how many bushels of grain were delivered?

- **Default**: Your lease may include a list of actions that count as defaults in the terms of the lease, specifying whether part or all of the listed defaults can be cured or waived by the other party.

- **Ability to Assign or Sublease**: The lease should state whether the tenant can assign or sublease its obligation to another farmer.

- **Notice**: Include notice provisions, to specify how and when to give notice of default, notice of intent to terminate the lease, or any other notice needed to make the terms of the lease work.

- **Termination**: The lease should include procedures for terminating the lease, either voluntarily or involuntarily (for example, in case of a default).

- **Miscellaneous Provisions**: Miscellaneous provisions can include just about anything legal that you'd like to include as an important term of your lease. With farm tenants, common provisions include *indemnity clauses* or *hold-harmless agreements*, requiring the tenant to pay any damages that are assessed against you, if someone sues you or you are cited by the government, based on something the tenant has done on the land. They may also include a *choice of law* (New York), *choice of forum* for disputes (e.g., New York Supreme Court of Suffolk County), *Alternative Dispute Resolution* clause (e.g., requiring non-binding mediation through the *New York State Agriculture Mediation Program* ("NYSAMP") and then binding arbitration), *confidentiality clause*, and *severability clause*. In many cases, it is beneficial for the lease to state that the landlord and tenant are not in a partnership or joint venture.

Termination of Farm Property Leases

When *terminating* a farm lease, landlords must give proper *notice* under the terms of the lease and New York law. The failure to follow laws regarding notice to a farm tenant may result in an automatic renewal of the lease under the current terms. Because of this- you are highly encouraged to work with an attorney to make sure you *strictly comply* with these requirements.

Possession and Title to Growing Crops

Tenant farmers who review their leases may note that if they have been noticed off (terminated from renewal) properly, *March 1* is likely the *last day of possession*. Every day after that, the tenant may be assessed a liquidated damage payment to the landowner pursuant to the farm lease.

Tenants with crops still in the ground may not be able to harvest until after March 1. Each respective party (and their legal counsel) most likely has different beliefs about what the result should be there:

- Landowners believe tenants must abandon the crop left (which the landowner most likely plans to harvest and keep); and

- Tenants believe they have as much time as they like (perhaps even after spring planting on the acres that the tenant did renew on).

However, neither side is entirely correct. This issue turns on the nature of the relationship between the parties. As long as the tenancy is for a *certain period*, the tenant will probably not be permitted to harvest the crops after the last day of the lease. See Triggs v. Kahn, 167 N.YS.2d 262, 264 (N.Y App. Div. 1990). However, if the tenancy is not for a certain period and the tenant has been given "the right to harvest any annual crop already sown before the indefinite term is brought to an end[,]" the tenant might retain the right to harvest the crops under the *doctrine of emblements*. See Jacob H. Rottkamp & Son, Inc. v. Wulforst Farms, LLC, 844 N.Y.S.2d 600, 605 (N.Y. Sup. Ct. 2007). Please note that this only applies to *annual crops*.

In situations like this, *common sense* can help. A couple of stalks of corn left in the corner of the field, or maybe even a partial row left to help with snow drifting, can likely be declared abandoned by the tenant and taken by the landowner. Conversely, twenty (20) acres left in the field is still property of the tenant, who has a reasonable right to harvest in peace.

The Landlord's Lien

A landlord's lien used to be superior to other creditors' claims; however, it does not arise automatically because of a landlord-tenant relationship in New York. Landlords who want to retain title to the products of the land against the tenant's other creditors must explicitly include a provision to that effect in the lease.

Both the landlord and tenant should memorialize their intent to create such a *security interest*. The sooner the landlord in this situation files a *UCC-1 statement* with the *NYS Department of State*, the more likely courts are to protect his or her position for payment. Ideally, this filing should be made when the lease is signed.

New York landlords should be *cautious when relying on security interests*. The validity of UCC -1 statements is often the subject of protracted litigation. Accordingly, New York courts have commented that landlords may find more effective protection in the form of *insurance*. See e.g., Badillo v. Tower Ins. Co. of New York, 686 N.Y.S.2d. 363 (N.Y. Ct. of Appeals 1999).

Liability for Tenant Activities

When is a landowner legally liable for harm that is caused to others by a tenant's activity on leased farmland? For example, a tenant who spreads manure or pesticides on the property might create a nuisance that affects a neighbor, who then wants to sue you because you have more assets or better insurance against which to collect. Will you have to pay? What can you do to protect yourself from liability?

The general principle is that everyone who creates a nuisance or participates in maintaining the nuisance is liable. This means that landowners cannot avoid liability simply by leasing their land to tenants – what matters is whether the landowner knew about how the tenant was likely to use the property when the lease was signed or renewed.

How does all of that affect what you do with your farm property leases? In practice, landowners should review leases with an eye towards seeking *indemnification* and *hold harmless agreements* from any tenant who accepts *manure* under a manure-management plan or manure-easement arrangement, because you face at least the potential for legal liability to third parties for any nuisance created, when a tenant uses manure as part of the operation.

Pricing Leases to Tenant Farmers

When *pricing leases*, some *flexible, nonstandard arrangements* can be made. This lets the landowner in on some of the profit that can flow from *swings in the market*. This concept is called *"flex leasing."* Generally, the tenant and the landowner agree on a *base price* and on *trigger points, set by third-party standards* (such as posted county price or crop insurance price rate), which may result in additional payments to the landowner.

For example, **actual price** multiplied by **actual yield**, which is divided by a **base price** multiplied by a **base yield**, will result in per acre rent payment that is likely to reflect some of the upward or downward movement in the market.

Renting the Farm House and Buildings

When you decide to rent out a farmhouse and accompanying buildings and acreage, you are entering into a separate profession: the *residential landlord*. Residential tenants have rights that are very different from those of tenants who are renting bare ground. If disputes arise, judges are simply not as sympathetic when you wear a *landlord's cap* as opposed to your seed corn cap. A rental agreement in writing, signed by the landlord and the tenants, should always be performed.

Important Lease Terms

As with the acreage leases discussed above, a written *residential lease agreement* should outline every important aspect of the agreement, including:

- *term* of the agreement (i.e. the length of the lease),
- *amount of rent*,
- *due date* for payment of the rent (e.g., first of the month),
- amount of the *security deposit*,
- name and address of the *manager or landlord*,
- list of which *utilities* are paid by which party, and
- any special requests or requirements by either party.

These could include provisions limiting the number of occupants, assigning responsibility for **mowing and snow removal,** or listing **maintenance** that either party plans on having finished prior to occupancy. If the tenant is to be responsible for property maintenance, the lease must say so.

Residential Security Deposits

The security deposit that you require on a residential lease must be kept intact in a separate, *interest-bearing bank account*. In addition, the bank in which it is deposited must have a place of business in New York. Within thirty (30) days of termination, the landlord must *return the deposit* to the tenant, unless there are damages to the property and the landlord takes proper steps to collect them against the security deposit.

> It is generally a good practice to do a **walkthrough** before a tenant moves in and prior to the tenant leaving to identify any damage.

If there are damages for which part of the deposit is retained or unpaid rent, the landlord can keep the appropriate amount of the deposit only if he or she:

- *Submits a written statement* to the tenant, specifying *why* the deposit was kept; and
- *Allows* the *tenant* to *inspect* the property and *submit a statement* of damage.

As a landlord, if you don't provide the written statement to the tenant explaining why you did not return deposit money, you forfeit the deposit and any rights that you have to that money. It is the responsibility of the tenant to provide a *forwarding address* to which the deposit can be sent. The tenant's failure to do so can result in the tenant forfeiting any right to the deposit.

Warranty of Habitability

As a landlord, it is *your legal responsibility* to provide the property to the tenant in a *habitable condition* and to *maintain the habitability* of the premises. This means making any needed *repairs* and ensuring that all *electrical, plumbing, sanitary, heating, ventilating, air-conditioning, and other facilities* are properly working. If the tenant is to be responsible for the maintenance of the property it should be so stated in the rental agreement.

In the event the landlord fails to provide a *habitable residence*, the tenant has a right to terminate the agreement. If the tenant chooses to continue the agreement and make any needed repairs, he or she has the right to *deduct the costs* of those improvements from the rent (i.e., rent abatement).

After the rental agreement has been signed, the landlord may adopt new rules as long as they are in *writing* agreed to by the tenants. The new rules will apply to all tenants living on the property with the purpose is to create a better and safer living environment.

Inspecting the Premises

Unless there is an emergency, the landlord must give the tenant at least 24 hours notice of intent to enter a residential dwelling to inspect it, or for any reason other than an emergency. The tenant *must* let the landlord enter the dwelling if the tenant has received a fair warning that the landlord will do so or in case of an emergency.

For example, if you see water seeping out of the house in the general vicinity of the bathroom, you may reasonably suspect a water leak, which is an emergency, and you can legally enter the house right then, without providing 24 hours notice. On the other hand, if you're simply curious to see whether your tenant's housekeeping skills are up to snuff by your standards, you must provide the notice.

Tenant Obligations and Terminating the Lease

In addition to paying the rent on time, a tenant must keep the premises as clean and safe as possible, including disposing of all garbage and other waste. The tenant must do all that is possible to keep appliances and other facilities in good working condition.

Generally, a tenant cannot use the premises for anything other than for housing—the landlord must approve any other use. Any other use must be approved by the landlord. The tenant must also notify the landlord of any extended absences from the premises.

Non-Payment of Rent

The tenant must pay rent when it is due. When and *if a tenant fails to pay rent* in a timely manner, your *first step* as a landlord will be to *serve* a *three-day notice to pay rent or quit (leave the premises)*. If another three days then passes with no payment of rent, your *second step* is to begin the *eviction process*.

A written notice must be *personally served*, hand-to-hand, so the tenant cannot claim that a legally required notice was not given.

On the other hand, if you've served a three-day notice, and the tenant has showed up within the three days and paid the *full rent, plus any necessary associated costs and fees* that came out of your pocket, then you must accept it and allow the tenant to stay. If it happens again, it is important to note that any time a tenant is late with the rent, a new three-day notice to cure or quit must be served.

If you allow the tenant to remain on the property without paying rent for 30 days, you take the risk that you could lose your ability to file a *forcible entry and detainer action*. However, a claim for the *rent* can still be made in New York *small claims court* if it is less then $5,000.

Terminating the Lease

When the landlord gives *written notice of termination and notice to quit*, the documents must be *served* on the tenant personally. To terminate a rental agreement, whether the party terminating it is the landlord or tenant, notice of termination must be given an appropriate amount of time, as set forth in New York law,

Let's say rent is due on the 1st day of the month in a month-to-month lease. If you serve a 30-day notice on March 15th, the tenant has until April 30th to leave the premises (not April 15th).

before the anticipated date of termination. For month-to-month leases (or subleases), notice should be given 30 days end of term.

If a *lease is for a one-year period or more* and *notice of termination is not timely* given to the tenant, the lease will be *automatically renewed*. In other words, the tenant will continue the lease on the same terms as before, except that the tenancy will then become a *month-to-month* tenancy. Therefore, if a one year or longer lease term is coming to an end, and the landlord doesn't want to continue renting to the current tenant, it is important to make sure that notice of termination is given to the other party at least thirty (30) days in advance of the termination date.

Eviction Proceedings

There are different eviction procedures in New York depending on whether you are dealing with a holdover or nonpayment proceeding. When seeking to reclaim possession, the landlord must first decide which type of summary proceeding to initiate. If the party occupying the property is no longer a "tenant," the landlord should commence a *"holdover" proceeding*. Otherwise, a *"nonpayment"* proceeding is appropriate. A landlord should consult an attorney for help with this decision.

> In the above example, if your tenant is still on your property on May 1 after personally serving the notice on March 15, then he/she is a "holdover."

If you prevail on a *holdover action*, the court will issue a warrant to the sheriff directing him to *restore possession* to the petitioner. The official must give the occupants at least 72 hours notice before executing the warrant during daylight hours.

To protect yourself, you should either *videotape* the move-out or take *photographs* as you go along, including pictures of the tenant's personal property after removal. If items are expensive, it could be prudent to take photos before you ever touch the objects, as well, to avoid claims of unreasonable damage.

The tenant's possessions can only be removed to the *public right-of-way*. Under *no circumstances* should the tenant's possessions be left inside the property or taken to an offsite storage unit.

Beware of "Self-Help"

Self-help for a landlord is a bad idea. You *cannot* simply enter the premises and start moving the tenant's things out to the sidewalk, unless you have been through the appropriate legal steps to evict the tenant. If the tenant is still in possession of the rental unit past the date the court sets in the order.

> Note that **NY Real Property Actions and Proceedings Law** ("RPAPL") § 853 authorizes **treble damages** for wrongful entry or detainer, especially if violence or threats thereof are involved. For urban farmers and food entrepreneurs in New York City, please note that a wrongful eviction from residential lease may be considered a Class A misdemeanor in some circumstances. See NYC Administrative Code § 26-521.

If the *tenant abandons* the rental property, the law gives you the right to seek new tenants. The first tenant's rental agreement is considered legally terminated on the date that the new tenants sign a lease.

A Landlord's Checklist

Here is a brief checklist, summarizing important matters that typically trip up a residential landlord:

- Always provide *24-hour notice* prior to entering the rental unit, except in emergencies.

- In a month-to-month or longer lease, give at least thirty (30) days' notice of termination of the lease *from the end of the term*. Let's say a month-to-month lease ends on the last day of the month. Timely notice for a lease ending on October 31 would be on or before September 30 the month before.

- A one-year lease does not simply terminate; the landlord must *give thirty (30) days' notice* if he or she will not be continuing the lease agreement, or it will renew automatically.

- A written agreement cannot be changed unless the parties agree upon the changes. This includes an *increase in rent*.

- If the landlord wants to increase the rent at the expiration of the lease term, he or she must provide *thirty (30) days' notice* of termination and rewrite and execute a new lease, with the new terms.

- Failure to pay rent should result in a *three-day notice* being served on the tenant in every situation. Do not let a tenant slide, or you could lose the ability to collect for that month.

> Your tenant fails to pay July rent, but you don't serve a three-day notice to quit. In August, the tenant again fails to pay rent, so you serve a three-day notice to quit, hoping to force payment of rent for both July and August. Your tenant will not be required by law to pay the July rent in order to cure the defect.

- When serving the tenant with any notice, do it in person with a witness or *hire a process server* to do it.

- *Get everything in writing* and make sure all parties are aware of their responsibilities.

- If the landlord is *retaining any of the deposit*, then the landlord is required to provide a written explanation to the tenant within 30 days. Failure to do so will terminate the landlord's rights to the deposit.

Leasing Animals

Bull Leases

As noted in the Chapter on Contracts, agreements can be made for one head of livestock. To illustrate this, here are some terms to think about in your bull lease between the bull owner (the lessor) and cow man who will be leasing the bull (the lessee):

- **Term:** The term of the breeding season should be listed (e.g., March 1 to June 30, July 1 to September 1).

- **Number of Bulls**: Note the number of bulls leased from the lessor plus any other bulls leased from other cattlemen during the breeding season.

- **Payment**: The lease should note the amount owed, due date, payment instructions, type of payment accepts, interest and/or penalties for late payments. In some cases, the bull owner may request a deposit be made on the bull that will be returned upon the safe return of the animal to his/her farm or ranch.

- **Bull Owner Representations**: The lessee may request that certain representations be made such as bull health, body condition score, fertility, breed registration, pedigree, structural soundness, libido, genetic DNA markers, strength with *Expected Progeny Differences* ("EPD's"). If genetic DNA markers are relied upon by the lessor, there should be clause indicating that the bull owner is not liable if the genetic testing company made a mistake.

- **Lessee Representations on Cow Herd**: The lessor may request the certain representations be made such as herd health, fertility (especially if there is a penalty for low conception rates), and number of cows that the bull(s).

- **Health**: It might be appropriate to add more detail about the health of the bull and the cow herd of the lessee including health certification from a licensed veterinarian or special tests that need to be performed.

- **Delivery of Bull to Cow Herd**: Who will pick-up and/or drop-off the bull(s) and payment for same? Will there be a penalty for late pick-up or drop off after the breeding season? How will the bulls be transported?

- **Movement of Bull from Lessee's Farm**: Will the lessee farmer or rancher be allowed to move the bull during the lease term?

- **Death, Injury or Illness of the Bull**: who will be liable for the death or injury of the bull (i) before the lease date, (ii) during transportation or (iii) during the breeding season term? The bull owner should be promptly notified in these instances, including if the bull is missing.

- **Injuries to People**: The lease should discuss potential liability (and indemnification) from an injury to a family member, farm employee, farm visitor or child from the bull.

- **Insurance**: Will either party be required to carry insurance?

- **Performance**: The lessee farmer or rancher may wish to be compensated if the bull has a breeding rate under a predetermined level. If this provision is added, it is important that the lessor have a provision relating to conditions such as a drought, weather extremes or deficient grazing that may affect the bull's performance.

- **Management**: The lessee should promise to use *good management practices*, proper animal handling techniques.

- **Feed and Nutrition**: The lessee cattlemen should provide the bull(s) with *adequate feed and dietary supplements*. Any special feed or nutrition requirements should be memorialized. The bull(s) should not be allowed to be returned to the owner in state of malnutrition. In this instance, the lease should explain what the lessee's responsibility or liability would be (e.g., payment for veterinary expenses and or feed during the recovery period).

- **Right of Inspection**: Will the bull owner have the *right to inspect the bull* during the breeding term at the lessee's farm or ranch?

- **Ownership of Bull**: The lease should specifically state that the title and registration papers, if applicable, will remain with the bull owner to prevent a later dispute about ownership.

- **Option to Purchase**: On that note, the lease may provide an option for the lessee to purchase the bull at the end of the term at a mutually agreed upon price. Perhaps the lessee is only given the option of first refusal to purchase the bull for 30 days after the termination of the lease.

- **Title of Progeny**: The lease should specifically state that the lessee owns the progeny sired by the bull and that no profits are to be shared from their sale.

- **Relationship of the Parties**: The bull lease should specifically state that the parties are not forming a partnership or joint venture.

- **Termination**: The lease should include a provision allowing either party to terminate the bull lease with adequate notice with certain conditions.

- **Confidentiality**: In every contract between cattlemen, including bull leases, the parties should ask themselves whether there is any information that they may wish to remain secret (e.g., payment terms). This is sometimes addressed in a separate Non-Disclosure Agreements (See Chapter 5).

- **Choice of Law**: Contract law is state law so it is especially important to address this if the contract is between cattlemen across state or country lines.

- **Dispute Resolution**: In every contract, it's prudent to consider how the parties would like to resolve any disputes that may arise between them (e.g., non-binding mediation, binding arbitration, and/or choice of court forum) and whether a prevailing party should pay for attorneys' fees. If the parties select a method of *Alternative Dispute Resolution* such as mediation or arbitration, the parties should still be able to get to court *in an emergency*.

Horse Leases

There are many different types of leases for mares, geldings, and stallions. Generally speaking, you might also enumerate *payment for shoeing*, using the *horse's farrier*, or *training expenses*. It may also be important to have a provision stated that the lessee does not have the right to sub-lease the horse and that *no other riders* are authorized to ride the horse unless expressly agreed upon in writing. Provisions pertaining to the *care of the horse*, especially hoof care, are important to memorialize in the contract. It's recommended that the horse lease specify that the horse is to stay at the *stable location* or *farm* absent express written permission. Insurance is particularly important in the horse industry so the lease should specify the burden to have *mortality insurance*, major medical insurance or loss of use insurance.

Additionally, the lessor may also request a provision indicating that he or she is not responsible for injuries resulting from elements of nature that can *scare a horse* such as thunder, lightening, rain, wind, wild and domestic animals, insects and reptiles. If the horse will be used for *horse-back riding*, perhaps the lessor should be responsible for injuries resulting from *irregular footing* on particularly *rough terrain*.

Other Livestock Leases

There are countless number of leases that involve livestock ranging from a *breeding male* like a bull, boar, ram, or stallion to allowing a livestock producer to *rent pasture on farmland*. In the seedstock industry, one livestock producer may allow another producer to lease particular animals and *travel with them* around the *show circuit* to help with marketing.

No matter the transaction (big or small), it's important to think through the details and what should be memorialized in the agreement. Remember—contracts are not about whether you trust to the other person. To the contrary, it's about *risk management* and ensuring everyone involved in the transaction is on the same page.

Leasing Farm Equipment

Farmers lag behind other industries in renting equipment instead of owning it (16 percent versus 32 percent), in spite of the many benefits of leasing equipment, which include tax deductibility of the payment, cash flow, keeping up with the latest technology, and not clouding the balance sheet with another asset and liability. Many modern farm operations are catching on to the fact that leasing equipment can make sense under the right circumstances. For example, equipment leases may be the best option for farm operations in situations like these:

- When you only need the equipment for a *short period of time* or it will be obsolete in a few years;

- When your ability to *deduct the cost of purchase* is limited by income and other deduction rules; or

- When at the end of a projected use period, the equipment will have *low residual value*.

Beware of Lease-To-Own Contracts

If, at the end of the term, the piece of equipment can be bought for little to no cost or can be bought for a set price that is not related to its residual value, it may be treated as a *disguised sale* by the IRS. Other warning signs include having a lease period that exceeds *75 percent of the useful life* of the item or having the lease payments equal nearly the cost of acquisition. The IRS has a rule called the *20/20 Test* to help it determine if the lease is truly a sale. The 20/20 Test comes from ensuring that *20 percent value remains* in the equipment at then end of the lease and at least *20 percent of the useful life* of the equipment remains at the end of the lease. Having the IRS determine how an item is treated for taxes is rarely a good thing for the tax filer.

Additional Resources

Don Pershing and J.H. Atkinson, "Figuring Rent for Existing Farm Buildings" Publication No. EC-451 available at http://www.extension.purdue.edu/extmedia/EC/EC-451-W.html (last visited May 19, 2013).

Iowa State University Cooperative Extension, "Improving Your Farm

Lease Contract" File C2-01, FM 1564 (June 2011) available http://www.extension.iastate.edu/Publications/FM1564.pdf (last visited May 19, 2013).

Erin Herbold-Swalwell, "Farm Leases" National Business Institute Webinar (August 6, 2013) available for purchase at http://www.nbi-sems.com/ (August 17, 2013).

Iowa State University Cooperative Extension, "Lease Alternatives for CRP Land" available at http://www.extension.iastate.edu/Publications/CRP2.pdf (last visited May 19, 2013).

James Oltjen, Daniel Drake and Mark Nelson, "Beef Cow Share Lease Arrangements" available at http://ag.arizona.edu/arec/pubs/rmg/6%20ranchbusinessmanagement/53%20beefcowsharelease96.pdf (last visited May 19, 2013).

J.H. Atkinson and David C. Petritz, "Pasture Leases" available at http://www.extension.purdue.edu/extmedia/EC/EC-623.html (last visited May 19, 2013).

Jason Foscolo, "The Sustainable Lease Agreement, a Legal Tool for Land Stewardship," Cornell Small Farms Program available at http://smallfarms.cornell.edu/2013/01/07/the-sustainable-lease-agreement-a-legal-tool-for-land-stewardship (last visited July 11, 2013).

JULIE I. FERSHTMAN, EQUINE LAW & HORSE SENSE (1996) and MORE EQUINE LAW AND HORSE SENSE (2000).

Kelly Phillip Erb, "TaxGirl" Blog at Forbes.com, at http://www.taxgirl.com (last visited July 11, 2013).

LeeAnn E. Moss and Bernie Erven, "Managing Landlord-Tenant Relationships: A Strategic Perspective" Publication FR-0004-01, available at http://ohioline.osu.edu/fr-fact/0004.html (last visited May 19, 2013).

National Agriculture Law Center's Reading Room for Agriculture Leases available at http://nationalaglawcenter.org/readingrooms/agleases/ (last visited May 19, 2013).

New York Farm Bureau, "Farmer's Guide to Oil & Gas Leases," available for purchase at
http://www.nyfb.org/legal/NYFB_s_Legal_Library_54_pg.htm (last visited July 17, 2013).

New York Civil Court, "How to Prepare for a Landlord-Tenant Trial" (May 2006) available at
http://www.nycourts.gov/publications/L&TPamphlet.pdf and "Housing (Landlord-Tenant)" FAQ, at
http://www.nycourts.gov/courthelp/faqs/housing.html (last visited August 17, 2013).

University of Nebraska-Lincoln Department of Agriculture Economics, "Farm Lease Calculator" available
http://agecon.unl.edu/resource/farmcalc.html (last visited May 19, 2013).

Rusty Rumley, "Agricultural Contracts and the Leasing of Land" available at
http://nationalaglawcenter.org/assets/articles/rumley_contractsandleases-ppt.pdf (last visited May 19, 2013).

Rusty Rumley, "Bull Leasing Contracts" available at
http://nationalaglawcenter.org/assets/articles/rrumley_bullleasing.pdf (last visited May 19, 2013).

University of California Cooperative Extension, "Farm Leases and Rents" available
http://sfp.ucdavis.edu/pubs/Family_Farm_Series/Farmmanage/leases/ (last visited May 19, 2013).

University of Georgia Cooperative Extension, "How Do You Negotiate an Equitable Crop-Share Lease?" available at
http://www.ces.uga.edu/Agriculture/agecon/pubs/equitable.htm (last visited May 19, 2013).

U.S. Department of Agriculture, "Your Cash Farm Lease" Miscellaneous Publication No. 836 available at
http://www.montana.edu/extensionecon/dynamicsinag/cashfarmleasepub836.pdf (last visited May 19, 2013).

Cari B. Rincker & Patrick B. Dillon

CHAPTER 7

FARM ANIMAL LAW

Animals are at the core of many New York farm operations -- even the grain farmer is likely to have a few animals or a farm dog around. Furthermore, most farmers are bound to encounter wild animals that impact the operation. There are a myriad of laws that affect domestic, companion and wild animals at the state and federal level. In particular, New York livestock producers should understand farm animal welfare law in New York and what they can do to build a defense today.

Livestock Animal Welfare Law

This section gives an overview of livestock animal welfare in New York. Livestock animal cruelty is a *crime* – each of the below violations are either a misdemeanor or felony in New York and should be taken very seriously. Farms that have issues with livestock animal cruelty should work with both an *agriculture* and *criminal* lawyer creating a powerful legal team with complementary knowledge bases.

Abandonment of Animals

Section 355 makes it a misdemeanor to *abandon* an animal or "leave it to die in a street, road or public place" or allow a *disabled animal* to lie in a public place for more than three hours once he/she receives notice that it has been left disabled.

129

28-Hour Law

There is a *28-Hour Law* at both the federal and state level. When transporting animals for more than 28 hours, livestock must be given five consecutive hours of rest along with available food and water. Therefore, if you are transporting horses from Buffalo, New York to Phoenix, Arizona, make sure to plan for *adequate* rest for the animals after a day on the road.

Poisoning Animals

Poisoning farm animals is a crime in New York. *Farmers do not need to know that the substance itself is poisonous* as long as he/she intended for the livestock to be exposed to the substance. This includes toxic levels of drugs that would otherwise be beneficial. Livestock producers should work closely with a veterinarian to avoid an accidental overdose.

Selling Diseased Animals

It is a crime in New York to willfully sell any horse or livestock "animal having the disease known as glanders or farcy, or other *contagious or infectious disease* dangerous to the life or health of human beings, or animals. . ." See N.Y. Agric. & Mkts Law § 357.

Horses

There are a statutory provisions in the New York Agric. & Mtks Act specific to horse breeders. Under Section 359-a(1), every vehicle utilized for the transportation of more than six horses shall meet the following requirements:

- The interiors of compartments containing horses shall be constructed of *smooth materials*, containing no sharp objects or protrusions which are hazardous;

- The floors shall be of such construction or covered with *abrasive material* so as to prevent horses from skidding or sliding;

- There shall be sufficient apertures to insure *adequate ventilation*;

- There shall be *sufficient insulation or covering* to maintain an adequate temperature in the compartment containing horses;

- *Partitions* of sturdy construction shall be placed a *maximum of ten feet apart* in vehicles which do not have stalls;

- *Doorways* shall be of sufficient height to allow *safe ingress and egress* of each horse contained in the compartment;

- Each compartment containing horses shall allow for *sufficient clearance* above the poll and withers of each horse in the compartment;

- *Ramps sufficient for loading* and unloading horses shall be provided if the vertical distance from the floor of the compartment containing horses to the ground is greater than fifteen inches; and

- There shall be at least *two doorways* for ingress and egress which shall not be on the same side.

Additionally, if you are transporting more than *six horses* on a highway then the horse trailer cannot have more than *one tier*.

Furthermore, it is a misdemeanor for a horse owner to *cut* the "bone, tissues, muscles or tendons of the tail of any horse, mare or gelding, or otherwise operates upon it in any manner for the purpose …of docking, setting or otherwise altering the natural carriage of the tail…" See N.Y. Agric. & Mkts Law § 368(1).

Under section 358, it is crime in New York for any person holding an *auctioneer's license* to willfully *sell a disabled horse* to another person that could not be worked without violating the animal cruelty statute. It is important for horse breeders to work with their veterinarian when they might suspect a potential issue.

Misdemeanor vs. Felony Animal Cruelty

There are several animal welfare crimes in New York offering misdemeanor liability for offenders. In New York, a person guilty of a misdemeanor may be imprisoned for one year or less and/or receive a $1,000 fine. If animals are seized then the producer will be liable for the reasonable costs to care for those animals. The only animal welfare crime with felony liability is *Buster's Law*, discussed below. Felonies are punishable by imprisonment (two years or less for each count).

Failure to Provide Adequate Food, Water, Shelter & Veterinary Care

The primary animal cruelty law in New York placing misdemeanor liability on livestock producers for the neglect of their farm animals provides the following:

> A person who overdrives, overloads, tortures or cruelly beats or **unjustifiably** injures, maims, mutilates or kills **any animal**, whether wild or tame, and whether belonging to himself or to another, or **deprives any animal of necessary sustenance, food or drink, or neglects or refuses to furnish it such sustenance** or drink, or causes, procures or permits any animal to be overdriven, overloaded, tortured, cruelly beaten, or unjustifiably injured, maimed, mutilated or killed, or to be deprived of necessary food or drink, or who willfully sets on foot, instigates, engages in, or in any way furthers any act of cruelty to any animal, or any act tending to produce such cruelty, is guilty of a class A misdemeanor . . . .

See N.Y. Agric. & Markets Law § 353 (emphasis added).

New York courts have interpreted the term *"sustenance"* to include *shelter and veterinary care*. Put simply, the misdemeanor animal cruelty statute in New York requires livestock producer to give the animals *necessary* food, water, shelter and veterinary care. Please note that this statutory provision applies to *all animals* including livestock, horses, and dogs.

Failure to Provide Food or Drink to an Impounded or Confined Animal

Under NY Agriculture & Markets Law § 356, persons caring for *"impounded or confined"* farm animals must ensure the livestock have a "sufficient supply of good and *wholesome air, food, shelter and water"* or they will be subject to misdemeanor criminal liability. The statute also allows the public to enter onto the property and supply adequate food and water if that person believes the animal has gone 12 successive hours without necessary food and water.

"Buster's Law": Aggravated Animal Cruelty

Buster's Law, which places *felony liability* for *companion animal cruelty* (excluding horses), rarely applies to livestock producers. Buster's Law defines "aggravated cruelty" as an action: (i) to cause **"extreme physical pain"** or (ii) that is **"especially depraved or sadistic."** N.Y. Agric. & Markets Law § 353-a. Livestock producers should be primarily concerned with misdemeanor liability for the failure to provide "necessary" food, drink, shelter and veterinary care pursuant to Section 353 as this provision only applies to companion animals.

> Buster was a cat whose owner poured kerosene on him and lit a match. These are the kinds of depraved acts that the statute proscribes. Stabbing a horse to death might be considered aggravated animal cruelty.

"Peace Officers" May Search and Seize Farm Animals

In New York, duly incorporated animal societies, principally the *New York Society Preventing Animal Cruelty* ("SPCA"), are able to obtain warrants as "peace officers" to search a farm upon showing reasonable cause to a magistrate that there has been a violation to the New York animal cruelty law. It can be confusing for New York livestock producers to know to handle visits from non-police officers. Since *"peace officers"* can search and seize livestock with a valid warrant, New York livestock producers are encouraged to seek legal counsel and take the following steps to protect their constitutional rights when a non-police officer would like to visit the farm:

1. **Ask for Identification**: The New York SPCA has similar authority with the search and seizure of farm animals in New York as police officers. Members from other animal societies may not have this same authority.

2. **Ask for the Warrant**: If the visitors to your property do not have a warrant, you have the right to ask them to leave. If they do not cooperate then you may contact your local law enforcement.

3. **Read the Warrant**: If the visitors have a warrant, then please take time to carefully read the warrant. Pay special attention to the scope of the warrant. For example, if the warrant is to investigate potentially abused dogs in the backyard, then the peace officers should not investigate horses in your barn.

> When dealing with a member of the SPCA **without a warrant**, farms should treat them like a **police officer** without a warrant. Sometimes, **cooperation is best policy**. Farms should discuss various scenarios with an attorney to develop a strategy and train employees accordingly.

4. **Ask if the Visitor Has Camera/Video Equipment**: If you decide to let visitors on your property without a warrant, ask if the visitors have camera/video equipment, including but not limited to smartphones. Peace officers have the ability to use camera/video equipment during their search. If the visitors do not have a warrant then you have a right to ask them to leave all cameras and smartphone equipment in their vehicle.

5. **Take Notes During the Farm Inspection**: Write down the *date, time*, names of the visitors, what organization the visitors are from, whether there was a warrant, what was inspected, and when the visitors left. Note whether there were any changes or *damages*

made to the property (e.g., feed pans knocked over, livestock locked away from access to water) and the *condition of the animals that were inspected* (e.g., visual indicators of sickness, approximate body condition score, signs of heat or stress).

> Smartphones can make it easy to take notes on the fly; however, if you do not have a smartphone then you have the right to slow down the inspection process for you to get an old fashioned pad of paper. Don't be afraid to ask for time to get writing utensils.

Furthermore, it is imperative that New York livestock producers have a relationship with an attorney that they know and trust. With the help of your attorney, *memorialize a farm protocol* for how to react to farm visitors—whether they are police officers, members of the New York SPCA, or from the general public. Said protocol should be incorporated in the farm's employee handbook and employees should be trained accordingly.

Your attorney will be the one who you call to defend you against farm animal cruelty charges so he/she must help you plan a defense strategy before an issue arises. To illustrate, livestock owners should have a working relationship with a veterinarian and a *Cornell University Extension Specialist*. Compliance with their recommendations should be documented.

In addition, it is prudent that livestock owners not only keep accurate feeding, breeding, and health records but livestock farmers should also participate in voluntary livestock animal welfare programs (e.g., *New York State Cattle Health Assurance Program* ("NYSCHAP")). Let your attorney counsel you as to the proper strategy for your specific situation.

Five Defensive Moves

Livestock producers must take the following *preemptive steps* to help build a defense against animal cruelty charges and mitigate the likelihood of being prosecuted:

1. **Document Compliance With Animal Care Recommendations**: New York livestock owners should have

a good working relationship with Cornell University extension specialists, nutritionists, veterinarians, and other livestock experts. Conduct regular farm visits with these experts to ensure your livestock are properly cared for. Document these visits and any recommendations given to you. Keep a record of noted improvements and observations. Archive these records in a place that is protected against a natural disaster.

2. **Follow Animal Care Guidelines**: Many livestock commodity groups have voluntary programs that livestock operations can participate in. NYSDAM also has some voluntary programs for horse breeders and other livestock producers (e.g., NYSCHAP). With the counsel of experts, livestock operations could also develop their own animal care handbook used internally on the farm. Furthermore, livestock owners should train farm employees in proper animal care and handling. It is recommended that proper animal handling techniques be memorialized in the employee handbook.

3. **Prohibit Farm Employees from Using Video Cameras**: In an employment contract, livestock owners may require employees to agree that they will not bring any recording devices on the farm. This would help reduce the likelihood that undercover employees would distribute an edited video shedding a false light on a livestock operation while giving the producer legal recourse if an employee does so. There is no "Ag Gag" law in New York.

4. **Use Media To Tell Your Story**: Farmers are encouraged to participate in social media like Facebook, Twitter, and blogs and work with local radio stations and newspapers to help educate the public on proper farm animal care. Update your farm's website and post pictures and videos putting your livestock operation in a positive light.

5. **Talk to Your Community About Your Livestock Operation**: Get involved in your community and help educate the general public on your farm's sound production practices.

By following these recommendations, New York livestock producers can reduce the likelihood that they will be prosecuted criminally for farm animal cruelty while helping to bridge the gap of understanding between livestock producers and consumers.

Highway Accidents Involving Livestock

In some situations, the owner of livestock or horses could be liable for personal injuries or property damage resulting in a highway accident between an animal and a driver. If the court finds that your animals had a propensity (or past-history) to wander onto public highways, then you might be *strictly liable* for those damages. However, if a court applies a *negligence* theory to your case, then the owner will be liable if he/she had reason to know of the animal's propensity to wander onto the highway and failed to take **reasonable steps** to prevent it.

Many Western states are *"fence-out"* states -- i.e., the property owner has the duty to "fence out" livestock from their property (or at least some types of livestock such as cattle and bison). When driving through Wyoming, Colorado, and New Mexico, a driver in a rural area might see a cattle crossing sign or a warning that livestock may be on the highway. Midwestern and Eastern states (like New York) take a diametrically opposite view due to our more dense population-- we have *"fence-in"* laws where livestock owners have the affirmative duty to "fence in" their livestock on their property.

If you have an issue with livestock that repeatedly wander off your property, you should speak to a professional, such as a Cornell Cooperative Extension Specialist. Once proper fencing is installed, a livestock owner should periodically inspect the fencing to note any breakage or gaps that need repair.

Bees

You're required to register your apiaries with NYSDAM, which can help avoid accidental damage to your hives by pesticide applications from other operations. In addition, all hive owners must post a conspicuous sign providing notice of where the beehives are and contact information (in order to protect them), as well as the beekeeper's identification number. Also, beekeepers may not keep an infected colony and must report any infection, infestation, or exposure of colonies in their control to NYSDAM.

If you are applying pesticides to your own property and you have neighbors who keep bees, be aware of the damage that can be caused by pesticide drift from your operations. Pesticides must be used in such a manner as to prevent contamination to adjacent lands. Before applying pesticides, you must provide at least 48 hours' notice to abutting property owners. The notice must include any warnings – including any potential risks to bees – listed on the pesticide label.

Beekeepers in New York may be subject to *tort liability*. In People v. McOmber, 206 Misc. 465, 469-470 (NY Sup. Ct., Lewis Co. 1954) the court held that honey bees may be kept but the owner has the duty to keep the bees so that they do not "annoy, injure or endanger the comfort, repose, health or safety of any considerable number of persons or to render a considerable number of persons insecure in the use of their property." See generally Patricia Salkin in the American Bar Association's webinar "Counseling the Local Food Movement" (May 2012).

Companion Animals

Dogs

A *dog owner* is liable for the action of his/her dog. Don't post "Beware of Dog" signs; believe it or not, if your dog was to *injure someone*, such signs might be used against you in court, as an admission that you knew you were dealing with a problem animal. Your best advice is to *control your animals*. You may *kill* a dog that is *attacking or attempting to bite a human being*; however, you may not use any more force than is reasonably necessary to repel the imminent attack.

Every dog must have a *rabies* vaccination. The law requires that a dog receive its first rabies vaccination no later than four months (three months in New York City) after its *date of birth*. The second vaccination (i.e., the first booster shot) must be within *one year* of the first. Subsequently, dogs must receive booster shots at least annually or every three years depending on the type of vaccine administered. Any dog, cat or other animal which has *bitten or attacked* a person must be *reported*. If rabies is suspected, animal-control officials can order the owner to *confine* the animal or it can be *impounded* by animal-control officials, who can hold the dog for *ten (10) days* and may then humanely destroy it. If the dog is returned to its owner, the owner must *pay fees* for impoundment.

Anyone who keeps or harbors a dog can be held strictly liable if the dog causes injury to another person. You do not have to own the dog or even be negligent in order to be liable. Instead, plaintiffs can recover from injuries sustained as a result of a dog bite simply by showing that: (1) the dog that bit the victim had a *vicious propensity*, and (2) the persons who harbored the dog or otherwise exercised dominion over it had *knowledge* of the dog's propensity or, in the alternative, a *reasonably prudent person* would have discovered it. See Palumbo v. Nikirk, 59 A.D.3d 691, 874 N.Y.S.2d 222 (2d Dep't 2009); Gannon ex rel. Gannon v. Conti, 86 A.D.3d 704, 926 N.Y.S.2d 739 (3d Dep't 2011). You could also be held liable for damages to other property caused by your dog, if you allow it to run loose in violation of the law.

New York Pet Shop Lemon Law

Article 35-D of the *New York General Business Law* ("GBL") governs the sale of cats and dogs. It is colloquially referred to as "*The Pet Shop Lemon Law*." Section 753(1) gives purchasers a remedy if within fourteen (14) days of the purchase of the cat or dog a licensed veterinarian officially certifies that the companion animal was "unfit for purchase" due to illness, congenital malformation or disease. This certificate from the vet is required for relief under the NY Pet Shop Lemon Law. If you are in the animal hospital within two weeks of purchase, ask the veterinarian for this certificate.

If the vet does certify the pet as being "*unfit for purchase*", then the purchaser has three different options under section 753(1):

- the right to return the animal and *receive a refund*;

- the right to return the animal and *receive a replacement animal*; or

- the right to retain the animal and be reimbursed for *reasonable veterinary costs* for the purposing of curing the pet.

New York courts have held that the *veterinary costs cannot exceed the purchase price of the animal*. Additionally, there are also potential causes of action against the pet shop for deceptive trade practices, false advertising, fraudulent/negligent misrepresentation and common law contract claims. However, from a practical standpoint, NY Pet Shop Lemon Law claims are oftentimes in *small claims court.*

Wild Animals

Game Animals

Farmers are just like any other citizen, when it comes to the rules of the *New York Department of Environmental Conservation* ("DEC"). These rules include *Big Game Hunting Regulations*, and a farmer must obey New York hunting rules for game animals. Even if the farm provides the lion's share of the food for most of the game animals in question, the farmer gets no special treatment.

The number of deer a hunter may take depends on which licenses and privileges the hunter has purchased. Check your paperwork for deer type tag and privilege information, including details on the length of hunting season. Hunters may also apply for a *Deer Management Permit* ("DMP") which allows them to take one antlerless deer per permit, in addition to deer that may be taken with other types of big game tags.

Don't carry a loaded shotgun or other firearm in your combine – it's just a bad idea. Aside from the obvious potential for firearm accidents, you may be violating both *game laws* and *criminal laws*. Your combine is a *motor vehicle* and the rules that affect carrying firearms in motor vehicles apply to you, even if you are only going 5 mph.

Endangered Species

When it comes to animals that belong to an *endangered species*, most people know that you cannot shoot, capture, or kill one of them, but many are not aware that you cannot modify the environmental situation or habitat of an endangered species, which will have the same effect as killing them. In fact, you are never allowed to hunt with the aid of bait or over any baited area when hunting big game, upland game birds, turkey or waterfowl.

Certain types of *big game* – including deer, bears, and turkeys –

must be reported to DEC when harvested. The harvest must be reported within seven (7) days. You can now report your harvest either by telephone or through the web.

Disposal of Dead Animals

Death loss is part of the livestock operation. Owners of dead animals have *72 hours* to dispose of the carcass in a *sanitary manner*. Sanitary disposal is the owners' responsibility whether the carcass is located on the owners' premises or elsewhere. Animals must be buried at least three feet below ground. Do not discard the carcass of an animal in a body of water.

Veterinarians

Veterinarians provide a crucial service to any livestock operation; however, vets are human and sometimes make mistakes. If you're disgruntled over a mistake made by your vet and you think you'd like to sue him or her, you should consider the fact that you will face two main challenges with *veterinary malpractice cases*:

- It is hard to find a veterinarian who will testify against another veterinarian (but you can be sure that every vet within 100 miles will find out that you sued a vet); and

- *Animals are personal property*. You usually cannot recover pain and suffering or damages based on sentimental value.

If you're not dissuaded, then it's still up to you to prove veterinary malpractice. The burden of proof in a veterinary malpractice action is always on the plaintiff. In order to win, you'll have to be able to prove each of following *four elements*:

- A veterinarian's acts or omissions failed to meet the *standard of care*;

- Acts or omissions were *negligently performed*;

- Negligently performed acts or injuries caused the *animal's injury or death*; and

- As a result, the *plaintiff was damaged*.

See <u>Akins v. Glens Falls City School District</u>, 53 N.Y.2d 325, 333, 441 N.Y.S.2d 644, 648, 424 N.E.2d 531, 535 (1981).

The professional duty of a veterinarian usually begins with *obtaining a history of the animal* (which assistants can be used to develop) and a *physical examination*. The veterinarian is required to use professional learning, skill, and care, during the initial contact, the diagnosis of the problem, the decision and execution of treatment, and follow-up care.

The vet's act has to have *caused injury or death*. If you are calling a vet, the animal is likely sick already. You have to establish that the vet's act is the reason for the injury or death, not just that the steer died when the vet gave it a shot.

Other *miscellaneous legal considerations* that may be used against vets include:

- **Res ipsa loquitur:** This Latin phrase translates to, *"the thing speaks for itself,"* and legally, it is used to mean that some mistakes are so obvious that the average person can figure out that the vet was responsible.

- **Administrative Action for Malpractice:** A person may file an action against a veterinarian with the state administrative licensing board that oversees veterinarians. This action is not likely to result in compensation for damages to the complaining party unless clearly demonstrated.

- **Negligence:** If the actions in question are not within the realm of malpractice, then there may be common negligence. For example, if a veterinarian was overseeing the loading of a bull into a head gate and did not properly secure the head gate, the standard of care is that of regular negligence. Since you don't have to be a vet to load a bull into a gate, the claim would not be one for professional negligence, or malpractice.

- **"Bailment" Law:** When a veterinarian *boards* or *transports* animals, the vet is acting as a *"bailee"* of an animal, which may give rise to a claim for negligent care of the animal while in custody. This is like when you give your coat to a coat-check. You aren't giving the coat away permanently, and you expect it to be returned in about the same condition that you gave it to them. For example, an insured veterinarian was bailee of an horse who died from poison while in his custody. A claim based upon a bailment does not require an expert witness, making it more practical and cheaper to pursue. However, just because the animal dies or is injured while in the custody of a vet doesn't make the vet liable for the death.

Fixing "Broken Windows" On Your Farm

On a final note, to help prevent farm animal welfare issues, livestock producers should fix "broken windows" on their farm. The Broken Windows theory can be used to help the public image of livestock producers.

In way of background, on page 141 in the book "Tipping Point", Malcolm Gladwell describes the **"Broken Windows"** theory as follows:

> Broken Windows was the brainchild of the criminologists James Q. Wilson and George Kelling. Wilson and Kelling argued that crime is the inevitable result of disorder. If a *window is broken* and left unrepaired, people walking by will conclude that *no one cares* and *no one is in charge*. Soon, more windows will be broken, and the sense of anarchy will spread from the buildings to the street on which it faces, sending a signal that anything goes. In a city, *relatively minor problems* like graffiti, public disorder, and aggressive panhandling, they write, are all the equivalent of broken windows, *invitations to more serious crimes*[.]

(Emphasis added).

The removal of graffiti from the streets and subway cars of New York City was a long process, extending from 1984 to 1990. Subway turnstiles were fixed to deter fare-beating while encouraging enforcement. Then in 1994, Mayor Giuliani was elected, and Chief Bratton at the *New York Police Department* ("NYPD") instructed his officers to crack down on *"quality-of-life"* crimes such as the "squeegee men," who came up to drives at intersections washing their windows and demanded a tip, and folks who urinated in public – you know, the *petty crimes*.

And guess what happened? Crime rate in NYC significantly decreased. To explain, in 1992, there were 2,154 murders in New York City and 626,182 serious crimes; but after the "tipping point", murders dropped 64.3% (to 770) and total crime dropped by almost 50% (355,893). It's really quite profound when you think about how those "little things" made such a powerful difference in the reduction of serious crimes. Gladwell explains that the "Broken Windows" theory and the "Power of Context" are one and the same. They are both based on the premise that "an epidemic can be reversed, can be tipped, by tinkering with the smallest details of the immediate environment."

So why does this matter for average New York farm families who are going about their lives trying to make a living off of the land? It is recommend that farms fix the "Broken Windows" on their farm as a preventative measure and a tool to build a positive public image. "Broken Windows" are the things that you *see all the time but don't think about* – but those "Broken Windows" may be giving negative messages to your neighbors and community about your farming operation. Here are some examples:

- **Online**: When is the last time you did a Google search on your farm? Do you need to clean up your online listing? Perhaps your farm needs a website that properly showcases its beauty and humane animal handling practices. It might be prudent to set up Google alerts for your farm and name to easily monitor things said about your farm/business online.

- **Your Property**: When is the last time you have driven around the periphery of your farm and really looked at it the way that general public sees it? Do your fence lines need to be fixed/mowed? Is there a pile of junk in your backyard that needs to be cleaned up? Do you have several sick animals near a public highway? When is the last time that you looked at your farm on Google Earth and viewed the aerial photo? This may also lend some ideas on how the property can be cleaned up for the public eye.

- **Your Reputation**: What is your reputation like in the local community? If an animal activist came to your hometown and asked people about your farm, what would be said? Are there things you can do to help build your reputation in your own local community? (e.g., sponsor a baseball team, volunteer for a civic organization, become a school board member, coach a soccer team, donate extra food to the local homeless shelter).

- **Your Paperwork**: Get your paperwork in order. Are you running your business as a DBA but have forgotten to file a Certificate of Assumed Name? Do you have farm employees and independent contractors sign an agreement prohibiting unauthorized photography or video? Has your limited liability company or corporation adhered to the corporate formality requirements in New York? Are you complying with federal and state environmental laws? Does your business have all the necessary permits? Is your farm property insured? These are just a few examples.

It's the little things that can have a *profound effect* on people and shape their impressions. To explain, the general public might draw the conclusion that the farmer who meticulously cares about his fence line likely takes good care of his/her animals, making sure they have adequate food and water. Alternatively, the dairy farm with a great online presence which *"opens its barn doors"* via social media is likely cognizant of the *animal handling techniques* used on the premises by its employees. The farm that remembers to follow through on legal formalities likely pays attention to details that matter to consumers. It's that kind of attention to detail and broken windows that can make the biggest difference for your farm and the agriculture community as a whole.

So, pay attention to *"broken windows"* on your farm. In the words of Malcolm Gladwell, they truly are the little things that make the big difference.

Additional Resources

Animal Agriculture Alliance, "Animal Welfare" information available at http://www.animalagalliance.org (last visited January 11, 2013).

Cari Rincker, "Overview of New York Livestock Law," Morrisville State College, December 4, 2012, slides available at http://www.slideshare.net/rinckerlaw/overview-of-new-york-livestock-law (last visited July 3, 2013.

Cari Rincker, "Using Social Media to Advocate for Agriculture," 4-H Workshop: Oneida County, New York (April 6, 2013), slides available at http://www.slideshare.net/rinckerlaw/using-social-media-to-advocate-for-agriculture (last visited July 3, 2013).

Cari Rincker, "When Activists Come Calling- Know Your Rights," 11 Annual Stakeholders Summit for Animal Agriculture Alliance in Washington, D.C. (May 3, 2012), slides available at http://www.slideshare.net/rinckerlaw/when-activists-come-calling-know-your-rights (last visited July 3, 2013).

Cari Rincker, "Finding the Right Balance: Technology vs. Tradition" New York Farm Bureau Young Farmers & Ranchers Leadership Conference (March 12, 2011), slides available at http://www.slideshare.net/rinckerlaw/technology-vs-tradition-finding-the-right-balance (last visited July 3, 2013).

Cari Rincker, Erica Beck, Sharon Breiner, Chelsea Good and Crystal Young, "How To Guide for Beef Bloggers" (February 2011) available at http://www.jdsupra.com/legalnews/how-to-guide-for-beef-bloggers-16667/ (last visited January 11, 2013).

Cari Rincker, Jessica Bussard, Chelsea Good, Matt Hardecke, Dani Heisler, Christopher Labbe, Sara Thissen, and Katy Wunsch, "How to Facebook Guide for the Beef Industry" (February 2011) available at http://www.jdsupra.com/legalnews/how-to-facebook-guide-for-the-beef-ind-16591/ (last visited January 11, 2013).

Jena Swanson, Jesse Bussard, Cari Rincker, Brandi Buzzard, and Katy Star, "How to Get LinkedIn: Guide for the Beef Industry" (November 2012) available at http://www.jdsupra.com/legalnews/how-to-get-linkedin-guide-for-the-beef-17213/ (last visited January 11, 2013).

Jena Swanson, Cari Rincker, Allen Livingston, Chris Labbe, and Sara Thissen, "How-To-Tweet-For-Beef Guide" (February 2011), available at http://www.jdsupra.com/legalnews/how-to-tweet-for-beef-guide-16213/ (last visited August 31, 2012).

JOAN SCHAFFNER AND JULIE FERSTMAN, "LITIGATING ANIMAL LAW DISPUTES: THE COMPLETE GUIDE FOR LAWYERS" (2009).

JULIE I. FERSHTMAN, EQUINE LAW & HORSE SENSE (1996) and MORE EQUINE LAW AND HORSE SENSE (2000).

National Agriculture Law Center, Reading Room on "Animal Welfare," at http://new.nationalaglawcenter.org/research-by-topic/animal-welfare/ (last visited August 18, 2013).

New York State Department of Agriculture & Markets, Laws and Regulations affecting livestock, available at http://www.agriculture.ny.gov/AI/Laws_and_Regulations.html (last visited January 11, 2013).

USDA National Agriculture Library, "Farm Animals" available at http://awic.nal.usda.gov/farm-animals (last visited January 11, 2013).

USDA Animal and Plant Health Inspection Service, "Animal Disease Traceability" available at http://www.aphis.usda.gov/traceability (last visited January 11, 2013).

CHAPTER 8

INTELLECTUAL PROPERTY

Farmers and food entrepreneurs are great inventors. Every year, they come up with thousands of creative brands and innovative ideas to increase speed, efficiency and profitability. Many great thinkers, however, have lost the profits from ideas stolen by others. If you don't know how to legally protect your great idea or mark, almost anyone can lift it and profit from your hard work. It's important for farms, agri-businesses and food entrepreneurs to have a candid discussion about their brand and any potential intellectual property that they might need to protect.

The term *"intellectual property"* ("IP") refers to the intangible, legal right to protect your ownership rights as the creator of a unique invention, expression of an idea or business mark. There are three basic types of IP: *copyrights*, *trademarks*, and *patents*.

Copyrights

Copyright is a form of intellectual property protection provided to the authors of "*original works of authorship*," including literary, dramatic, musical, artistic, and certain other intellectual works, both published and unpublished. Any expression, however, once written down in unique form, qualifies for copyright protection. Copyright protection comes into being as soon as an expression is recorded in some manner (in writing, in audio recording, etc.). In some cases, it is suggested to file with the *U.S. Copyright Office*.

Generally, the law gives the owner of copyright the exclusive right to reproduce the copyrighted work, to prepare derivative works, to distribute copies of the work, or to publically perform or display the work.

The copyright protects the *form of expression*, rather than the *subject matter* of the writing. A description of a machine could be

149

copyrighted, as could photographs taken of the machine once built, but this would only prevent others from copying the exact description or using your photographs without permission; it would not prevent others from writing a description of their own or from making and using the machine.

Marketing materials, like *advertisements* for farm products, also receive copyright protection of both the text and the photographs or videos used, preventing others from exactly duplicating your unique advertisements.

> A book describing a feeding nutrition system would be copyrightable, but the actual feeding system would likely not be covered by a copyright. The owner could obtain patent for a useful, non-obvious process.

Trademarks

Put simply, a *trademark* is an identifying mark for consumers in connection with particular goods or services. A trademark can take place in many forms including a word, name, symbol, device, sound, fragrance or "trade dress" of a food product packaging. When this mark is used in commerce, it helps distinguish the origin of the goods or services.

A *service mark* is the same as a trademark except that it identifies and distinguishes the source of a service rather than a product. The terms, "trademark" and **"mark"** are commonly used to refer to both trademarks and service marks. The purpose of the trademark or service mark is to inform the public about the source of goods or services.

Trademark registration can take place at the federal level with the *U.S. Patent and Trademark Office* ("USPTO" or "PTO") under the *Latham Act* or the state level with the *NYS Department of State* ("DOS" or "NYSDOS"). If the good or service is used in interstate commerce (i.e., outside the state of New York), then it may be registered with the USPTO. Trademark registration with the USPTO greatly enhances legal protections to the trademark owner.

That said, a person or business does not have to register a trademark in order to have intellectual property rights. This is referred to as a *"common law"* trademark right. Before registering a mark with the USPTO or NYSDOS, a business can usually use the small ^{SM} **(service mark)** or ™ **(trademark)** symbol (so long as they are not infringing on another mark). Once a farm or food business has a registered mark, it can use the ® **(registered trademark)** symbol.

When starting an agriculture or food business, it is important to run a public record search to make sure the company is not infringing on somebody's intellectual property rights for similar goods or services. If the mark is *confusingly similar* to another brand or mark, you may be infringing on somebody else's mark. With common law trademark claims, it's typically *"first in time, first in right."* In other words, whoever is using a mark first in a particular market for a class of goods or services, wins.

In some cases, it is recommended that clients hire a professional trademark searcher who will look at USPTO trademarks (both dead and active), state trademark registrations in all 50 states, Internet searches, ownership of website domains (even if inactive), and other public records.

> For example, a food technology company wanted to file a federal trademark application for a software program to be sold nationally. The Internet search and USPTO search both came up clean. However, the professional trademark searcher found a similar name of a trademark filed in Oklahoma by another food technology company. This computer program only served Oklahoma customers. Although the software programs were different, the public might be confused on the product.

In this instance, the professional search was helpful to prevent possible trademark infringement of the Oklahoma company. The USPTO will only run a search with the USPTO and will not investigate state trademark registrations or common law trademark claims.

The "Principal Registry"

Although a farm or food entrepreneur does not have to have a federal trademark or service mark to have enforcement rights under common law, admission to the USPTO principal registry offers several advantages. First, in a trademark infringement lawsuit, the fact that a trademark is on the Principal Registry is evidence that the mark is valid and owned by the registrant in connection with the goods or services. Second, even if the USPTO ultimately denies an application to the principal registry, it will give the mark priority over someone who has not applied for a mark. Third, once a mark is on the Principal Registry for five years, it is incontestable under 15 U.S.C. § 1065. Fourth, under 15 U.S.C. § 1124 it strengthens the ability to block the importation of an infringing good.

Distinctiveness

During the application process, the reviewer will determine whether a mark (1) is inherently distinctive, (2) is distinctive and has acquired a secondary meaning, or (3) is so lacking in distinctiveness that it cannot distinguish from the goods or services from another party.

If a mark is deemed to be *"merely descriptive"*, then the USPTO will allow the applicant to apply for the Supplemental Register. The owner of the mark will still enforce rights of the mark. After showing exclusive, continuous use of the mark for five years, the applicant can then apply to the Principal Registry.

In order to be accepted onto the USPTO principal registry, the mark must be *distinctive*. Categories of protectable marks are (1) *arbitrary or fanciful*, (2) *suggestive*, (3) *descriptive*, or (4) *generic*. Marks that are arbitrary, fanciful or suggestive are considered "distinctive" and protectable. If a mark is *"merely descriptive"* then the mark is only protectable if they acquire distinctiveness through a *"secondary meaning"* (i.e., different than its natural meaning). Generic terms are so highly descriptive that they are incapable of acquiring distinctiveness.

For example, the words "farm", "food" and "agriculture" are generic words that are not, by themselves, distinctive and won't be a protectable trademark with the USPTO. However, Rincker Cattle Co. or Smith Homemade Jellies would likely be considered descriptive – last names (or surnames) are considered inherently descriptive. Overtime, the requisite distinctiveness could be acquired for the principal registry. An example of this might be with Yellow Pages – at first glance, the term is descriptive but overtime it has gained a secondary meaning. On the other hand, Apple has an arbitrary meaning for computers but would be generic for a brand of apples or apple-flavored candy. The best (and most easily protectable marks) are fanciful – like Kraft® cheese or Aunt Jemima® for syrup. Suggestive marks are still strong marks, but have a descriptive component, like Agvance® software.

"Nonfunctional"

In order to register a mark with the USPTO, the mark must be nonfunctional. A product feature is "functional" if it is essential to the use or purpose of the good or affects the cost or quality of the good. The purpose of this requirement is two-fold: (1) to distinguish trademarks from patents, and (2) to put everyone on an even playing field to prevent exclusive use of a feature that would put competitors at a significant non-reputation related disadvantage. See Qualitex Co. v. Jacobson Products Co., 514 U.S. 159, 165 (1995). This is referred to as the *"functionality doctrine"*. The trademark examiner will determine whether the mark is nonfunctional and is only used as a brand identifier.

Use in Trade

In order to have a trademark right, one must use the mark in connection with the offering of goods or services to the public. When a party discontinues the use of a mark with no intent to resume such use, then that person or business has abandoned the mark.

> Cari opened a photography business after law school titled "Blackacre Ranch Photography." She did not register the mark but gained a common law claim to the mark with photography services in agriculture. She took cattle pictures and sold them in interstate commerce (i.e., across state lines and internationally). However, since opening her law practice, Cari has not had time to take professional photography. She hasn't taken professional pictures for several years and has shut down her website at www.blackacrephotography.com. However, she still has a Twitter and Facebook account for Blackacre Ranch Photography. Even though she is not actively using the mark in trade right now, she *likely* has not demonstrated the requisite intent to abandon the mark indefinitely.

If a trademark is not registered, then the owner of the mark only has exclusive rights to use the mark in market and geographic space where the party is actually using it. If a trademark is registered with the USPTO, then the owner has a presumptive exclusive right to use the mark throughout the United States. This is one reason why, if eligible, a farm or agri-business should protect its trademark right with a federal registration.

Interstate Commerce

If a farm, agri-business or food entrepreneur wishes to register a mark with the USPTO, then the mark must be used in *interstate commerce*. The term "interstate commerce" essentially means that the goods or services are being sold across state lines to other U.S. states, foreign countries, or Tribal Nations. If goods or services are only sold within the state of New York, then this would likely be considered *intrastate commerce* (instead of inter-state commerce).

The movement of goods or services in interstate commerce has to involve more than just one rare event. Importantly, a farm or agri-business selling products only in New York may still enter interstate commerce.

> Erica is a pumpkin farmer in Upstate New York and is an inspirational, paid public speaker for women in agriculture. She speaks mostly in New York but has been paid to speak in Japan and a few Midwestern states. Her public speaking business has entered interstate commerce.

Intent to Use

Perhaps you aren't selling your goods or services in interstate commerce *yet* but hope to *soon*. You may be able to file an *Intent to Use* (the mark in interstate commerce) application with the USPTO. You cannot have a registered mark with the USPTO until you are using the mark in interstate commerce; however, the Intent to Use application will preserve your rights to the mark once you are registered back to the filing date. Once approved by the USPTO, you will need to *file extensions* in a *timely matter*. You will need to use the mark in interstate commerce within three years.

Registration Process with the USPTO

Farmers and food entrepreneurs should consult with an attorney before applying for a trademark with the USPTO. You should be prepared to give your attorney the following information:

- Date that the mark was first used and the date that the mark was first used in interstate commerce (unless filing an *intent-to-use* application);
- A drawing of the mark (e.g., logo if applying for a design mark); and,
- Specimen showing the mark used in interstate commerce.

You should discuss with your attorney the specific class(es) of *goods and services* in which you use the mark. For example, if you want your mark to be protectable for homemade food products and t-shirts, then both classes of goods should be applied for. Each class of goods and services requires additional filing fees, so please discuss priorities with your attorney.

If the good or service is not used in interstate commerce, then a farm or food entrepreneur may apply for a trademark with the NYS Department of State.

Trademark License

Once a trademark is registered with the Principal Registry, a farm, agri-business or food entrepreneur can license use of the trademark to another person or entity using the same class of goods or services. For example, if a farm selling produce directly to consumers trademarked "eFoodie" for the name of its blog and for the e-commerce side of the business, it could license use to other business entities (perhaps within the same family business) to use eFoodie in the same way.

Trademark Assignments

If a farm, agri-business or food entrepreneur sells his/her business to another person or entity (including a family member), then a trademark assignment should take place with the USPTO to avoid an abandonment of the mark. Assignments of registered marks (or even marks that are pending application) must be in writing between the parties subsequently filed with the USPTO.

Trademark Infringement

The burden is on the owner of the trademark to enforce trademark rights, including marks registered with the USPTO or NYSDOS. The mark does not have to be *exactly* the same in order to constitute trademark infringement. The standard is whether the use of the mark is *likely to cause confusion or mistake* to decieve the public. You don't have to have a registered trademark for another person or entity to infringe upon the use of your mark – you will just have a more difficult burden of evidence.

The Second Circuit in <u>Polaroid Corp. v. Polarad Elecs. Corp.</u>, 287 F. 2d 492 (2nd Cir. 1961) looked at the following factors when deciding the likelihood of confusion between marks: (1) the strength of the senior mark, (2) degree of similarity between the two marks, (3) proximity of the products or services, (4) likelihood that the prior owner would "bridge the gap", (5) evidence of actual confusion, (6) the defendant's good or bad faith in adopting the mark in question, (7) the quality of defendant's product or service, and (8) sophistication of the buyers.

> In a trademark infringement suit against another "Blackacre Ranch Photography", Cari would likely need to show the court that her mark was well established in the industry and that folks in the livestock industry might have hired the other business for photography services instead of Cari, believing they were working with Cari's business. It would strengthen Cari's argument that the other business knew about her business if a Google search of "Blackacre Ranch Photography" showed Cari's business.

There are no hard and fast rules with trademark infringement. Note that a mark is only good for a certain class of goods or services. In the above example with the farm using eFoodie for the name of their blog and e-commerce business selling food products direct to consumers, use of iFoodie for an iPhone application selecting restaurants in New York City likely would not infringe upon the mark. Farms, agri-businesses and food entrepreneurs should contact an attorney before commencing enforcement of a trademark (e.g., sending a cease and desist letter).

Take home points: Trademarks and service marks are important to protect. If practicable, a farm, agri-business or food entrepreneur should register all eligible marks with the USPTO (if used in interstate commerce) or NYSDOS (if used only in the state of New York) for both standard character marks (e.g., "eSaleBarn) and design marks (i.e., the logo). While the trademark application is pending (or before the application is made), farms and agri/food businesses should use the ^{SM} (for service marks) or ^{TM} (for trademarks) symbols, putting the world on notice that they claim the mark for their business. If you are a business start-up, run a thorough Google search and USPTO search (and, if appropriate, hire a professional searcher) to see if there are any trademarks that you might infringe upon. Once you have a trademark or service mark, it is important to protect your intellectual property rights.

Patents

A *patent* for an invention is the grant of ownership rights to the inventor, issued by the USPTO. Generally, the term of a patent is *20 years* from the date the application was filed.

A patent grants "the right to exclude others from making, using, offering for sale, or selling" the invention in the United States or "importing" the invention into the United States. What is granted is not the right to make, use, offer for sale, sell or import, but the right to exclude others from making, using, offering for sale, selling or importing the invention. Once a patent is issued, the government is done; you are on your own to protect your patent.

Types of Patents

There are *three types of patents*: (1) utility patents, (2) design patents, and (2) plant patents. Each discussed below.

- *Utility patents* may be granted to anyone who invents or discovers any new and useful process, machine, article of manufacture, or composition of matter, or any new and useful improvement thereof.

> The word **"process"** is defined as an act or method, and primarily includes industrial or technical processes. The term "manufacture" refers to articles that are made. The term "composition of matter" relates to chemical compositions and may include mixtures of ingredients, as well as new chemical compounds. These classes of subject matter taken together include practically everything that is made by man and the processes for making the products.

- *Design patents* may be granted to anyone who invents a new, original, and ornamental design for an article of manufacture.

- *Plant patents* may be granted to anyone who invents or discovers and asexually reproduces any distinct and new variety of plant.

Patent law specifies the general field of *subject matter* that can be patented and the conditions under which a patent may be obtained.

Usefulness

The subject matter (i.e., the thing you want to patent) must be *"useful."* The term "useful" refers to the condition that the subject matter has a **useful purpose** and also includes a requirement that the patent **works**. A machine that does not perform its intended purpose would not be called useful and will not be patented.

You cannot patent *laws of nature* (e.g., gravity), *physical phenomena* (e.g., fire), or *abstract ideas* (e.g., freedom of speech); however, you may have copyrights of your own, unique *expression* of an idea (see below for more about copyrights). A patent cannot be obtained upon a mere idea or suggestion. The patent is granted for the new machine or manufacturer and not upon the idea or suggestion of the new machine. A complete description of the actual machine or other subject matter for which a patent is sought is required.

Novelty and Non-Obviousness

For an invention to be patentable, it must be *novel* (in other words, it must be *new* or unique). An invention is *not new if:*

- The invention was known or used by others in United States, or patented or described in a printed publication anywhere in the world before the invention by the applicant; or

- The invention was patented or described in a printed publication anywhere in the world or in public use or on sale in the United States more than one year prior to the application for the patent.

The subject matter for which a patent is sought must be sufficiently different from what has been used or described before, so that it may be said to be *nonobvious* to a person having ordinary skill in the area of technology related to the invention. For example, the substitution of one color for another or changes in size are ordinarily not patentable.

Seed Saving

Patented seeds are typically protected as *Utility Patents* or *Plant Patents* and *allow the patent owner to exclude others from using them for 20 years.* Case law in the 1980s widened the scope of patentability to "anything under the sun that is made by the hand of man," including living organisms.

The main thing that crop producers need to know is that, if you paid a premium for genetics, most likely the terms include an *agreement* that *prohibits you from saving seed.* The producers could be subject to random audit to show that the seed you planted yielded in the normal range and it was marketed or stored.

The *Plant Variety Protection Act* ("PVPA"), administered by the *USDA*, offers a few exemptions to the protections of the patent holder, including:

159

- *Breeders or researchers* may be able to use the seed in *developing a new variety*; and

- *Farmers* may be allowed to save seed for *replanting* if they *lawfully purchased* the seed.

The second exemption does *not* give farmers the *right to resell the protected seed*, but only to replant for personal use.

A *producer* can, however, save *public varieties seed*. This seed can be saved, but public varieties are much more limited because university devote more research budgets studying traits of *Genetically Modified Organisms* ("GMO's") – or GM seed. Additionally, the public varieties do not have the yield potential and traits desired by most producers, who are attempting to beat razor-thin margins to remain profitable.

Look at the labels of the products you purchase, and be wary of the ability to pick up GMO seed without having to pay a technology premium. Better yet, **just don't do it**. Companies invest heavily in developing their products and they are likely to invest heavily in defending their investments.

Additional Resources

Cari Rincker, "Protecting the Agri-Business: Managing Contracts, Trademarks and Non-Disclosure Agreements" (June 24, 2013) Fifth Annual Ohio Agriculture Law Symposium, slides available at http://www.slideshare.net/rinckerlaw/protecting-the-agribusiness-managing-contracts-trademarks-and-nondisclosure-agreements (last visited July 3, 2013).

Cari B. Rincker, "Protect Your Brand: Trademarks for New York Food and Agriculture Operations," New York Farm Bureau, The Legal Edge (July 2013) available at http://www.nyfb.org/img/topic_pdfs/file_a11dx3eo31.pdf (last visited July 12, 2013).

Devin Morgan, "Your Agricultural Assets, More Than Fields and Barns," available at http://www.eatdrinklaw.com/index.cfm/feature/254_50/your-agricultural-assets-more-than-fields-and-barns-for-farmshedcny.cfm#

(last visited July 11, 2013).

Devin Morgan, "Who Owns Your Farm's Name?" available at http://www.eatdrinklaw.com/index.cfm/feature/196_50/who-owns-your-farms-name-for-farmshedcny.cfm# (last visited July 11, 2013).

U.S. Copyright Office, "Frequently Asked Questions about Copyright," available at http://www.copyright.gov/help/faq/ (last visited July 16, 2013).

U.S. Patent and Trademark Office, "Frequently Asked Questions About Patents," available at http://www.uspto.gov/faq/patents.jsp (last visited July 16, 2013).

U.S. Patent and Trademark Office, "Trademark Process," available at http://www.uspto.gov/trademarks/process/index.jsp (last visited July 16, 2013).

CHAPTER 9

LIABILITY AND INSURANCE

Insurance is all around us. Farmers, agri-businesses and food entrepreneurs use insurance everyday to manage a myriad of risks: health insurance, life insurance, property insurance, liability insurance, crop insurance, motor vehicle insurance, and even vacation insurance.

An insurance policy is a contract, drafted by a team of lawyers and reviewed by an army of risk-analysis specialists and accountants, all employed by the insurance company and working with an eye toward profit. Because of this, it is important to clearly understand the terms of your insurance- what you have and what you do not. Food and agriculture lawyers can review your insurance policies to help determine whether you have ample coverage for your particular operation.

Even so, insurance is an important risk management tool for farms and food operations. In order to accurately determine what types of insurance coverage you need, it's important to understand liability concerns with your business. This Chapter highlights potential liability issues affecting farms and food operations and the types of insurance products available that can mitigate risk.

"Liability"

With insurance, it is important to understand the concept of *liability*. In a word, liability means *responsibility*. Liability can be based on *intentional, voluntary actions* (like assaulting someone by punching them). Liability can also arise over things one might consider "accidents," where there is *negligence*--the failure to take reasonable steps to avoid causing harm that you could have foreseen, like failing to keep a good eye on a burning field and "accidentally" burning down your neighbor's barn. Finally, you can face *strict liability* for harm that is caused by your failure to follow the law - even where the resulting harm is likely not what the law was intended to prevent.

Let's say you have a completely toothless, clawless and harmless old pet tiger. The law says that all captive tigers must be caged. As you might expect, this law is designed to prevent harm to others. However, your tiger doesn't have the capability to cause harm to your neighbor's livestock (or personal injury to your neighbor, for that matter). Nevertheless, if you violate the law by allowing your tiger to roam free, and its nap on your neighbor's car roof leaves a deep dent, you'll be held **strictly liable** for the cost of repairs.

Premises Liability

If your farm or food business brings members of the public onto your property, then *premises liability* becomes a potential issue. Examples include: roadside stands, farmers' markets, pick-your-own produce, agri-tourism, on-farm livestock or horse sales, farm tours, or cooking classes in your kitchen. The *standard of care* and potential liability issues differ according to the class of persons on the property (e.g., trespassers, children, licensees, or invitees).

1. Trespassers

Generally speaking, a property owner is *not liable to trespassers for physical harm caused by his/her failure to exercise reasonable care* (e.g., a trespasser is hunting in your pasture and trips on a cattle guard). However, a land owner who knows or has reasons to know that trespassers constantly intrude upon a limited area on the farm may be subject to liability for bodily harm caused by his/her failure to exercise reasonable care, especially with *artificial conditions* on the property (e.g., a farmer who knows neighbors repeatedly trespass on one part of his cattle pasture for hunting may want to put reflective material on the cattle guards).

> If a landowner is aware of potential trespassers, he/she should consider all **potentially dangerous conditions**. For example, perhaps the owner should warn trespassers of certain animals like bulls that may be hazardous to city folk. Farmers should remove the keys from tractors. Landowners should keep all chemicals and other potentially dangerous items in buildings.

2. <u>Children</u>

Landowners have a special duty to children who come onto the land. More specifically, the property owner will be subject to liability for physical harm to children who have trespassed on the property if:

- Bodily harm is caused by an artificial condition;
- The landowner had reason to believe that children trespass on the place where the injury took place;
- The artificial condition has the ability to cause an unreasonable risk of death or serious bodily harm to children;
- The children, due to their age and intelligence, do not realize the danger;
- The utility to the landowner for maintaining the dangerous risk and burden to eliminate the danger is outweighed by the risk to children; and
- The landowner fails to exercise reasonable care.

This is oftentimes referred to as the *"Law of Attractive Nuisance"* on a farm. Landowners should look at things through the eyes of a child to help discern possible dangerous conditions (e.g., farm machineries, water ponds).

3.   Licensees

The word *"licensee"* describes a person who has been invited onto property that is not open to the public. *Friends* and other social guests are considered licensees. A landowner will be subject to liability to his licensees for physical harm caused by his/her failure to exercise reasonable care for their safety if the dangerous condition was known or should have been known and the guest should not be expected to know the danger. In these instances, the landowner has the duty to *make the dangerous condition safe* or *warn the visitors* of the risk involved.

> If a farm has a BBQ for all of its family and friends, then the farm has a duty to warn its guests of any dangerous conditions on the property (e.g., roosters, farm equipment, bad steps on a backyard deck).

4.   Invitees

Landowners owe the *highest duty of care to an invitee*, or members of the public that enter the land for the purpose of business dealings. Examples include the following: (1) farmstands, (2) pick-your-own produce, (3) cooking classes, (4) on-farm horse or livestock sales, (5) corn mazes, (6) hay rides, (7) petting zoos, and (8) farm tours.

In these cases, the landowner will be subject to liability for physical harm caused by invitees by a condition on the land if he/she failed to exercise reasonable care and he/she knew or should have known about the harmful condition and it would be expected that the public would not discover the dangerous condition. Landowners have the duty to warn invitees of potentially dangerous conditions.

> Landowners who have members of the public come on their property should use barriers to prevent the public from entering areas of the property that may be potentially hazardous. There should be signs warning invitees of potential hazards.
> Landowners with pets should be particularly mindful of potential injuries (e.g., dog bites).

Products Liability

Products liability is the legal *responsibility* for personal injuries and property damage caused by defective products. Potential liability attaches to every set of hands that touch a food product until it gets to the consumer. Farms and food entrepreneurs selling food directly to the consumer increase their likelihood for potential products liability issues.

States differ in the products liability theory they employ – New York is a *strict liability* state. To illustrate, if a consumer at a pick-your-own farm picks and then consumes berries and becomes ill because the berries were contaminated, a New York court will likely hold the producer strictly liable for the consumer's injuries.

> Due to potential products liability, farms that sell food products directly to the consumer should pay special attention to food safety and products liability insurance. Additionally, they should form a business entity, like a limited liability company, that would help limit personal liability.

Picking the Right Insurance Policy

Remember that an insurance policy is a contract between the insurance company and the insured. In this contract, the insurance company has the *duty to indemnify* you and the *duty to defend* you against a lawsuit brought by a third party relating to the covered risk. Meanwhile, you will have the *duty to pay* premiums, the *duty to cooperate* and the *duty to disclose* to the insurance company any relevant information about the operation.

The insurance company's duty to defend is carried out by hiring an attorney chosen by the company and controlling that attorney's right to settle. In other words, if you are dead set against settling, the insurance company has the right to do so. Additionally, once the company pays out its policy limits, it has no further duty to defend you.

The purpose of an insurance policy is to shift the financial risk of the food and agriculture operation to the insurance company. More specifically, the insurance company will pay any *covered claim* (up to the limit) and *defense costs* in a lawsuit (including attorneys' fees and court costs). Virtually every business should be covered by a liability insurance policy; however, it can be challenging to decide which policies adequately cover an agriculture or food business.

Knowing the lay of the land of insurance is important to farm operators, agri-businesses and food entrepreneurs, both big and small. You might be tempted to save money on *insurance premiums* (the cost of the insurance) by hand-selecting only *limited coverages* that you think you are likely to need with *high deductibles* (the out-of-pocket amount you're responsible for if a loss occurs). *Inadequate amounts* of insurance won't pay out what you will need to stay up and running if a loss occurs.

Insurance policies are normally either *"claims-made"* or *"occurrence-based."* *Claims-made* policies will only cover the insured for claims made within the window of time the insurance policy is in effect so long as the claim itself is made within a specified time. Alternatively, an *"occurrence-based"* policy covers anything that happens within a certain window of time and will "pay out" *regardless of when the claim* is made to the insurance company.

Exclusions from Coverage

What you see in big print is often modified, updated and changed in the fine print. An insurance contract almost always carves out *exclusions from coverage.* Exclusions are losses that the insurance policy simply will not cover. Most policies do not cover losses that result from *intentional acts*, such as theft by employees over a certain amount, assaults, or alcohol-related events. Other exclusions may relate more specifically to the type of insurance involved. For example, a typical *farmowners policy* might not be adequate to insure against losses suffered from the flooding of a nearby creek.

Read through your insurance policy carefully, *before* you pay the premium. When in doubt, ask your insurance agent to point out language that provides the coverage you need. No matter what an agent orally tells you that you're buying, when a loss occurs, you are going to be stuck with the coverage is provided in the written insurance policy. If you wait until a loss has occurred before you take the first look at your policy, you may be surprised to find that coverage for your loss is excluded. Farmers and food entrepreneurs can utilize a food and agriculture lawyer for an insurance review.

Most insurance contracts can be confusing. It is not unusual for insurance companies to issue *standard-form policy* documents that appear to include common exclusions from coverage, accompanied by *"riders,"* which are additional pages that are attached to the policies and may actually provide for a coverage excluded in the main document. These riders are part of your policy, and the entire policy, with riders, should be kept in a safe location.

Know the type of coverage you are getting. For example, *basic coverage*, *broad form coverage*, and *special coverage* on farm buildings are each designed to cover different kinds of losses.

- *Basic coverage* is intended to compensate you for losses from causes like fire, lightning, explosion, windstorm, hail, riot or civil commotion, aircraft or vehicle, vandalism, theft, sinkhole collapse, and volcanic action.

- *Broad form coverage* would include all of the above and add additional coverage for damage from causes like the weight of ice, snow, or sleet, falling objects and accidental discharges of water.

- Purchasing *special coverage* would get you the protection included in the basic and broad coverage, but special coverage also offers what is called *open peril coverage*, under which other causes of damage are covered unless they are *specifically excluded* under the farm policy (like, for example, a flood loss).

Types of Insurance

There are many different kinds of insurance that farms, agribusiness and food entrepreneurs should consider. The most common types of insurance for food and agriculture operations are as follows:

1. **Farmers Comprehensive Personal Liability ("FCPL") Policy** (a/k/a farmowner's insurance): Most farms use a farmowner's insurance policy to cover the ordinary risks of a farming operation. This type of policy normally only covers activities ancillary to farming (i.e., not agri-tourism or cottage

food operations). Farmers should pay special attention to the exclusions section in this policy to see what is *not* covered. To illustrate, sale of *processed* vegetables or meat products at a farmers' market or roadside stand may not be covered. Furthermore, injuries to the policyholder or family member of the policyholder are normally excluded. Finally, the policy likely excludes property damage by the insured him/herself.

> The FCPL will set an amount of coverage for bodily injuries and property damage. A farmer should make sure there is enough coverage in these two areas.

2. **Commercial Insurance Policy**: A commercial insurance policy or endorsement is appropriate for operations engaging in business outside the scope of the *basic farmowners insurance policy*. For example, most farmowners policies cover products liability for the sale of raw food products, whereas the commercial insurance policy may cover personal injuries (such as slip and falls and other types of injuries not related to defective products) resulting from the sale of *processed* food products (e.g., slicing vegetables, cutting meat products, making beef jerky). Additionally, a commercial insurance policy should be purchased if a business is being run out of a home, has agri-tourism activities, or engages in on-farm poultry slaughter.

> There are a myriad of liability issues surrounding agri-tourism and agri-tainment. For example, children may climb hay bales in a hay maze that could cause serious injuries. An adult sitting on a straw bale could discard a cigarette and cause a fire. A scared child in a haunted "barn" around Halloween could fall and break an arm. Small children could jump off a moving wagon giving hayrides. A child could get kicked by a farm animal during a petting zoo. If you participate in any agri-tourism activities, pay special attention to possible safeguards to mitigate liability and make sure you are properly insured.

3. **Products Liability Policy**: Products liability policies help provide coverage for liability resulting from an illness or death due to contaminated food products sold by the purchaser. It is highly suggested that farms involved with the direct marketing of food products to consumers, schools or restaurants have products liability insurance. Farms selling raw milk should also consider a products liability policy.

4. **Homeowner's Insurance**: Homeowner's insurance usually *does not* cover business activities. Therefore, you should consider a commercial policy if you have a home business office, cottage food operation, a rooftop garden, offer in-home cooking classes, or sell produce from your home.

5. **Motor Vehicle Insurance**: Food and agriculture operations should pay special attention to their auto insurance policies if vehicles are used to transport goods, livestock or special equipment. Talk to your insurance agent – you may need a *commercial automobile policy*.

6. **Cyber Liability Insurance**: This is a fairly new type of insurance, relatively speaking, and it addresses risks associated with doing business over the Internet (or e-Commerce). Covered risks can include privacy issues, infringement of intellectual property (trademark or copyright infringement), stolen credit card information (from PayPal, Google Checkout or other online credit card processor) or computer viruses.

7. **Environmental Insurance**: After a Phase I and Phase II *Environmental Assessment* ("EA") on a farm property, environmental insurance can be a useful risk assessment tool if there is high environmental risk on certain parts on the farm property. The real estate transaction may require the seller to purchase the environmental insurance if remediation is needed.

8. **Pollution Insurance**: Pollution insurance covers losses as a result of the sudden release of specified contaminants. This type of insurance may be appropriate for farms with a manure storage tank or *underground storage tanks* ("UST's"). Additionally, pollution insurance will be useful for farms with

potential water, dust, or odor problems that may, over time, cause injury to others.

> Pollution claims from livestock production (such as a chemical release from hog confinements) and business activities other than farming (e.g., selling soap, lemonade stands, quilt shops) are typically excluded from a Farmers Comprehensive Personal Liability Policy. In these cases, a separate pollution insurance policy should be considered.

9. **Crop Insurance**: Federal crop insurance is subsidized by the U.S. Department of Agriculture ("USDA") *Risk Management Agency* ("RMA"). It protects the producer against crop losses due to natural disasters such as drought or flood. It is available for nearly every type of commodity ranging from sweet corn to raisins. Crop insurance is discussed later in this chapter.

10. **Livestock Insurance**: There are two types of livestock insurance: (1) *private livestock insurance* and (2) *RMA reinsured livestock insurance* (similar to our federal crop insurance programs). Federal livestock insurance through the RMA will only protect the producer against losses caused by natural disasters such as flood and drought whereas private livestock insurance may offer wider protection. For example, some policies may protect against theft of a prize bull from the National Western Stock Show in Denver, Colorado. It is available for several livestock species including cattle, swine, and sheep.

11. **Equine Insurance**: A standard farmowner's policy will typically cover small-scale equine boarding; however, there are special equine insurance policies for horse training, riding schools, trail riding and horse racing. Equine insurance is discussed in more detail below.

Special Riders (or Endorsements)

There are many special activities on agriculture or food operations that require amendments to the underlying policies. These amendments are oftentimes referred to as "riders" or "amendments." Examples of these special activities may include *agri-tourism*/agritainment, petting zoos or other activities where the *public is in direct contact with animals, equine, custom farm work, on-farm poultry slaughter*, production of *processed foods*, use of *ATV's*, and the transportation of *frozen genetics* (e.g., embryos, semen). It is always best to have a candid discussion with the insurance company about all of the proposed activities and carefully review all proposed riders.

Umbrella Insurance

"Umbrella insurance" is a special additional coverage for liability not covered by your existing policies. The name "umbrella" improperly infers that umbrella insurance adds coverage in the "holes" of existing insurance policies; instead, umbrella insurance should be viewed as a "**top hat**." It essentially raises your already existing limits and existing coverage. For example, if you have a $1 million farmowner's insurance policy with the $2 million umbrella, the umbrella policy would protect the farm against a $2 million court judgment. Umbrella insurance *does not "fill in holes"* in your existing insurance policies – *it simply increases the limits*. From a practical standpoint, umbrella policies are typically the most affordable way to get higher policy limits.

How Much Coverage Does a Farm or Food Business Require?

It depends on your budget and risk appetite. There isn't an equation to determine the best possible coverage. Most farms and food entrepreneurs should have *at least* $1 million in insurance coverage. It is recommend that farmers and food entrepreneurs have enough in insurance to cover their assets. When deciding the proper limit, farms and food entrepreneurs should consider the types of activities and legal liability they are undertaking.

Documentation

Documenting Property Losses, *Before* They Occur

Documenting details is important when it comes to making claims against an insurance policy, and many insurance contracts require it. Even if you experience damage that would clearly have been covered by your insurance policy, you may be out of luck if you haven't specifically documented the *existence and value of an asset* to the company and you have no proof of what you've lost. In fact, not only could your insurance claim be denied, but you could also lose other benefits, such as *casualty loss tax deductions* on your income-tax returns.

> For example, a homeowner was denied a casualty loss deduction by the IRS because, while the homeowner had pictures of a fire that destroyed his home, the homeowner had no pictures of the items he claimed to have lost in the fire. This prevented determining the value of the items.

A simple way to avoid this problem is to take a *pre-loss inventory* of your items, using free *inventory forms* available online from providers like www.knowyourstuff.org or helpful computer programs such as Bento (which can synch with your smartphone). You can upload *pictures*, assign what *room* the item is in, and add items like *serial numbers* and *purchase prices*. All of this information is *stored* online, plus you can *print* the document and *file* it with your insurance agency.

As one local agent suggests, no adjuster is going to pay for 20 leisure suits based solely on your word, but a picture of 20 leisure suits is hard to argue against. If nothing else, take a few minutes and *use your smartphone to photograph* your shop tools, manuals and other assets. Many of your smaller items that you are not likely to remember about in the event of a large loss are still expensive to replace. Use the phone to take a photo of the data plate with the serial number of your equipment, large and small. Then transfer it to a memory stick and throw it in your personal safe.

Your agent should be kept up to date on your *new purchases*, as well. If you add a John Deere 4440 to the farm inventory, make sure to tell the insurance company; otherwise, it will be a lot harder to make a claim when a tree falls on it or it is stolen. Your agent can help you by binding the company when you acquire new property, but you should report it quickly because some policies allow you just thirty (30) days to get property listed on your policy after it is acquired.

Documenting Accidents and Damages

If you're in an accident or if someone else notifies you that they intend to make a claim against your insurance, you should take time as soon as possible to *make written notes* of every detail you can remember, including anything said by the other people involved. If it is at all possible, *take photographs* with your smartphone.

> For example, photos taken at an accident scene, including both close-ups of damage, as well as distance photos showing the relative positions of vehicles and any other relevant factors, can make all the difference in the world when an insurance claim is made or a lawsuit is filed against you. Sometimes, photographing property damage can prevent a claimant from later claiming that there was more damage than there really was or from inflating the value of the thing damaged.

Borrowing and Lending Equipment

If you let your neighbor use your semi tractor and trailer, and he gets into an accident while using them, your insurance (not your neighbor's) is going to pay the claim. The only way to shift this responsibility is to insist on having a *written rental agreement* that clearly assigns the responsibility to the neighbor leasing your equipment. Although many neighbors may want to "make it right," seeing the highly estimated cost of repair often dampens that initial offer.

Keeping Insurance Information Handy

Consider taking a picture of your policy declaration page and

insurance agent's telephone number with your smartphone. Leave it on there. If you have an accident on the road with a tractor, you may not have insurance cards or a glove box to put them in. Also, if one of your employees gets in an accident, it is an easy way to get the information to the investigating officer quickly.

Crop Insurance

The federal crop insurance program is a subsidized insurance program that provides financial protection to producers against crop losses caused by natural disasters such as drought or flood. The primary purpose of federal crop insurance is to promote the economic stability of agriculture through a sound delivery system regulated by the federal government.

Background

The *Federal Crop Insurance Act* ("FCIA"), first passed in 1938, aimed to promote economic stability in agriculture by offering producers access to crop insurance, but historically, participation was low, until the passage of the 1994 *Federal Crop Insurance Reform Act* ("FCIRA"), the creation of the *U.S. Department of Agriculture's Risk Management Agency* ("RMA") in 1996, and the 2000 Agricultural Risk Protection Act ("ARPA"). The result has been a combination of additional subsidies and access to additional types of coverage, causing participation to rise dramatically.

In addition, agricultural operations now have greater access to many insurance providers; currently, there are fifteen (15) insurance companies known as the *"Approved Insurance Providers"* ("AIPs") with federal approval to offer crop insurance policies. Those policies are reinsured by the *Federal Crop Insurance Corporation* ("FCIC"). Put simply, *"reinsurance"* is a contractual agreement where one insurer transfers (or "cedes") all or a portion of the risk it underwrites to another insurer. The relationship between the FCIC and the AIP is governed by the *Standard Reinsurance Agreement* ("SRA").

A copy of the *Common Crop Insurance Policy, Basic Provisions* for the 2011 crop year (11-br) (Released April 2010) is located online at http://www.rma.usda.gov/policies/2011/11-br.pdf. Crop insurance policies are available for over one hundred crops and vary from one county to another.

> Examples of covered commodities include (but are not limited to): Almonds, Avocados, Bananas, Barley, Blueberries, Cabbage, Canola, Chile peppers, Citrus (e.g., oranges, lemons, grapefruit), Coffee, Cranberries, Corn, Cotton, Dry peas, Figs, Flax, Sweet Corn, Tomatoes, Grapes, Macadamia Nuts, Mint, Mustard, Oats, Onions, Papaya, Peanuts, Pasture/Forage, Pears, Pecans, Peppers, Popcorn, Pumpkins, Raisins, Rice, Rye, Safflower, Soybeans, Silage, Stonefruit (e.g., cherries, apricots, peaches, nectarines, plums, prunes), Sugar Beets, Sugarcane, Sunflowers, Tobacco, Trees (e.g., Mango Trees), Walnuts, and Wheat.

Maps for each commodity type and lists of counties may be found at http://www.rma.usda.gov/data/cropprograms.html.

Multi-Peril Crop Insurance ("MPCI") is the only type of crop insurance available through the federal crop insurance program, which aims to protect farmers against loss of production below a calculated coverage level, which is determined by using the farmer's actual production history. The farm operator cannot pick and choose which fields will create the production history.

Crop Insurance Administration

Although on the surface a crop insurance policy is a two-party arrangement between an agricultural producer and an insurance company, the federal government has a pervasive role through the USDA and two of its agencies: (a) the *Federal Crop Insurance Corporation* ("FCIC") and the (b) *Risk Management Agency* ("RMA"). RMA manages FCIC; therefore, RMA is oftentimes is used to refer to the relevant federal agency.

- **RMA's Role**: RMA's role is deeply embedded in contract law. For instance, RMA determines all policy terms and premium rates, establishes all loss adjustment procedures, and has the final word on what constitutes a *"good farming practice."* This situation can affect a farmer in several ways, beginning with

177

timely payment of a claim and continuing through remedies sought if a claim is denied. Farmers and their counsel work with RMA regional offices rather than directly with FCIC.

- **FCIC's Role**: The FCIC has the power to establish the prices, terms, and conditions for federal crop insurance contracts and to oversee the delivery of crop insurance to eligible producers.

Types of Coverage

- **Multiple Peril Crop Insurance Policies**: Standard MPCI policies insure producers against yield losses caused by natural disasters (e.g., drought, excessive moisture, hail, wind, frost, insects, disease); however, in some circumstances, coverage for fire (excluding arson) and hail can be deleted. MPCI policies must be purchased *before* you plant. One policy per county protects the operator from covered causes of loss.

- **Yield Loss Policies**: Yield-based policies provide financial protection to producers for yield losses and, depending on the particular crop insurance policy, is measured by the *quantity or the value of their yield*. You will select the amount of average yield (*Actual Production History* or "APH"), which is insured between 50-85%. Payment is made by the AIP on the amount of yield which is short of the insured (guaranteed) yield. The APH is equal to the sum of actual, proven yields divided by the number of years in the database (4 to 10 years).

- **Revenue Loss Policies**: Revenue-based policies provide financial protection to producers for revenue losses caused by declines in yield or price. There are several types of revenue-based policies, each defining "revenue" differently.

  1) **Group Risk Income Protection** ("GRIP"): producers are paid indemnities when the average county revenue for the insured crop falls below the revenue chosen by the farmer.

  2) **Adjusted Gross Revenue** ("AGR"): insures the revenue of a producer's entire farm, rather than an

individual crop, by guaranteeing a percentage of gross farm revenue.

3) **Crop Revenue Coverage** ("CRC"): provides revenue protection based on price and yield expectations by indemnifying losses below the guarantee at the higher of an early-season price or the harvest price.

4) **Income Protection** ("IP"): provides financial protection to producers against reductions in gross income when either a crop's price or yield declines from early-season expectations.

5) **Revenue Assurance** ("RA"): farmers are allowed to select a dollar amount of target revenue from a range defined by 65-75% of expected revenue.

The majority of crop insurance policies are either yield loss or revenue loss policies.

Types of Losses Covered by Crop Insurance

Crop insurance covers losses by "natural" causes. *Natural causes* may include drought, excessive moisture (such as natural flooding or hurricanes), hail, wind, frost, insects, damage from wildlife, and disease. Examples of unnatural causes that will not be covered include arson, bioterrorism, wind from helicopters, damage from livestock, and flooding from the *Army Corps of Engineers*. Furthermore, the crop damage must have occurred while the crop was in the field.

Losses due to a producer's **neglect**, failure to reseed "to the same crop in such areas and under such circumstances as it is customary to reseed," or *failure "to follow good farming practices*, including scientifically sound sustainable and organic farming practices," are not insured losses under the crop insurance program. 7 U.S.C. § 1508(a)(3) (emphasis added). As noted above, the RMA is responsible for making "good farming practices" determinations and is subject to an administrative appeal procedure that does not involve the reinsured company.

Examples of a failure to follow "good farming practices" can include when a farmer (1) allowed cattle to graze corn during a growing season, (2) did not apply any cultivation or spraying to control weeds, or (3) did not seed the crop.

The farmer will not be able to receive an insurance payout if he/she misrepresented to or concealed important information from the insurance company.

Denial of Insurance Claim

If you receive a denial letter from your insurance company, *don't just sit on it.* You only have a limited time to react to this denial (i.e., *statute of limitations*). A farmer must commence arbitration *within 1 year* after the denial of the claim. Judicial review must take place within *1 year* after the binding arbitration decision. New York law also has statute of limitations for tort and contract claims.

Equine Insurance

A horse owner can easily get lost in the menu of equine insurance policies. The most common type is *Equine Mortality Insurance.* This type of insurance normally requires proper notice to the insurance company if the insured horse becomes ill or injured. The horse owner is also required to give the horse "proper care and attention." Common endorsements (or riders) for *Equine Mortality Insurance* include *Loss of Use, Major Medical, Surgical-Only,* and *Agreed Value* (instead of *Actual Cash Value*).

The insurance policy may give very specific notice requirements. The policy might require *immediate* notification via telephone or that the horse owner front veterinary expenses. If you believe you may have an insurance claim, pay special attention to the requirements in your policy.

Other types of insurance applicable to equine operations include the following:

- Herd Policy,
- Limited Equine Mortality Insurance,
- Specified Perils,
- Stallion and/or Mare Infertility Insurance,
- Prospective Foal Insurance,
- Equine Professional Liability,
- Individual Horse Owner's Liability, and
- Event Liability Insurance.

Additional Resources

Agriculture Marketing Resource Center, "Best Management Practices in Agritourism" available at http://www.agmrc.org/media/cms/AgritourismBestManagementRE VJune201_6F2297595C6F1.pdf (last May 19, 2013).

Cari B. Rincker, Allen H. Olson, Beth Angus Baumstark, William K. Crispin, Julie I. Fershtman, Charles D. Lee, Michael D. Martin, P. John Owen, "Crop and Livestock Insurance from the Ground Up," American Bar Association Continuing Legal Education Webinar (January 25, 2012), available for purchase at http://apps.americanbar.org/cle/programs/t12crg1.html (last visited December 27, 2012).

Cari B. Rincker, Dr. Stan Benda, Derrick Braaten, Jason Foscolo, Neil Hamilton, Erin Hawley, Leon Letter, Jesse Richardson, Jr., Rich Schell, Patricia Salkin, "Counseling the Local Food Movement," American Bar Association Continuing Legal Education Webinar (May 10, 2012), available for purchase at http://apps.americanbar.org/abastore/index.cfm?section=main&fm= Product.AddToCart&pid=CET12LFMCDR (last visited July 1 2013).

Karen R. Krub, "Pasture, Rangeland, Forage Insurance Program (September 11, 2009) available at http://www.flaginc.org/wp-content/uploads/2013/03/PstrRngldFrg.pdf (last visited May 19, 2013).

Karen R. Krub, "Individual Crop Insurance" (September 11, 2009) available at http://www.flaginc.org/wp-content/uploads/2013/03/IndCrpIns.pdf (visited May 19, 2013).

Karen R. Krub, "Group Risk Crop Insurance" (September 11, 2009) available at http://www.flaginc.org/wp-content/uploads/2013/03/GrpRskCrpIns.pdf (last visited May 19, 2013).

Lynn A. Hayes and Karen R. Krub, "Livestock Indemnity Program" (2009) available at http://www.flaginc.org/wp-content/uploads/2013/03/LIP.pdf (last visited May 19, 2013).

Lynn A. Hayes, "Livestock Risk Protection Insurance," (September 11, 2009) available at http://www.flaginc.org/wp-content/uploads/2013/03/LvStkRskProtect.pdf (last visited May 19, 2013).

National Agriculture Law Center's Reading Room on Landowner Liability available http://nationalaglawcenter.org/readingrooms/ (last visited May 19, 2013).

Public Health Association of BC, "A Farmer's Guide to Hosting Farm Visits" available at http://www.phabc.org/modules.php?name=Farmtoschool&pa=showpage&pid=2#.UZklyys6Wds (last visited May 19, 2013).

CHAPTER 10

FARM PROPERTY LAW

Farming by its very nature depends on real property. Learning the legal lingo of *real property law* and the basics of acquiring, using, and disposing of real property can be as crucial for a farmer as learning the difference between diesel and gasoline. This Chapter gives a cursory overview of farm property law.

Real Estate

Types of Deeds

Property ownership is most often conveyed or transferred by either a *Warranty Deed* or a *Quitclaim Deed*. A warranty deed is the best kind to get if you are a buyer purchasing a piece of real estate. With a warranty deed, a seller "warrants" good ownership of the property, free and clear of any outside claims or faults. If something should come up later that questions the validity of good title to the property, the seller remains liable. In other words, the seller will remain responsible if a title issue presents itself.

In contrast, a seller who gives a quitclaim deed simply abandons ("*quits*") whatever ownership interest or claim, if any, that the seller has on a piece of property. The seller may or may not have good title. The seller makes no warranty of ownership. The quitclaim deed also puts the risk of *surprises* on the buyer.

Warranty deeds are the preferred method to transfer title when buying real estate. However, while the quitclaim deed may sound risky, this kind of deed is perfectly adequate in some situations. In fact, it is the standard deed used in certain circumstances and it can even be used to cure some types of existing problems with title to a piece of land.

Property laws affecting title can be quite complex. A buyer should consult an attorney who can determine the validity of the seller's ownership interests after reviewing a title opinion.

Types of Real Property Ownership

Joint Ownership of Property

You can own a piece of real estate jointly with another person or persons. Joint ownership means that each co-owner owns a given interest in the entire piece of real estate – usually, each owns an equal, but not necessarily.

What does it mean to co-own property jointly with someone? Even if two people each own an equal interest in a piece of property, there is no physical "half" of it that one can fence off and keep from the other. Instead, each co-owner has the right to use an undivided interest in the whole property along with the right to one-half of the proceeds if the property is sold. If the joint owners cannot agree on how to use the property, *a "partition" lawsuit* can be filed in court by one of the joint owners where a judge is asked to put an end to the joint ownership and force the sale of the property.

There are *different forms* of joint ownership. The rights and obligations that result from them depend on the language that is used in your deed. Here are different forms of joint ownership and a few notes about the rights of the co-owners in each situation:

- **Joint Tenants with Rights of Survivorship ("JTWRS")**: If one co-owner dies, the surviving co-owner(s) automatically own the deceased person's interest. If you are the survivor, you need only file an affidavit when the other co-owner dies in order to take good title to his or her portion.

- **Tenants in Common ("TIC")**: This form of joint ownership does not include survivorship rights for the co-owners. If one co-owner dies, his or her Last Will and Testament likely controls what happens to his or her interest.

- **Life Estates**: In this arrangement, a person has ownership rights in a piece of property that last only for the length of time that the person is alive. A life interest is not perpetual, and it is generally followed by a *"remainder"* interest granted to some other person(s).

> For many years, a life estate to the surviving spouse with a remainder interest to the children was a **cheap, effective way** to pass real estate without a lot of complex will-drafting. It allowed a widow to continue to benefit from the land, while ensuring that the children ultimately took title to it. Further, the life estate ensured that a second spouse and that spouse's children didn't "get their hands on" family assets, usually farm ground. The elder generation essentially got to behave as if the ground was still entirely theirs (rent collected, taxes paid, military and homestead exemptions applied) until their deaths.

Property rights are said to be like a *bundle of sticks*. Each aspect of property (right to use, responsibility to pay taxes, mineral rights, wind farm rights) is one of the sticks in the bundle. Owners or co-owners with full ownership rights (called a *"fee interest"*) hold the entire bundle of sticks. Under a *life estate*, one person holds onto the *right to occupy* and use the property along with the *responsibility to pay the taxes* (the life estate holder). Another person(s) (remainderman) hold(s) the rest, and when the first person dies, those property right "sticks" transfer to the second person(s).

The *remaindermen* have some rights even while a life estate holder is still alive. For example, the remaindermen can prevent "waste" of the value of the property, such as logging trees from the property or the demolition of good quality buildings. As a caveat, enforcing these rights can sometimes turn into an expensive litigation battle. In such cases, it is suggested that the remainderman first try to use an agriculture mediator to help resolve the dispute.

Problems with Life Estates

Court rulings and modern realities make life estates less appealing than they might seem. First, while the transfer occurs upon the life estate holder's death, the remaindermen cannot take those sticks without clearing a *Medicaid lien* on the property. The value of the life estate holder's interest is figured just prior to his death. This can mean that despite transfer of substantial interest in the farm prior to death, a life estate holder can be made to pay back part of monies advanced for care in a long-term care facility.

Second, the *tax basis* for a life estate property is established at the time of transfer-- not at death. If it was not a sale with a retained life estate, then the remaindermen get the transferor's presumably low basis in the property, instead of the higher "stepped-up" basis that they would have received had the property been transferred via probate proceedings. This means that more *taxable income* will be recognized if and when the remaindermen sell the property.

It gets even more tangled and snarled when folks *retain* a life estate to their spouse, then a *life estate to their children* and make the *grandchildren the remaindermen*. This can run afoul of *federal gift tax law*, because the gift to the grandchildren is a gift of a future interest and there is no *gift tax exclusion* is available for such a gift. Thus, the life estate may still have some applicability, but its use as a quick and easy way to avoid planning is fading.

Easements

Sometimes, one piece of property acquires an *easement* to *make use of or cross over* another property. Easements can be for travel, access, drainage, noise, smell, or any number of things that could otherwise burden the property subject to the easement. Easements are just another stick in the bundle of sticks that make up property rights. These rights can be given freely or they can be taken from the other property, as a *matter of right*.

Easements are usually agreed upon between the parties; however, there are also *proscriptive easements*. Proscriptive easements are the kind that can be taken from another property without agreement. This idea is akin to adverse possession.

A good easement contains the *legal descriptions* from the recorded deeds of both the properties involved. It should be written as specifically as possible, with an eye towards preventing future problems.

> An easement to allow "access to the pasture" is vague. Does it mean access to drive cattle across the parcel? Can a party use farm equipment when the pasture is torn up? An easement that is 15 feet wide was probably great in 1948, but now is too small to allow passage of larger, modern farm implements. The easement should address who has to maintain the property and how costs get shared.

The best course is to have an attorney prepare a written easement. A poorly-written easement that leaves room for confusion is likely to lead to conflicts later that will have to be settled in court, and that situation will produce much larger attorneys' fees, other costs, and potential business losses for all involved.

Purchasing Property

All *property purchase agreements* need to be in writing, or they are not enforceable. All binding agreements follow a simple formula of **Offer + Acceptance + Consideration** (payment of the purchase price) **= Binding Contract** (think back to Chapter 4 on Contracts).

> Neither "I will buy your farm today" or "I will buy your farm for $10,000 *someday*" are valid contracts.

Oftentimes when evaluating the value of the farmland one forgets to think about the value of buildings, dwellings, well, tile, fences and improvements, and dates of possession. Unless otherwise agreed upon, if you buy real estate, the *crops growing* on the farm property pass with it.

- **From the buyer's standpoint**, a portion of the purchase price should be allocated to the *residence* (which cannot be depreciated), buildings, fences and wells (which are depreciable to the buyer), and then a portion to the bare ground.

- **From the seller's standpoint**, it would be best to have as much of the purchase price as possible allocated to the residence. This is because the seller receives favorable tax treatment as a capital gain (and in some cases, could be completely excluded from gain tax). The seller wants no more assigned to the buildings, fences, tile and well than they have remaining on the depreciation schedule, as the excess assigned to those items will be treated as ordinary income, which is not as favorable as a capital gain.

Adverse Possession

When does "**the back forty**" become "**the back forty-two**"? The subject of acquiring title to property by *adverse possession* always seems to generate interest and discussion, but when the facts and the law are peeled back far enough, adverse possession is rare. Adverse possession is the *acquisition of title (not use) to property* by possession. From a practical standpoints, courts make it difficult to obtain property through adverse possession. A plaintiff must prove each of the elements.

The party claiming title by adverse possession must have *clear and convincing* evidence that establishes *hostile, actual, open, exclusive, and continuous possession, under claim of right or color of title, for at least 10 years* (the statute of limitations in New York). Each of these *required elements* for adverse possession presents a separate hurdle:

1. **Hostile Possession**: Hostility refers to *words or acts* that show a person claims a right to use the land. Where no formal declarations of intent are made, hostility can be demonstrated by acts characteristic of an owner, rather than those of a mere user, such as maintaining and improving land. Interestingly, payment of taxes is not essential to the acquisition of title by adverse possession. Permissive use of land is not considered to be hostile or under a claim of right even if it continues over a long period of time. So if your neighbor knows you cut through his yard and waves to you when you do it, then the hostility is defeated.

2. **Actual Possession**: For there to be actual possession, the claimant need not live upon land, enclose it with fences, or stand guard. It is enough if the claimant *treats the property like his/her own ground.* That said, the conduct required to claim a building is different from the conduct required to claim a wooded lot. A *claim of ownership* may be shown by receiving the rents, issues, and profits of the property, by improving it, or by paying for insurance on the property.

3. **Open/Notorious Possession**: This requires proof or showing that the true owner *should be aware* somebody else is claiming the ground. In other words, it is not done in secret. Erecting signs and buildings or cropping the land are all things that should indicate to the true owner that someone is using the ground.

4. **Exclusive Possession**: The possession of the property must be exclusive. *A mixed, shared or scrambled possession is not exclusive* and will not ripen into title. Again, when you cut across the neighbor's yard and he uses the same route, you are not establishing possession.

5. **Continuous Possession**: This element of adverse possession requires a *type of claim* and a *holding period* of 10 years. The two types of claims are *Claim of Right* or *Color of Title*, discussed below.

   • A **Claim of Right** is described as "I think the land is mine." Good Faith is essential. If the person claiming adverse possession didn't believe the land was theirs, then the Claim of Right basis for adverse possession fails. An example of this can be found in a case in which a woman attempted to claim a strip of her neighbor's land by adverse possession. The court denied her claim because she knew it was not her property, even though she had treated the property as her own for 30 years.

   • **Color of Title** is a document-based claim, summed up as, "somebody gave me a document that says the property is mine." An example could be a mistyped deed, title, or last will, which leads you to believe you own part of the neighboring property, a title document which appears to grant you title, but in reality is no title. Such a document, taken in good faith, gives you a toehold to a claim of adverse possession. So if you take a deed for the southwest quarter of the southwest quarter of Section 6 and live on it and hold it for ten years, even though you were only sold the southern half of the southwest quarter of the southwest quarter of Section 6, you may have a claim.

6. **For Ten (10) Years**. This is a simple math problem (usually). Consider a scenario in which you have maintained an abandoned railroad right-of-way as your own for years and otherwise meet all the elements for adverse possession. Under Claim of Right, you thought the land was yours when the tracks were pulled up; or, under Color of Title, the strip was conveyed to you, when really belongs to an out-of-state investor. Five days before the end of the 10 years, the investor's summer intern comes out and says, "Thanks for taking care of that. We are putting in a new ethanol spur line here, so you can take your last crop off." The ten-year period is most likely not met and you are out of a strip of land.

Sound simple? Consider this real-life example from a court case:

A disputed strip of land was between parcels owned by two hunting clubs. The disputed land was included in the plaintiff's title description, as demonstrated by a survey performed more than 10 years before the plaintiff brought suit to quiet title. Both parties provided evidence of use of the disputed area by hunters. Both owners placed deer stands in the disputed area and both removed stands placed by the other party. Although a barbed-wire fence existed in the disputed area, the fence had not been maintained by either party and was not continuous.

The court held that the defendant failed to prove exclusive use of the disputed area; therefore, title remained with the plaintiff as record titleholder. Here, the defendant should have spoken up loud and often, if it believed it had title to that disputed strip. Waiting ten years to raise a fuss about the issue probably weighed heavily against any claim it asserted on the property.

Acquiring title through adverse possession is a lot harder than just claiming that the fence post was moved ten years ago and now you own what's inside it. You'd make a better investment of your time and money by having conversations with the neighbors to buy their property if you want to buy it. Alternatively, if a dispute arises hire an agriculture mediator to "get in the middle" to facilitate a discussion.

Tax Planning in Property Transactions

Capital gains tax is generally lower than ordinary income tax rates. The tax is computed on an amount equal to the difference in your *basis* in the property and the amount you get when you sell or dispose of the property. There are variations, but that is the essential rule.

Basis has a specific legal definition. Simply put, it is amount you pay for a property you purchase; however, there are a variety of things that can push your basis up or down affecting your ultimate tax liability when you get rid of the property. For example, if you acquire property by some means that is not a purchase, you may get a *transferred basis* related to the cost paid for the property by the previous owner, or you could get a *stepped-up basis* related to the value of the property at the time you receive it.

A *step-up in basis* is a concept that allows a person who receives property from an estate to pay capital gains tax on only the difference between the *value at the date of the donor's death* and at the *date of sale*. On the other hand, if the property is gifted to the same person while the donor is still alive, the cost basis that the gift-giver paid for the property *transfers* to the new person.

- Let's say a farm was bought in 1950 for $300 per acre and given to the next generation during the owner's lifetime, in 2011, when the market value was $10,000 per acre, the gift donee would get a transferred basis of $300 per acre. If the donee sold the property at current market price, he/she would pay capital gains tax on $9,700 per acre.

- On the other hand, if the next generation inherited the property in 2011, the recipient would get a *stepped-up basis* of $10,000/acre. If the recipient sold the property for $12,000 an acre in 2014, only $2,000 per acre would be subject to capital gain tax.

The IRS allows you to *delay paying capital gains taxes* on a sale by conducting a *"like kind" exchange*. This is a process where you give up one piece of property and acquire another similar property in exchange. The basis from your *old property* is transferred to the *new property* and you delay paying capital gains tax until you sell the new property. However, with careful tax planning developed by an attorney and/or accountant, you can exchange into another property, and then hold that until death, when your heirs will receive a step up in basis and pay lower capital gains tax.

When you pay for property, you need to use a real estate agent or an attorney to close the transaction. This ensures all the terms of your agreement are enforced, and that the transaction is properly recorded. If there is a mortgage on the property at the time of purchase, the bank's lawyer will prepare a HUD-1 settlement statement showing how the purchase price, along with credits and additional expenses, are allocated.

Fence Law

In New York, property owners grazing livestock are required to *erect, maintain and repair* the fenceline. Under *New York Town Law* § 300, each owner of two adjoining tracts of land is required to erect and maintain a fence to keep his/her grazing animals separate, unless they agree (*in writing*) to let their lands lie open to allow the animals to graze on either property. If one of the owners has not kept animals in the past five years, then that owner is not responsible for erecting, maintaining, or repairing a division fence. In New York, a livestock farmer has the responsibility to "fence in" his/her livestock. Taking time to inspect your fence (and taking notes in a journal) is a good plan for livestock owners.

Additionally, NY Town Law § 303-5 vests in town officials known as "fence viewers" the power to **investigate** and determine who is responsible for *refusing or neglecting* to make or maintain a division fence, and to assess the actual damage caused by such neglect. Moreover, under § 307-8, if livestock from an adjoining property damages the property of an owner who was at fault for failing to make or maintain his fence, then the failure to maintain the fence precludes recovery for damage from the strayed animal. Failure to maintain your fence will also preclude the owner of purebred stock from bringing a cause of action against the owner of a stallion, buck, or boar who strays and damages that stock.

Under NY Town Law § 309, *barbed or other wire* may be used in the construction of any division fence, provided that such fence be constructed as follows:

- Have at **least four strands of wire**;

- With posts and supports no further than fourteen feet apart (or such distance that the local officials prescribe); and

- Built as a reasonably sufficient enclosure for holding the particular kind or class of cattle or animals usually pastured on either side of the fence.

Under section 309, if an *unrepaired fence* is unsafe, then it shall be the duty of the owner or owners to *immediately repair* it.

Finally, under N.Y. Real. Prop. Acts. § 843, *if you erect any fence or structure taller than ten feet in height* for the purpose of excluding the adjacent land's *enjoyment of light or air*, then your neighbor may have a private nuisance claim against you.

Wind Farms

As the real estate truism states– in wind development, the key is *location, location, location*. The first question that every landowner should ask themselves is whether their property is suitable for a wind farm. Wind speed is the most obvious factor in determining suitability of a property. Wind speed data is available through the *National Renewable Energy Laboratory* ("NREL"); however, some agriculture producers choose to hire an environmental consultant to receive scientific data on their property's wind potential.

That said, wind speed is just one factor in determining whether your land is marketable to wind developers. Rocky terrain and protected federal and state lands serve as constraints for wind developers. Proximity to transmission lines can also make a property more marketable. Finally, location also determines federal, state, and local legal frameworks and available economic incentives for wind developers.

Once property is determined to be suitable for wind development, it is recommended that neighboring area agriculture producers form a landowner association with one another in order to increase their collective bargaining power with wind companies. The larger block of acreage that can be bundled among landowners, the more marketable the property will be to a wind developer. Additionally, this gives farmers greater leverage to negotiate increased revenues and more favorable wind lease terms. Also, landowner associations provide an opportunity to spread out legal fees among several agriculture producers making it more affordable to retain an attorney to review and negotiate terms in the wind lease. Finally, cooperation among several producers helps improve transparency, ensuring all landowners get the best possible terms in their lease.

When negotiating a wind lease agreement, there are typically four major stages of wind development: (i) development period, (ii) construction period, (iii) operational period, and (iv) termination period. The duration of each of the stages should be narrowly defined in the lease.

- **Development Period**. In this initial stage, the wind company evaluates the property for its potential by completing the following activities --- wind assessments, environmental review, economic modeling, permitting, and securing financing. During this stage, other than installing a meteorological tower on the property to measure the wind, the wind developer typically makes little use of the property itself.

- **Construction Period**. During the construction period, wind turbine generators, steel towers, foundations, concrete pads, anchors, fences, and other fixtures will be installed in the pasture or field. If construction does not commence within the specified time, the lease should terminate automatically, or the wind developer may tie-up the land for forty plus years without ever constructing a turbine on the property.

- **Operational Period**. Next, during the operational period, wind energy is being generated on the property, transmitted to available markets, and sold for profit. The operational period may last up to 50-60 years.

- **Termination Period**. In this phase, the party ends and the wind developer ceases to produce wind energy. Here, the wind developer is obligated to remove his/her equipment from the farmer or rancher's property. This is commonly referred to as *"decommissioning."* Decommissioning may be limited to a few months, while remediation may take several years to adequately complete.

Since a farmer's property will be significantly encumbered by a wind lease, an agriculture producer should make sure he or she is adequately compensated. There are no clear-cut rules with financial revenues as the market varies due to *geographic location, total acreage, wind speed, terrain, proximity to transmission lines,* and available *economic incentives* for the wind developer. Due to the uncertainty in the market and whether a wind developer will actually develop a piece of property, agriculture producers should try to secure as much money as possible up front.

With wind lease negotiations, knowledge of the potential of the wind project is key to understanding value. One way to get a lot of information easily is to obtain a copy of the *Power Purchase Agreement* ("PPA") between the wind company and the electric company, which will have the electrical sale rate and the estimated production capability. An inflation factor should be built into any kind of fixed-payment arrangement.

Conditions of use can also affect the value of the contract. Look to the agreement to see if the power company has any duty to actually put up a tower, or if it is simply locking out competitors from entering an area. A hard-fought right to a percentage of the production generated is not worth anything if no duty to actually produce wind energy on the site actually exists.

Landowners should also be aware of *Renewable Energy Credits* ("REC") - an important, but sometimes overlooked, second source of revenue from a wind project. In some cases, the power is sold to one source, and the REC can be sold to an entirely different company, which may need the REC to offset the non-renewable energy it is creating from other power production plants. Changing federal and state laws are steadily increasing the value of REC to energy companies and thus increasing the value to a sharp landowner.

If helping your local community is of greater value to you than the money to be gained from the contract, make sure that the company you're doing business with will actually be helping to meet that goal. For example, a national company will not likely have an impact on the local economy, as the profits from wind generation will flow to its shareholders. Some communities have created locally-owned wind production projects as a way to keep the value-added resource of wind production dollars in the community. For some, this distinction may be critical in deciding which company to sign with.

Financial terms in a wind lease should be periodically *adjusted for inflation*. Before signing a wind lease, farmers should consider the following *financial terms*:

- **Minimum Rent**. Landowners should ideally negotiate for an annual minimum rental payment which should periodically increase each year during the development period. This helps ensure a guaranteed amount of money each year for the livestock farmer or rancher, regardless of fluctuations in the market or wind production.

- **Construction Bonus**. Agriculture producers should negotiate a "construction bonus" in addition to the annual minimum rental payment for the time during which the developer commences construction on the wind farm.

- **Royalties**. After construction, when the wind turbines become operational and generate electricity for sale by the wind developer, farmers and ranchers will typically receive an annual royalty--oftentimes a percentage of the gross revenues. The royalty percentage should also periodically increase and include a percentage of any money received by the wind developer in lieu of the sale of electricity.

- **Termination Fee**. Farmers should negotiate to receive a "termination fee" if the wind developer terminates the lease agreement prior to construction. This is appropriate since the farmer or rancher loses revenue for the period necessary to negotiate with another developer.

- **Attorneys' Fees**. Especially if a landowner association is formed, farmers and ranchers should not be shy to ask the wind developer to pay for all or part of legal expenses necessary during negotiation or litigation that may arise out of the wind lease.

- **Payment for Other Uses**. Among the other uses for which an agriculture producer can expect payment include the following: roads, transmission lines, substations, meteorological towers, and payments for access to in-holdings if the land includes a large amount of federal or state land within its boundaries.

Agriculture producers should also reserve the right to conduct an audit from time to time to verify that they are receiving the amount of money guaranteed to them under the terms of the lease agreement.

The *length* of the wind-energy lease should be considered, with a view to the fact that land-use decisions made now may have a long-term impact on the availability of the land for later, profitable use by you or your heirs. Most leases are for a period of 20 years or longer, but some attempt to reach into perpetuity.

The lease agreement should not only *identify the uses* for the wind developer, but it should also *reserve all other uses* to the agriculture producer (e.g., farming). For example, the agreement should reserve all rights to mineral exploration and development to the landowner, as well as all water, hunting, fishing, and solar rights. Furthermore, farmers may wish to protect part of his/her property from development such as the riparian areas, irrigation ditches, or boulder formations.

Most wind lease agreements will include an *indemnification provision* requiring both parties to defend and hold each other harmless from claims for any future loss or damage arising from the various uses of the property. *Beware of this provision* as farmers are not on an equal playing field with wind developers. To explain, any loss to the landowner arising from the wind developer's use and occupation of the land may total in the thousands or tens-of-thousands of dollars; however, any loss to the wind developer arising from the landowner's use and occupation of his own land may total in the millions or tens-of-millions of dollars.

As expected, wind energy development will inherently increase the property value on a farm. Due to this fact, agriculture producers should make sure that the lease agreement assigns any increase in property taxes to the wind developer–otherwise, the increase will be the burden to the landowner. In addition, any utilities necessary for the construction or operation of the wind farm should be the responsibility of the wind developer.

Without question, the wind lease agreement will specify whether the landowner and the wind developer may assign the contractual rights and obligations to third parties. Almost always, wind developers will request freedom to sublease, assign, and mortgage their rights without the consent of the landowner. These broad rights may be necessary in order for the wind developer to obtain financing; however, farmers should demand to be notified each time the lease is transferred to another party to understand who is responsible for any default of the lease agreement.

The landowner should require the wind developer to *keep the land free and clear of all liens* related to the wind farm. It should be the responsibility of the wind developer instead of the landowner to contract and make payment for all labor and materials related to the construction of the wind farm. Additionally, the wind lease should not hold the farmer responsible if the wind developer cannot afford to pay for labor and materials.

One of the most important provisions of any wind agreement is the *default and termination clause*. Most wind leases allow the wind developer the ability to terminate the lease at any time and for any reason, while the landowner has little autonomy to terminate the agreement. Farmers and ranchers should negotiate to have the ability to terminate the lease if the wind developer defaults in any way, such as fails to: pay rent, maintain adequate insurance, pay taxes, or meet any other obligation in the contract.

In the event of default, or termination of the lease, the landowner should specify how much time the wind developer is permitted to remove the wind turbines from the land. Payment must also be established during this time period. In order to prevent the wind developer from simply walking away from the project, farmers or ranchers should demand a *"decommissioning security"* to be paid as soon as the wind turbines become operational.

Designating proper *reclamation* provisions is one of the most important aspects of the wind lease agreement. Reclamation is necessary during construction, operation, repairs, and after the project has been removed from the land. Agriculture producers cannot rely on the governmental authorities to protect their property so reclamation must be adequately explained in the lease itself. This is particularly important if the landowner's property has any unique characteristics or wildlife habitats that need to be protected.

Reclamation measures should identify the means by which to keep track of the original condition of the property, either through photographs or an assessment prepared by a range professional. Moreover, other reclamation measures should discuss the following issues:

- identification of improvements that should be removed,
- instructions on depth of soil removal,
- description of stockpiling of topsoil and storage during construction,
- decompaction of the soil,
- reclamation of roads,
- vegetation,
- erosion,
- seeding,
- noxious weeds,
- dust control, and
- trash removal.

The above-mentioned issues are the most important to properly negotiate with a wind energy company before entering into this type of long-term agreement. However, there are several miscellaneous issues that may need attention, such as a *forum selection clause*, *arbitration clause*, *condemnation*, or discussion of what happens to land included in a **conservation reserve program** ("CRP") or in any other governmental program. All agriculture producers are encouraged to contact an attorney to review a wind lease before entering into an agreement that may potentially impact his or her land for decades to come.

Additional Resources

Jessica A. Shoemaker, "Negotiating Wind Energy Property Agreements" (2007) available at http://www.flaginc.org/wp-content/uploads/2013/03/WindPropertyAgrmnts20071.pdf (last visited May 19, 2013).

Jessica A. Shoemaker, "Farmers' Guide to Wind Energy: Legal Issues in Farming the Wind" (June 2007) available at http://www.flaginc.org/wp-content/uploads/2013/03/FGWEcomplete.pdf (last visited May 19, 2013).

Monika Roth and Jacob Schuelke, "Guide to Starting a Farm Business in New York State" (November 13, 2004) (Property Tax Exemptions, Financing Options) available at http://ccejefferson.org/wp-content/uploads/2009/09/GuidetoStartingYourFarmBusinessinNew YorkState.pdf (last visited July 24, 2013).

Oklahoma State University Cooperative Extension, "Wind Energy Leasing Handbook" Publication No. E-1033, available at http://nationalaglawcenter.org/assets/articles/rrumley_windenergyha ndbook.pdf (last visited May 19, 2013).

Stoel Rives, LLP, "The Law of Wind: A Guide to Business and Legal Issues" available at http://www.stoel.com/webfiles/LawOfWind.pdf (last visited May 19, 2013).

Stoel Rives, LLP, "The Law of Solar Energy: A Guide to Business and Legal Issues" available at http://www.stoel.com/showindustry.aspx?Show=1634 (last visited July 24, 2013).

CHAPTER 11

ENVIRONMENTAL REGULATION

There are numerous federal and state environmental laws that affect how New York farms are managed. Farmers must work within this regulatory framework to protect environmental resources and ensure compliance. The following is a review of key regulations designed to protect water, air, land, and wildlife. Farms should seek assistance from an attorney and environmental consultant if issues arise.

Water

The Federal *Clean Water Act* ("CWA") was enacted in 1972 with the goal of protecting the country's waterways from pollution. *Environmental Protection Agency* ("EPA") is charged with enforcing the CWA at the federal level. Meanwhile, the *New York Department of Environmental Conservation* ("DEC") works at the state level to protect New York's water resources. While states must adhere to the regulations imposed by the CWA, most states have also enacted additional legislation that addresses water quality issues locally and often with more stringent requirements. The two key laws in New York impacting water quality are the *New York Water Resources Law* ("WRL") and the *New York Water Pollution Control Law* ("WPCL").

Sources of water pollution are generally classified as being either point or nonpoint. *Point source* water pollution is discharged from a *discernable and identifiable source* such as a pipe, ditch, well, or concentrated animal feeding operation ("CAFO"). *Nonpoint source* pollution is caused by nonspecific, more diffuse sources, such as when land runoff, rainfall and seepage spread agricultural chemicals and waste, salt from irrigation systems, or sediment to surrounding groundwater and waterways.

The EPA regulates point source pollution through the *National Pollutant Discharge Elimination System* ("NPDES"). A NPDES permit is required to lawfully discharge any pollutant into navigable waters. In New York, the EPA has delegated the responsibility of issuing permits for point source discharge into state waters to the NYDEC, which issues a *State Pollutant Discharge Elimination System* ("SPDES") permit in lieu of a NPDES. See N.Y. Envl. Conserv. Law § 17-0101 et seq. Depending on the activity and the water body involved, additional permits may be required. As previously mentioned, CAFO's are treated as point sources, and resultant water pollution requires permitting. For example, a farmer operating a CAFO that discharges water from a feedlot's lagoon into a stream must obtain the appropriate SPDES permit.

States typically regulate nonpoint source pollution through the implementation of best management practices. See 33 U.S.C § 1329. The NYDEC has implemented a variety of initiatives including permits, training, and education to abate nonpoint source pollution. *New York County Water Quality Coordinating Committees* ("CWQCCs") have also been established to address nonpoint source pollution concerns at the local level. New York's *Agricultural Environmental Management Program* ("AEM") is a voluntary, incentive-based program that helps farmers identify potential nonpoint sources of pollution and develop a plan to protect the environment while maintaining the farm's commercial viability.

Adherence to both state and federal water pollution control laws is imperative. Violation of these laws can result in administrative, civil, and criminal penalties. Violators can be fined up to $1,000,000 per occurrence and face up to 15 years in prison. See 33 U.S.C. §§ 1318 & 1319; N.Y. Envl. Conserv. Law § 17-0303.

Air

The Federal *Clean Air Act* ("CAA") was signed into law in 1970 and Congress enacted the last major amendments in 1990. The CAA charges the EPA with the protection and improvement of the country's air quality and the ozone layer. The *New York Air Pollution Control Act* ("APCA") empowers the NYDEC to administer the federal CAA programs and to adopt and enforce regulations for preventing, controlling, and prohibiting air pollution within the state. Similar to the CWA, the APCA requires that stationary sources of air pollution obtain an appropriate operating permit.

In 2009, The EPA implemented the *Mandatory Reporting of Greenhouse Gases* ("GHSs") rule. See C.F.R. 40 § 98(JJ). According to this rule, agricultural and livestock facilities with manure management systems are required to file a report with the EPA if the operation emits 25,000 metrics tons of carbon dioxide equivalent per year. GHS emissions resulting from enteric fermentation, rice cultivation, field burning of agricultural residues, composting, agricultural soils, and carbon storage do not trigger this reporting requirement. See Guide for the Agriculture and Livestock Sectors, Final Rule: Mandatory Reporting of Greenhouse Gases, September 2009.

New York law restricts the *open burning* of many materials. The burning of agricultural waste is permitted if:

- It is done *on-site* as part of a valid agricultural operation;
- The waste is *grown* and *generated on-site*; and
- The waste is capable of being *fully burned* within 24 hours.

See NYCRR Tit. 6 § 215.3(d).

Fertilizer bags, large plastic storage bags ("Ag bags"), offal, tires, plastic feed bags, and other plastic or synthetic materials are not considered agricultural waste and may not be burned in an open fire. Burning in barrels or modified barrels is also considered an open fire, therefore prohibited items may not be burned in such containers. See NYCRR Tit. 6 § 215.1.

Violations of the CAA can result in administrative, civil, and criminal penalties. The maximum civil penalty is $25,000 per day for each violation. The maximum prison sentence is 15 years. See 42 U.S.C. § 7413.

Land

Solid & Hazardous Waste

The Federal *Resource Conservation and Recovery Act* ("RCRA") was enacted in 1976 to protect citizens from hazardous waste by controlling the manner in which waste is disposed. The *New York Solid and Hazardous Waste Management Law* is the state counterpart to the RCRA, designed to safeguard the public while encouraging the conservation of energy and natural resources.

Both state and federal laws regulate the management of solid waste, hazardous waste, and holding tanks containing petroleum products and other chemicals by dictating how and where such waste must be disposed. Certain types of waste disposed of within the property boundaries of a farm are exempt from these regulatory requirements, including:

- Solid waste generated within the property boundaries of the farm;
- Animal and aquaculture manure, carcasses, and parts generated from farm activities; and
- Pesticide waste disposed of in accordance with the guidelines printed on the pesticide labeling

Although pesticide waste is excluded from the RCRA and the state law, the *Federal Insecticide, Fungicide, and Rodenticide Act* ("FIFRA") imposes restrictions on farmers regarding the management of pesticides.

Disposal of non-exempt waste may place a farmer into one of three RCRA generator categories: (1) Conditionally Exempt Small Quantity Generator, (2) Small Quantity Generator, and (3) Large Quantity Generator. Each classification carries with it corresponding requirements, such as:

- Obtaining an EPA identification number,
- Waste limits,
- Accumulation limits,
- Storage management,
- Reporting,
- Training, and
- Preparedness and prevention planning.

New York's Hazardous Substances Bulk Storage Act ("HSBSA") and *Chemical Bulk Storage Regulations* ("CBSR") govern the management of hazardous substances, excluding petroleum products, stored in underground, aboveground, and non-stationary storage tanks. Bulk storage of petroleum products are controlled separately under *New York's Resource Management Services*

Regulations ("RMSR"). Under these state laws and the RCRA, farmers are subject to specific maintenance, inspection, reporting, handling, and storage requirements for petroleum and hazardous chemicals.

Farmers must practice proper spill prevention, maintenance, and disposal of waste protocols. The improper handling of waste material, hazardous chemicals, or petroleum can result in administrative, civil, and criminal penalties. Farmers are encouraged to contact the DEC if they are unsure whether specific waste is hazardous to ensure proper compliance.

Pesticides & Chemicals

The EPA administers the *Federal Insecticide, Fungicide, and Rodenticide Act* ("FIFRA"). It is designed to control the sale, use, and distribution of pesticides. FIFRA requires that all pesticides used in the United States be registered and licensed by the EPA. All registered pesticides must be properly labeled with usage, storage, and disposal specifications. It is unlawful to use a registered pesticide in a way that deviates from the label specifications.

New York pesticide laws and regulations enforce FIFRA guidelines at the state level and apply to the agricultural application of pesticides and chemigation of crops, animals, soil, and commodities. The DEC oversees the registration, commercial use, purchase, and custom application of pesticides.

Similar to the EPA registration requirement, every pesticide product used, distributed, sold, or offered for sale within the state of New York or transported in intrastate commerce must be registered with the DEC. The DEC maintains a list of all restricted pesticides that require a use permit before being distributed, sold, purchased, possessed, or used within the state. All restricted pesticides must be stored, used, and disposed of in a manner that does not injure people, animals, property, or the environment. Grape vineyards are subject to special pesticide use regulations.

Wildlife

The goal of the Federal *Endangered Species Act* ("ESA") of 1973 is to create conservation programs and incentive systems to safeguard the nation's fish, wildlife, and plants. The *U.S. Fish and*

Wildlife Service ("USFWS") is tasked with overseeing ESA regulations. New York's various laws and regulations related to water pollution, waste management, and pesticides are tailored to protect wildlife, aquatic life, and their habitats.

The *New York Fish and Wildlife Law* ("FWL") and regulations prohibit the possession, importation, or sale of certain wildlife. The FWL gives the NYDEC the authority to regulate fish and wildlife resources while also enforcing fishing and hunting laws. Farmers hunting or fishing on their own farmland are exempt from NYDEC licensing requirements. See N.Y. Envtl. Conserv. Law §§ 11-0707. However, in accordance with the ESA and FWL, farmers may not kill, take, or wound any protected fish or wildlife on their farmland or elsewhere.

Farmers must also consider whether modifications made to farmland are considered a prohibited "taking" of protected animals. Under the ESA, the term "take" includes harassing or harming. See 16 U.S.C. § 1532(19). Therefore, such modifications that negatively affect the habitat of an endangered species may constitute a taking.

Animal Feeding Operations

An *Animal Feeding Operation* ("AFO") is a lot or facility that does not sustain crops or vegetation where animals have, are, or will be stabled, confined, fed, or maintained for at least 45 days in any 12-month period. A *Concentrated Animal Feeding Operation* ("CAFO") is an AFO with a prescribed number of animals. The number of animals stabled or confined in an AFO dictates whether the operation is categorized as a Large, Medium or Small CAFO.

Large CAFOs: Large CAFO's house a minimum of:

- 700 mature **dairy cows**, whether milked or dry;
- 1,000 **veal calves**;
- 1,000 **cattle other than mature dairy cows or veal calves** (cattle includes but is not limited to heifers, steers, bulls and cow/calf pairs);
- 2,500 **swine** each weighing 55 pounds or more;
- 10,000 **swine** each weighing less than 55 pounds;

- 500 **horses**;
- 10,000 **sheep or lambs**;
- 55,000 **turkeys**;
- 30,000 **laying hens or broilers**, if the AFO uses a liquid manure handling system;
- 125,000 **chickens** (other than laying hens), if the AFO uses other than a liquid manure handling system;
- 82,000 **laying hens**, if the AFO uses other than a liquid manure handling system;
- 30,000 **ducks** (if the AFO uses other than a liquid manure handling system); or
- 5,000 **ducks** (if the AFO uses a liquid manure handling system).

See NYCRR Tit. 6 § 750-1.2(21).

Medium CAFOs: Medium CAFO's contain:

- 200 to 699 **mature dairy cows**, whether milked or dry, except that an AFO that stables or confines 200-299 mature dairy cows, whether milked or dry so long as there is not a discharge;
- 300 to 999 **veal calves**;
- 300 to 999 **cattle other than mature dairy cows or veal calves** (cattle includes but is not limited to heifers, steers, bulls and cow/calf pairs);
- 750 to 2,499 **swine** each weighing 55 pounds or more;
- 3,000 to 9,999 **swine** each weighing less than 55 pounds;
- 150 to 499 **horses**;
- 3,000 to 9,999 **sheep or lambs**;
- 16,500 to 54,999 **turkeys**;

- 9,000 to 29,999 **laying hens or broilers**, if the AFO uses a liquid manure handling system;
- 37,500 to 124,999 **chickens** (other than laying hens), if the AFO uses other than a liquid manure handling system;
- 25,000 to 81,999 **laying hens**, if the AFO uses other than a liquid manure handling system;
- 10,000 to 29,999 **ducks** (if the AFO uses other than a liquid manure handling system); or
- 1,500 to 4,999 **ducks** (if the AFO uses a liquid manure handling system).

See NYCRR Tit. 6 § 750-1.2(21).

Small CAFOs

A small CAFO contains fewer than the prescribed number of animals required for classification as a Medium or Large CAFO, but is either designated by NYDEC as a CAFO or has requested a CAFO SPDES permit. See NYCRR Tit. 6 § 750-1.2(21). A recent change to New York CAFO rules permits a non-discharging AFO to house up to 299 mature dairy cows without being classified as a CAFO, and thus waiving the permit requirements on such operations.

CAFOs as a Point Source

As previously discussed, a CAFO is considered a point source subject to CWA and SPDES regulations, which subjects the CAFO to numerous requirements, including the following:

- CAFOs that do not discharge nor propose to discharge are eligible for a General Permit (GP-0-09-001) provided they file a Notice of Intent and either a *Comprehensive Nutrient Management Plan Certification* ("CNMP") for Medium CAFOs or *Annual Nutrient Management Plan Submittal* ("ANMPS") for Large CAFO's with the NYDEC.

- CAFO's that discharge or seek to discharge must obtain a *Clean Water Act SPDES General Permit* (GP-0-09-002).

- CAFO's may not be built within 100 feet of a stream or within the 100-year floodplain.

- CAFO's are required to submit an *Annual Compliance Report*.

- If the number of animals in a CAFO increases by 20%, the CAFO's CNMP must be updated and all maintenance standards must reflect the increase.

- Large CAFO's must send two individuals to *manure application training*.

See New York State Department of Environmental Conservation New York State Pollutant Discharge Elimination System ("SPDES") General Permit for Concentrated Animal Feeding Operations (CAFOs) (GP-0-09-001), June 12, 2009, at 3, 6-7 available at http://www.dec.ny.gov/docs/permits_ej_operations_pdf/eclcafofshe et.pdf (last visited May 11, 2013).

   The list above is simply a brief snapshot. CAFO operators must comply with many more regulatory requirements to avoid violating state and federal laws. Staying abreast of changing regulations and adhering to applicable rules is vital to a successful operation. Livestock producers with a CAFO should work closely with an agriculture lawyer and a CAFO environmental consultant to ensure compliance.

Additional Resources

Department of Environmental Conservation, "Permits for Concentrated Animal Feeding Operations (CAFOs)," at http://www.dec.ny.gov/permits/6285.html (last visited August 17, 2013).

Environmental Protection Agency, "Clean Water Act," at http://cfpub.epa.gov/npdes/cwa.cfm?program_id=45 (last visited August 17, 2013).

Megan Stubbs, "Environmental Regulation of Agriculture", Congressional Research Service Publication No. 7-5700, R41622 (February 22, 2013) available at http://www.fas.org/sgp/crs/misc/R41622.pdf (last visited May 18, 2013).

Monika Roth, "Guide to Starting a Farm Business in New York State," (November 13, 2004) (Chapter on Environmental Laws and Regulations), available at http://ccejefferson.org/wp-content/uploads/2009/09/GuidetoStartingYourFarmBusinessinNew YorkState.pdf (last visited August 17, 2013).

National Agriculture Law Center, Reading Room on "Animal Feeding Operations" at http://new.nationalaglawcenter.org/research-by-topic/afo/ (last visited August 17, 2013).

National Agriculture Law Center, Reading Room on "Clean Water Act" at http://new.nationalaglawcenter.org/research-by-topic/clean-water-act/ (last visited August 17, 2013).

National Agriculture Law Center, Reading Room on "Climate Change" at http://new.nationalaglawcenter.org/research-by-topic/climate-change/ (last visited August 17, 2013).

National Agriculture Law Center, Reading Room on "Environmental Law" at http://new.nationalaglawcenter.org/research-by-topic/environmental-law/ (last visited August 17, 2013).

National Agriculture Law Center, Reading Room on "Forestry" at http://new.nationalaglawcenter.org/research-by-topic/forestry/ (last visited August 17, 2013).

National Association of State Departments of Agriculture Research Foundation, "State Environmental Laws Affecting New York Agriculture", available at http://efotg.sc.egov.usda.gov/references/public/NY/NewYork.pdf (last visited August 17, 2013).

CHAPTER 12

LAND USE, ZONING AND THE RIGHT-TO-FARM

Land use and zoning law can greatly impact farms – both rural and urban – and food entrepreneurs. Before purchasing or renting a farm or starting a food business, one should sit down with a food and agriculture lawyer to ascertain whether there are any potential land use or zoning issues that should be addressed. Once a farm is up and running, it is important for producers to understand the New York Right-to-Farm Law and their right to commence mediation with disgruntled neighbors with nuisance complaints.

Background

The authority to regulate land use at the local level in New York is derived from the state's delegated *police power* to make laws necessary and proper to preserve *public security, order, health, morality and justice.* Local governments like zoning boards may promulgate land use regulations under its police power in the following four areas:

- *Type of Use* (e.g., agricultural, commercial, residential);
- *Density of Use* (e.g., height and width);
- *Aesthetic Impact of Use* (e.g., design and placement of structures on the land); and
- Effect of use on the community's *cultural and social values* (e.g., preservation of agriculture, encouragement of local food systems, prevention of urban encroachment on open land space).

In order for a land use regulation to be valid under police power, it must be:

- For a *public purpose*,
- Through means *reasonably tailored* to that purpose, and
- In a manner that *does not impose excessive costs* on individuals.

Local governments in New York must engage in a formal planning process where it promulgates a *comprehensive plan* (or "master plan"). Zoning ordinances are then promulgated pursuant to this comprehensive plan. The zoning code might prohibit agriculture production or other types of *commercial activities* (e.g., home-based food processing) in residential areas.

Land Use Issues with Urban Agriculture

Although land use and zoning issues can also affect agriculture in rural areas throughout New York state, an urban or suburban farmer should carefully review the zoning code. According to Dean Patricia Salkin at Touro Law Center in the "Counseling the Local Food Movement" webinar with the American Bar Association, there are several zoning mechanisms that can be used to promote *small-scale agriculture production* within city limits:

- **Comprehensive Plan**: As noted above, this is the over-arching plan upon which land use regulations are implemented. It sets forth the purposes and goals of the land use regulation in that county. It is important that the comprehensive plan itself emphasize the importance of small-scale commercial agriculture production within the city limits and the promotion of locally grown food and home-based food processing.

- **Zoning Ordinances**: If various types of urban agriculture and agri-tourism (or agri-tainment) are not addressed in the zoning ordinances/code, local governments may amend existing provisions allowing for same. Common restrictions in zoning ordinances include road setbacks, lot size, dimensions, signage size and placement, site plan requirements, screening, etc.

- **Definitions**: Local governments may consider adding/clarifying definitions used with urban agriculture such as "rooftop garden," "community garden," "green roof," "small scale urban agriculture," "animal harvesting facility," "food distribution facility" etc. (or whatever the appropriate terms are for that locality) to ensure that the definitions are clear to the community.

- **Uses Allowed "As of Right"**: Zoning ordinances typically describe the permitted uses, as of right, within a given district. As such, food production should be prescribed within certain districts as a matter of right.

- **Accessory Uses**: Accessory uses are incidental to the primary use of the building on which they are located. For example, a rooftop garden on a residential building in Brooklyn would be an accessory use. Local governments can amend zoning laws to allow small-scale production agriculture as an accessory use.

- **Special Use or Conditional Use Permits**: Some local governments allow for small scale agriculture production through *special use* or *conditional use permits*. Such uses are not allowed "as of right." Instead, they are subject to additional review by the local zoning board or legislative body.

- **Overlay Districts**: An overlay district may be used as a mechanism to *preserve* certain areas (e.g., historic area, hazard prevention) or to *promote* certain types of urban/suburban agriculture.

- **Home-Based Business Regulations**: Zoning ordinances may have an allowance for small-scale home-based food processing (cottage food operations) at residential locations and on-site farmstands.

Cities that allow for the use of *backyard chickens* may place specifications on the following: (1) number of hens, (2) setbacks for coops/pens, (3) number of roosters (if allowed at all), (4) neighbor consent, (5) pest control, and (6) feed storage. Local zoning ordinances that allow for *urban apiaries* may post regulations for the lot size and setbacks.

Agricultural Districts and the Right-to-Farm

NY Agric. & Mkts § 300 et seq. sets forth agricultural districts in New York. "The socio-economic vitality of agriculture in this state is essential to the *economic stability and growth* of many local communities and the state as a whole. It is, therefore, the declared policy of the state to *conserve, protect and encourage* the development and improvement of its agricultural land for production of food and other agricultural products." See NY Agric. & Mkts § 300.

Section 303 sets forth the standards for *creation* of "agricultural districts." Any owner or group of owners that owns the greater of: (1) at least *500 acres*, or (2) at least *ten percent* of the land proposed to be included in the district, is eligible to submit a proposal to the county legislative body. At a minimum, the proposal must include "a description of the proposed district, including a map delineating the exterior boundaries which shall conform to tax parcel boundaries, and the tax map identification numbers for every parcel in the posed district." NYSDAM may impose additional requirements for the proposal. After complying with *notice and hearing requirements*, the county legislative body may adopt a plan to create an "agricultural district." In order to be adopted, the plan must include "an appropriate *review period*," typically of *eight, twelve, or twenty years*.

The operative feature of New York's Right-to-Farm Statute is in Section 308, which bars private nuisance suits if "the Commissioner issues an opinion that a particular agricultural practice is sound[.]" Pure Air and Water Inc. of Chemong County v. Davidsen, 668 N.Y.S.2d 248, 249 (1998). The statute only applies to actions for *"private nuisance."* However, the same conduct which it protects could still be actionable pursuant to other theories, such as public nuisance, trespass, or violations of federal environmental statutes. See, e.g., Concerned Area Residents for the Environment v. Southview Farm, 843 F.Supp. 1410 (W.D.N.Y. 1993). It is also inapplicable to damages for any personal injury or wrongful death claims. Importantly, the Right-to-Farm statute is limited in scope primarily to land that is designated as an "agricultural district" and "used in agricultural production subject to an agricultural assessment" under section 306.

There is a *four-step analysis* for a New York Right-to-Farm determination.

- First, any person *may request an opinion* "as to whether particular *agricultural practices are sound.*" A "sound" agricultural practice is defined in section 308(1)(b) as one which is "necessary for the on-farm production, preparation and marketing of agricultural commodities."

- Second, the *NYSDAM will make this evaluation* on a case-by-case basis. In so doing, it is statutorily required to consider whether the agricultural practices are being "conducted by a farm owner or operator participating in" its *Agricultural Environmental Management Program* ("AEMP") as well as to "consult appropriate state agencies and any guidelines recommended by the advisory council on agriculture."

- Third, the *NYSDAM must provide notice* once it has issued an opinion. In addition to being *published in a newspaper* with general circulation in the surrounding area, the notice must also be provided in writing *directly to the property owner*, as well as to owners of adjoining property. NYSDAM's opinion becomes final unless it is contested by an aggrieved party within thirty (30) days of publication. A party contesting such an opinion faces an uphill battle; courts defer to an agency's expertise on such a decision, allowing it to stand unless it is *"arbitrary and capricious."*

- Fourth, *if the opinion deems a particular agricultural practice to be "sound," it cannot constitute a "private nuisance"* as a matter of law. Because parties have no vested property interest in the right to sue under a private nuisance theory, this result does not constitute an unconstitutional "taking." If someone does bring a private nuisance suit on account of a "sound" agricultural practice, the Right-to-Farm statute authorizes recovery for the *reasonable costs* attributable to defending against such a lawsuit.

By enacting the Right-to-Farm statute, New York's legislature intended to provide some *protection for farmland against encroachment from non-agricultural development.* Indeed, the legislature expressed particular concern about the potential for competition over land resources to result in a vicious cycle of rising farm taxes, inadequate investment in farm maintenance, and the ultimate idling of productive agricultural land. While reported cases on the subject are scarce, New York's Right-to-Farm statute has been recognized by academics as a relatively sensible approach to balancing these competing interests, at least as compared to similar statutes in other states.

Additional Resources

Cari B. Rincker, Dr. Stan Benda, Derrick Braaten, Jason Foscolo, Neil Hamilton, Erin Hawley, Leon Letter, Jesse Richardson, Jr., Rich Schell, Patricia Salkin, "Counseling the Local Food Movement," American Bar Association Continuing Legal Education Webinar (May 10, 2012), available for purchase at http://apps.americanbar.org/abastore/index.cfm?section=main&fm=Product.AddToCart&pid=CET12LFMCDR (last visited July 1 2013).

Hannah Koski, "Guide to Urban Farming in NYS" available at http://nebeginningfarmers.org/publications/urban-farming/ (last visited May 19, 2013).

Harvard Food Law and Policy Clinic, "Good Laws, Good Food: Putting Local Food Policy to Work for Our Communities," (July 2012) available at http://www.law.harvard.edu/academics/clinical/lsc/documents/FINAL_LOCAL_TOOLKIT2.pdf (last visited August 17, 2013).

National Agriculture Law Center, "States' Right-to-Farm Statutes" available at http://www.nationalaglawcenter.org/assets/righttofarm/ (last visited July 29, 2013).

CHAPTER 13

EMPLOYMENT AND LABOR LAW

Most farms, agri-businesses and food companies employ labor of one sort or another. Hiring others to work for you opens the operation to regulation from state and federal agencies that administer *labor laws*. It is important for all business owners, especially those involved in the agriculture industry, to have a solid grasp of employment law.

Classification of Workers

Employee vs. Independent Contractor

The distinction between *employee* and *independent contractor* is crucial in just about every area of law that affects the labor you hire to work on your farm operation (or elsewhere). Even *unpaid labor* such as *interns, apprentices, and community volunteers* may be classified as employees (and they usually are). As a general rule, *employees receive more benefits or protection from these laws* than do independent contractors. Employers who classify workers as independent contractors do not have to withhold federal and state income taxes for employees, nor do the employers have to pay Social Security taxes, carry workman's compensation insurance, or pay unemployment taxes for these workers.

It shouldn't be too surprising, then, that in most of these situations, the people you hire to work for you are first *assumed to be employees*. If you want to prove that your labor is not entitled to various labor law advantages (all of which generally require either more money or more work, or both, from the employer), it is usually *your burden to prove* that the person you hired was an *independent contractor*.

In general, the question of "employee vs. independent contractor" is one of *control over the details of the work:*

- If the *operator controls how, when and where* the other party works, it looks a lot like an *employer-employee relationship*.

- If the person you've hired sets his or her own *hours*, provides his or her own *equipment*, and does *similar work for other operators*, it begins to look more like an *independent contractor relationship*.

It is important to realize, too, that the "labels" you put on your relationship with your workers do not control their legal classification.

Who is an "Employee?"

When looking at any person who is working the farm – a paid worker, intern, apprentice or volunteer laborer- it is important to understand when state and federal laws will classify a person as an "employee." Broadly, the *Fair Labor Standards Act* ("FLSA") defines an **employee** as "any individual employed by an employer." 29 U.S.C. § 203(e)(1). The term "**employ**" under the FLSA means to "*suffer or permit to work*." 29 U.S.C. § 203(g). Federal tax laws use common law rules to determine whether a person is an "**employee**." See 26 U.S.C. § 3121(d)(2). For example, the IRS has historically looked at whether the principal has the right to *direct and control* the worker who provides services. See Internal Revenue Service, Publication 51 (Circular A), Agricultural Employer's Tax Guide (2010).

Alternatively, the *Migrant and Seasonal Agriculture Worker Protection Act* ("MSAWPA" or "MSPA") defines an "**agricultural worker**" as an "individual who is employed in agricultural employment of a seasonal or other temporary nature, and who is required to be absent overnight from his permanent place of residence." 29 C.F.R. § 500.20(p). Furthermore, a "**seasonal agriculture worker**" is defined as "an individual who is employed in agricultural employment of a seasonal or other temporary nature and is not required to be absent overnight from his permanent place of residence: (1) When employed on a farm or ranch performing field work related to planting, cultivating, or harvesting operations; or (2) When employed in canning, packing, ginning, seed conditioning or related research, or processing operations, and transported, or caused to be transported, to or from the place of employment by means of a day-haul operation." 29 C.F.R. § 500.20(r).

When is an Intern an Employee?

Interns are oftentimes classified as *migrant or seasonal agricultural workers*. To explain, interns usually do temporary agricultural work (e.g., summer or a semester). An intern's duties on a farm usually include field work. For these reasons, a farm intern would likely be considered a **"seasonal" worker**. To be considered a **"migrant" worker** under the MSPA, the intern also has to be absent overnight from his or her permanent place of residence (i.e., away from his or her home). If an intern opts to stay in employer-provided housing during the internship because there are few inexpensive housing options available, that intern is likely considered a **"migrant agricultural worker."**

Although some farms and food entrepreneurs may have a *contractual agreement* stating that the intern is *not an employee* and instead referring to him or her as a "volunteer," "trainee" or "independent contractor", courts have repeatedly set aside these agreements when this person should be classified as an employee. In other words, courts have held that an employee cannot waive his or her rights in a contract to FLSA benefits and will instead look at the *reality of the work arrangement.*

In order for a *"trainee"* or *"intern"* to be exempt from federal minimum wage requirements in the "for-profit" private sector of farms, agri-businesses and food companies, the following *six factor test* must be satisfied:

- The internship, even though it includes actual operation of the facilities of the employer, is similar to training which would be given in an *educational environment*;
- The internship experience is for the *benefit of the intern*;
- The intern does *not displace regular employees*, but works under close supervision of existing staff;
- The employer that provides the training derives *no immediate advantage* from the activities of the intern, and on occasion its operations may actually be impeded;
- The intern is not *necessarily entitled to a job* at the conclusion of the internship; and
- The employer and the intern understand that the *intern is not entitled to wages* for the time spent in the internship.

If all six of the above factors are met (i.e., not just a few of the factors but all six of them) an employment relationship does not exist under the FLSA and the farm or food employer does not need to pay the intern minimum wage. See U.S. Department of Labor, Wage & Hour Division, Fact Sheet #71: Internship Programs Under The Fair Labor Standards Act (April 2010).

From a practical standpoint, farms and agri/food businesses with an internship program should understand that it is unlikely that the intern will be classified as a "trainee" even if he or she is obtaining credit from an educational institution. Farms and food entrepreneurs with an unpaid internship program should carefully tailor their program to meet this test.

Who is an Independent Contractor?

Put simply, a worker must retain control over the manner and means to accomplish a project to be considered an independent contract. Courts look at a myriad of factors when deciding if someone is an independent contractor:

- skill required;
- source of tools necessary for the work;
- location of the work;
- duration of the relationship between the parties;
- whether the hiring party has the right to assign additional projects to the hired party;
- the extent of the hired party's discretion over when and how long to work; and
- method of payment.

See Cmty. for Creative Non-Violence v. Reid, 490 U.S. 730, 751-752 (1989) and Ernster v. Luxco, Inc., 596 F.3d 1000, 1003-1004 (8th Cir. 2010).

It is *unlikely* that a farm or agri-business intern will be classified as an independent contractor under FLSA. The nature of the internship itself rests on the fact that the intern is there to learn from the host farmer or food entrepreneur so that he or she may use the skills and knowledge gained from the internship on their own. Typically, an intern *does not come to the farm* or agri-business with the *skills necessary to complete his or her tasks independently* and will be subject to the *direction and supervision* from his or her host.

The intern will use the farmer's tools or the agri-businesses office space.

Who is a Volunteer?

In determining whether someone is a volunteer or an employee, courts look at the following factors:

- Whether the worker received *any benefits* including "in kind" compensation (e.g., food and lodging);
- Whether the activity is usually considered a *full-time occupation*;
- Whether the services are of a nature *typically associated with volunteer work* (i.e., helping the sick, elderly, indigent, handicapped or underserved communities); and,
- *Length of time* the individual is dependent on the food/agricultural employer.

See Tony & Susan Alamo Found. v. Sec'y of Labor, 471 U.S. 290, 301, 303 (1985).

It is *unlikely* that an *intern* on a farm or in an agri-business would be considered a *volunteer*. If the intern is receiving "in kind" compensation including food or housing, then this shows the court that the intern has an *economic dependence* on the employer. Additionally, working for for-profit farms or agri-businesses is not typically associated with volunteer work. Interns usually work full-time for several weeks or months at a time; however, if the intern only worked one day per week and provided his or her own housing then this person less likely to look like he/she is working in a full-time occupation to the courts. Ultimately, courts will look at the *totality of the circumstances* when making this determination.

Who is an Apprentice?

Apprenticeships are offered at several farms throughout New York. Although apprenticeships seem to be a nice way to give workers a *deepened educational experience*, they should be offered with cautious awareness of their regulation.

It is important to understand that formal apprenticeship programs are regulated by the *National Apprenticeship Act*

("NAA"). Certain parameters must be met in order for there to be a registered apprenticeship. For example, applicants are required to go through a formal training program and obtain a completion certificate.

Apprenticeships are available for the following:

- Agriculture Service Worker,
- Farm Equipment Mechanic I and II,
- Farm Worker, General, and
- Farmer, General.

As a caveat, apprenticeship programs are challenging for farmers because they require a classroom education component which can be challenging to properly administer.

Potential Labor Issues with CSA "Worker Shares" or Other Types of Volunteer Farm Labor

Many *Community Supported Agriculture* ("CSA") farms are using *"worker shares"* or *"half worker shares"*. Instead of paying for his or her share, a subscriber may volunteer between 4 to 6 hours a week for 20 to 30 weeks. A *"half worker share"* allows for smaller volunteer commitment for a *reduced fee*. CSA worker share programs oftentimes go through a *formal application process*. Additionally, some CSA's offer free shares in exchange for use of their space for the "drop off" points.

Although CSA's are most widely recognized for volunteer farm labor, some farms are enrolled in the *World Wide Opportunities on Organic Farms* ("WWOOF") matching volunteers ("WWOOFers") from around the globe that wish to work on a farm for temporary housing and food. Furthermore, many farms accept casual volunteers from their community (e.g., church, schools, non-for-profit organizations, "crop mobs") in exchange for food.

As noted above, FLSA defines "employ" as "to suffer to permit to work"—which would include almost any volunteer farm labor arrangement. However, this definition has been narrowed to *exclude* those who work without a promise or expectation of compensation but *only for his or her personal pleasure*. See Walling v. Portland Terminal Co., 330 U.S. 148 (1947).

Importantly, the FLSA defines a "volunteer" as "an individual who performs service for a public agency for civic, charitable, or humanitarian reasons, without promise, expectation or receipt of compensation for services rendered." 29 C.F.R. § 553.101. Although not clear-cut, it appears that this definition does not include working for for-profit private entities, like farms or food businesses, or volunteering in exchange of "in kind" compensation (e.g., a share in a CSA).

The court generally uses the following questions when deciding whether a volunteer is an employee:

- Is the volunteer working *in expectation of compensation* (including "in kind" compensation)?
- Is the *volunteer displacing paid employees*?
- Does the volunteer give the business any kind of *competitive advantage*?

In most cases, CSA worker share programs and other farm labor programs where the volunteers are being paid "in kind" compensation are utilizing employees under FLSA. That said, the 500-Man Day exception, as discussed below, will apply to many small scale farms. If volunteers are considered employees then this will contribute to the 500-Man Day calculation.

For example, a CSA share worth $800 is compensation under the FLSA in the amount of $800. However, that farm must keep an accounting of the "volunteer" labor hours to make sure that $800 surpasses the minimum wage requirement. This requires farms to keep accurate records of "in kind" compensation.

If a farm using volunteer farm labor wishes to be exempt from this requirement, **it must carefully craft the program with the assistance of an attorney**.

Minimum Wage and Overtime

Once it has been determined that a farm or agri-business worker is an "employee", then the minimum wage and overtime requirements under FLSA applies. The current federal requirements are as follows:

- **Adults**: $7.25 per hour (New York will incrementally raise to $9.00 in 2015).

- **Youth Age 20 and Under**: A federal minimum youth wage of $4.25 per hour applies to workers who are under the age of

20 for the first 90 consecutive days of their employment. A farm or food business may not intentionally displace other employees in order to hire employees under the age of 20. See 29 U.S.C. § 206(g).

- **Full-Time Students (a Department of Labor Certificate is required)**: Full-time students may be paid 85 percent of the federal minimum wage if certain requirements are met (e.g., ensuring that the student-worker is not displacing a worker who would be paid minimum wage, not performing work performed by regular employees). See 29 U.S.C. § 214(b)(2); 29 C.F.R. §§ 520.200-520.508.

Payroll can be paid at different rates (biweekly or weekly), but the issue of *overtime* pay comes into play if the employee goes *over 40 hours in a 7-day calendar week*, regardless if it is in one pay period or two. Employees must be paid *time-and-one-half their regular hourly rates* of pay for hours worked in excess of 40 per week. There are exceptions to this overtime requirement, some noted below.

You can encounter serious legal problems by failing to keep and maintain records of the names and permanent addresses of temporary agricultural employees, dates of birth of minors under age 19, or hours worked by employees. As costs rise for labor, more and more operations, even small ones, need to resist any and all temptation to skirt around the requirements of the IRS and federal wage laws. You have to keep a constant eye on these laws because some of them can change dramatically from year to year. The penalties for non-compliance are far worse than the burden of compliance. The bottom line on this is to **hire a bookkeeper and/or seek legal advice** to keep yourself informed about the current state of these regulations.

Exemptions to the Minimum Wage and Overtime Requirements

There are three primary federal FLSA exemptions most likely to apply to small-scale farming operations using farm intern labor. These include (1) *500 Man-Day Exemption*, (2) *Hand Harvest Laborer Exemption*, and (3) *Agriculture Overtime Exemption*.

1. 500 Man-Day Minimum Wage and Overtime Exemption

This exemption applies to smaller-scale farming operations with a limited number of employees. To explain, this exemption applies to farm employers that used *500 or fewer man-days* of agricultural labor during each *calendar quarter* of the preceding year. 29 U.S.C. § 213(a)(6)(g). See 29 C.F.R. § 780.305 (noting that 500 man-days generally equals *seven full-time employees*). Please note that this exemption only applies to *agricultural work* (including farming, livestock production, and ancillary tasks such as transportation to market or manning a table at a farmstand) See 29 C.F.R. § 780.11; 29 U.S.C. § 203(f); 29 C.F.R. § 780.105. Processing, packaging or delivery of *another farmer's crops or livestock* do not fall under this exemption. See 29 C.F.R. §§ 780.137, 780.141.

A "man-day" is any day on which any employee performs *one hour or more of agricultural work* for a specific farmer – not per farm. 29 U.S.C. § 203(u); 29 C.F.R. § 780.301(a); 29 C.F.R. § 780.304(b). Work performed by the farmer or his/her immediate family <u>does not count</u> as a "man day". 29 U.S.C. § 203(e)(3); 29 C.F.R. § 780.301.

In order to qualify for this exemption, the farmer must have *accurate time records* illustrating the number of hours worked by each employee during the prior calendar year. See 29 C.F.R. § 780.306.

2. Hand Harvest Laborer Minimum Wage and Overtime Exemption

This exemption applies to local hand harvest laborers and includes those who: (1) commute daily from their permanent residence, (2) are paid on a *piece-rate basis* in *traditionally piece-rated* occupations, and (3) are *engaged in agriculture* less than 13 weeks during the preceding calendar year. 29 U.S.C. § 213(a)(6)(C). This exemption does not apply to full-time workers who earn a livelihood from working on the farm. See 29 C.F.R. § 780.310.

3. Agricultural Overtime Exemption

This is a broad overtime exemption for agricultural workers from receiving federal overtime pay applicable to farms of any size for employment in agriculture production. See 29 U.S.C. § 213(b)(12). It is important to understand that this exemption only applies to

agriculture workers—there is a separate exemption for workers engaged in the transportation of fruits or vegetables in intrastate commerce. This exemption would not apply to a bookkeeper or someone who works at your roadside stand.

Tax Withholding

A variety of *taxes must be withheld* from the pay of an *employee*, including *federal income taxes, social security taxes, state income taxes, and local taxes* (e.g., Yonkers, New York City). The business is required to hold these funds and then periodically deposit them and report them to the government. The government views the responsible parties as agents of the government when performing these duties. Please note that state *unemployment insurance taxes* are paid by the employer.

Additionally, the employer must provide a *paystub* showing the deductions and other specific items withheld, and the employer must mail the employee a *W-2 form* at the end of the year, to file with his or her own income tax return. The only exemption from these requirements is for *children under 18* who are employed by their parents in a *non-corporate partnership or LLC farm business*.

The waters muddy if you use "in kind" compensation (e.g., food, housing). Non-cash wages are exempt from the *Federal Unemployment Tax Act* ("FICA"), income tax withholding, and social security. Furthermore, meals and lodging are generally excluded from the gross income of an employee if provided on the business premises for the convenience of the employer. See 26 U.S.C. § 199 and 26 C.F.R. § 1.119-1.

If your help qualifies as an *independent contractor* or is an individual (i.e., not a partnership, corporation, or LLC), *and you pay over $600* to them during the calendar year, you must follow *IRS 1099 reporting rules* and send the contractor a *1099 form* at the end of the year, to be filed with his or her own income tax return. This rule is oftentimes overlooked.

Farm Family Employment

Who is the Employer?

More than one person in a farm operation can qualify as an

"employer." In a farm family, it can sometimes be challenging to distinguish who is the **"employer"** and who is the **"employee."** More than one person in a farm can qualify as an employer—or a business entity, such as a general partnership or limited liability company may be considered the employer. If a number of family members run a farm together, those people might collectively be the employer.

Courts will generally look at how a business is running to determine who the employers and employees are. For example, courts look at (1) *financial stake* in the business, (2) *how profits are shared*, (3) *decision-making* authority (including supervision of workers, hiring/firing workers), and (4) *responsibility* in the day-to-day activities in a family farm or agri-business.

Ownership in the farm operation does not mean that the farmer-employer must own the real property that is being used for agriculture production. Courts look at the totality of the circumstances to determine financial stake. For example, is the land being rented? Who owns the livestock or farm equipment? Without a doubt, courts will consider the farming operation's organizational documents (e.g., Operating Agreement if it is a limited liability company, Partnership Agreement) and tax documents (e.g., a Schedule F on the tax return).

Family Employee Exemptions

After identifying the employer in a farming operation, the next step is to identify family employees. There are several exemptions that apply to family under federal and state labor laws. Some include the following:

- **Minimum Wage Exemption**: A farm employer's "immediate family" (spouse, children, and parents) are exempt from the FLSA's minimum wage requirement. Note that "immediate family" does not include brothers, sisters, aunts, uncles, grandparents, grandchildren, nieces, nephews, cousins, in-laws, etc.

- **Occupational Safety and Health Act ("OSHA") Exemption**: A farm employer's "immediate family" are exempt from OSHA, discussed more below.

- **Social Security and Medicare Exemption**: This exemption applies to a farmer-employer's children who are under 18 years old.

- **Federal Income Tax Withholding**: Farmer-employers need not withhold federal income tax from children who are under 18 years of age.

Generally speaking, farm employers are **not exempt** from their requirement to pay federal unemployment tax for all family member employees.

Children and Agricultural Employment

Hiring Your Own Children

Under federal law, children *under the age of eighteen* (18) can perform on-farm labor. See 29 U.S.C. § 212 and 29 C.F.R. Part 570. If you operate a farm, *any child of yours* can do any job on the farm. See 29 U.S.C. § 213(c)(2) and 29 C.F.R. § 570.123(c).

Work Hours and Duties

Under federal law, minor children who work in non-agricultural employment cannot be under fourteen (14) years of age, and are subject to the following basic rules, many of which turn on the age of the child laborer:

- **Children aged sixteen (16) years or older** can perform non-hazardous duties, with unlimited hours; and

- **Children aged fourteen (14) and fifteen (15) years** cannot perform hazardous duties, work in manufacturing jobs, or work in mining, and they cannot work during school hours on school days (with limited exceptions). See 29 C.F.R. § 570.2(b).

- **Children aged twelve (12) to thirteen (13) years** may only work on farms not owned or operated by their parents if (1) the farm that the child will work on also employs the child's parents, <u>or</u> (2) the child's parents have given express written consent. <u>See</u> 29 C.F.R. § 570.2(b). They also cannot work during school hours on school days.

- **Children aged eleven (11) years or younger** may not work on a farm unless the farm is owned and/or operated by the child's parents. <u>See</u> 29 U.S.C. § 213(c).

Children in *agricultural employment* may work:

- Up to 14 hours a week (in two-hour blocks) when school is in session; or

- Up to 20 hours a week (in maximum of four-hour blocks) when school is out.

In addition, children over the age of 14 may *de-tassel*, from *June through August*, with *no restriction on hours*.

> No matter how eager the child, don't ignore the work hours limitations for minor workers. Both **employers and parents** who allow a child to work in **violation of the child labor laws** may be punished by **fines**, or **jail time**, or both.

Teen-aged employees may drive a car or truck on farm property, operate garden-type tractors, clear brush by hand, hand-plant seeds or plants, weed, hoe and water plants, care for poultry and horses, pick produce, and help with milking operations. As a general rule, *minor children* (under the age of 18) *cannot* be employed to work in any of *these agriculture-related industries or tasks*:

- Logging,
- Power-driven woodworking machines,
- Power-driven metal punch machines,
- Slaughter,

- Meat packing or rendering plants,
- Circular saws,
- Band saws,
- Wrecking and demolition;
- Roofing,
- Excavating, or
- Operating forklifts, backhoes, or cranes.

Hazardous Work

Essentially, only children *over the age 16 may do hazardous work* in the agriculture industry. Hazardous work would include:

- Operating tractors over 20 horsepower ("PTO");
- Combining;
- Mowing;
- Corn- or cotton-picking;
- Trencher or earthmoving equipment operation;
- Being in stall with a bull, boar, stud horse, or a sow or cow with newborn offspring;
- Working from a ladder or scaffold at a height of over 20 feet;
- Felling, bucking, skidding, loading or unloading timber;
- Driving a bus, truck or automobile;
- Handling or applying toxic agriculture chemicals;
- Handling or using a blasting agent; and
- Transporting, transferring or applying anhydrous ammonia.

If the child is *under age 16*, he or she *cannot* work:

- Felling, bucking, stacking or loading timber;
- Working from a ladder or scaffold; or
- Transporting or applying NH3 or handling Category I toxic ag chemicals. See 29 CFR 570.71(a)(1-11).

The *U.S. Department of Labor* is active in seeking to restrict this list further, and you should consult with your attorney or the Department of Labor to find out the current *Ag Hazardous Occupation Orders* to ensure your operation can safely employ your youth employee.

Record Keeping

If you have a minor farm employee, ensure you have his or her full name, address, date of birth, and proof of age. Proof of age can be a copy of a birth certificate, driver's license, or a Form I-9.

Workman's Compensation

Before a farm operation pays someone to do something as an employee, *workman's compensation insurance* ("workman's comp") needs to be secured. Designed to protect workers injured on the job, this insurance provides *automatic benefits and medical coverage* to *employees* who are *injured* while working *"in the course and scope of employment,"* including benefits for treatment of the injury, temporary or healing period benefits, and permanent disability benefits.

Workman's comp represents a compromise. In return for the certainty of receiving automatic benefits for work-related injuries, a covered employee accepts the *limited remedy* of receiving *only the benefits* provided under the workman's comp law; he or she *cannot sue the employer* for negligence to recover traditional court-awarded damages.

Workman's compensation insurance to cover employees is required by law, but it is secured by you through a private insurance agent. While it is *not* necessary to cover true *independent contractors* with workman's comp, you'd better be able to prove that someone injured while working on your farm was not actually an employee. If you don't obtain coverage, there are consequences:

- First, there is *no "limited remedy" protection* for an employer who isn't carrying workman's comp insurance. You can be held personally liable for the employee's injuries, meaning that the *employee can sue you and can collect any judgment against your assets*. If an injury occurred while the employee was working for you, *you are presumed to be liable* for the injuries. The burden of proof will be upon you as the employer to prove that you aren't liable. This burden of proof is significant because it is a complete reversal from the usual injury lawsuit, which normally requires the injured person to prove that a defendant was at fault for causing his injuries.

- In addition, you could face *criminal liability* for failing to obtain workman's compensation insurance when you should.

While the owner of a company can *exempt* him or herself from the obligation to carry workman's comp insurance coverage, by applying to become *"self-insured,"* a decision to go this way is often pennywise and pound-foolish. As farming is consistently listed as one of the most dangerous occupations, it would be wise to consult your insurance agent before waiving this potential source of income protection.

A *workman's compensation claim* is handled under its own set of laws, requires the company to investigate, and has relaxed evidence rules.   An injured employee who feels that he hasn't received appropriate benefits or the right amount of benefits under workman's comp can file an *appeal* with the *New York Workman's Compensation Board.*

> For example, consider the possibilities if a hired worker lost an arm or a leg in a combine accident. Workman's compensation insurance would cover and provide medical treatment and perhaps a lump-sum benefit to an injured employee.   A court, on the other hand, could award a person with such injuries millions of dollars in damages for current and future medical expenses, pain and suffering, loss of the ability to have a normal relationship with a spouse, or even punitive damages, all of which could be collected against anything and everything you own.

A Quick Word on OSHA

The federal *Occupational Safety and Health Act ("OSHA")* covers the majority of workers in New York. It does not cover the self-employed, farms where only immediate family members work, or places covered by other federal agencies and laws.

Family Medical Leave Act ("FMLA")

With some limited exceptions, FMLA applies when an *eligible employee*, who works for an *eligible employer*, had an *eligible event* entitling him or her to 12 weeks of unpaid leave per 12 month period with the right to be restored to his or her former position with equivalent benefits, pay, etc. See 29 C.F.R. §825-214.

An *"eligible employer"* would be a farm or agri-business who employs at least *50 employees* (including part-time employees, temporary and/or seasonable employees, and employees who are currently on a leave of absence). These 50 employees must be employed *at least 20 weeks* of the year (those weeks do not need to be consecutive). Furthermore, the employer must employ these 50+ employees within *75 miles* of the location the eligible employee works at (measured by highway miles).

In order to be eligible, an employee must have worked for at least 12 months (including 1250 hours of work) as of the date that the leave starts. Please note that the burden is on the farm or agri-business employer to provide a *record* of the employee's hours worked – if there are no records then there is a presumption under the law that the employee worked the *necessary 1250 hours*. See 29 C.F.R. § 825.110(c)(3).

There are **four** main eligible events:

- The *birth* of a child;

- The placement of a child for *adoption*;

- The need to provide for the *care of a spouse, parent or child* who has a *serious health condition*; or

- The *employee's own serious health condition* that prohibits the employee from performing at least one of the essential functions of the job.

Eligible employers must display a *FMLA poster* and provide information about FMLA in their *employee handbook*. Furthermore, eligible employers must provide *notice of FMLA eligibility* to the employee within *1-2 days* after learning the employee's request for

FMLA leave (even if it is an oral request). There are also additional requirements regarding health benefits given to employees.

Employee Handbooks

Every farm, agri-business and food entrepreneur who hires employees should consider having an *employee handbook*. It helps give the employees an orientation to the business culture, helps manage expectations, and helps to minimize confusion. Furthermore, getting a employee handbook drafted by an attorney can be a nice way to "audit" your farm or food business to ensure compliance with federal and state employment and labor laws.

Additionally, employee handbooks can serve as *written evidence* that you informed an employee of a certain policy and are implementing certain procedures on your farm. For example, livestock operations are encouraged to memorialize animal handling techniques in their employee handbooks (and train the employees on these techniques). If livestock animal cruelty charges should ensue, the employee handbook can help build a *written defense* that the farm was properly caring for its animals. That being said, it is critical that farm and agri-business never depend on the employee handbook as a training tool—*hands-on training should always be performed* (and documented).

Employee handbooks have specific legal requirements, so farms, agri-businesses and food entrepreneurs are encouraged to work with an attorney. For example, there should be an *at-will employment disclaimer* (preferably signed by the employee). More specifically, the employee handbook should note that it *does not create a binding contract* as to the term or conditions of employment (except certain legal conditions regarding benefits or leave). Additionally, the employee handbook should also include an *Equal Opportunity and Nondiscrimination Policy* indicating that decisions will not be influenced by the employee's race, color, religion, sex, national origin, ethnicity, disability, veteran status, age, pregnancy, etc. As noted above, *"eligible employers"* should include a *Family Medical Leave Act* disclosure. Importantly, there should also be an express prohibition against *workplace harassment,* including procedures for reporting harassment.

The employee handbook should also cover the *Uniformed Service Employment and Reemployment Act* ("USERA") and *Consolidated Omnibus Budget Reconciliation Act* ("COBRA"). If minor children are employed, the handbook should note *child labor issues* mentioned above, including a prohibition from hazardous activities for minors under 16 years of age. Finally, a discussion on overtime pay (including limitations) should be included.

If the employees are using computers, consider implementing an *e-mail, Internet,* and/or *social media policy.* In some situations, it may be beneficial to have a *smartphone* policy to avoid unwanted photographs and videos. Additionally, a *confidentiality policy* is strongly encouraged in most cases.

The employee handbook should be tailored to the individual farm. In some cases, a discussion on farm safety, disease control, biosecurity, farm equipment/vehicles, food safety or farm visitors may be appropriate. As noted above, animal handling techniques could be included in the employee handbook.

The draftsman of an employee handbook should be careful to *avoid language suggesting a contract* between the farm/agri-business employer and employee—the employee handbook should be used as "guidelines". Information on discipline methods should also be omitted.

On a final note, the employee handbook can be a nice way to tell your employees the history of your farm or food business. After all, it may give them pride to be part of an operation with so much history or forward vision. Feel free to explain in the employee handbook how the agri-business has changed over the years and what values are important to its brand.

Practical Pointers on Being a Better Boss

Being a good boss primarily requires the employer to learn effective communication techniques, which boosts both *morale* and *efficiency* in the employer-employee relationship. Recognizing that the leader and the led are only two portions of a puzzle with several pieces, you must also consider the message and the goal when communicating with employees. Employees want *goals*-- if they are not clear on what your goal is then they will substitute their own understanding of the goal. When the goals don't match, conflict can result.

On your organizational structure, it is extremely important to understand how far your "aura" of control goes. In most organizations, about five or six people are the most that should report to one person. It is interesting that the lowest level of leadership in the military is a team of four to five solders lead by a team leader. Experience is the best litmus test for any recommendation. If every one of your employees reports directly to you and you have more than five employees, you probably need to reassess.

In dealing with problem employees, discipline needs to be consistent or it will not be perceived correctly. Employees can be harmed by unrealistic expectations, unclear guidance, improper or incomplete training, and/or the refusal to delegate authority to the actual decision maker.

If employees are not performing, make sure to do <u>something</u> about it. In a business, *ignorance is not bliss*. Until you address this issue it will have an impact on the business, the workers' happiness and their effectiveness. As an employer, you want to be friendly and fair, but you simply cannot be perceived as a "buddy" to any of your employees.

As you examine your work environment as a leader, some key concepts to consider are:

- Get rid of the thought "I can do it better and quicker."

- *Delegate every decision* down to the *lowest-ranked employee* capable of making the decision. Remember, you can delegate authority, but not responsibility. Once you have delegated a task, do not ever take it back, unless somebody or something (like profits) is about to be measurably hurt.

- Lead from the front.

- Acknowledge the work, no matter how trivial it might seem. We all want to feel like we are contributing to the team. However, avoid pandering and baseless praise. A simple acknowledgement goes a lot farther than empty rhetoric.

Additional Resources

Amanda Heyman and Jennifer Jambor-Delgado, "Farmers' Guide to Farm Employees," Farmers' Legal Action Group (August 2012) <u>available</u> at <u>http://www.flaginc.org/wp-content/uploads/2013/03/MILEguide.pdf</u> (last visited August 18, 2013).

Cari Rincker, Rachel Armstrong, Kimberly Clarke, Edward Cox, Karen Eichman, Maggy Gregory, Jennifer Jambor-Delgado, and Arthur N. Read, "Overview of Employment and Labor Law for Farms and Ranches" American Bar Association Continuing Legal Education Webinar available for purchase at http://apps.americanbar.org/cle/programs/t13oel1.html (last visited May 19, 2013).

Jennifer Jambor-Delgado and Amanda Heyman, "Farmers' Guide to Farm Internships" Farmers' Legal Action Group, Incorporated (February 2013) available at http://www.flaginc.org/wp-content/uploads/2013/04/Farm-Intern-Guide-FINAL-w-covers.pdf (last visited August 18, 2013).

New York Farm Bureau, "Farmers Guide to Labor & Employment Laws" (2nd ed) available for purchase at http://www.nyfb.org/legal/NYFB_s_Legal_Library_54_pg.htm (last visited July 17, 2013).

New York Farm Bureau, "Farmers Guide to ICE and Immigration Law Enforcement Activities: An Employer's Rights and Responsibilities," available for purchase at http://www.nyfb.org/legal/NYFB_s_Legal_Library_54_pg.htm (last visited July 17, 2013).

Cari B. Rincker & Patrick B. Dillon

CHAPTER 14

FREEDOM OF INFORMATION

You may find a time when you want to see the documents available to the public about yourself or your food or agriculture operation. There are two main federal statutes that guide the process of obtaining information from the federal government: (i) *Freedom of Information Act* ("FOIA") and (ii) *Privacy Act* ("PA"). In New York, requests can be made to state administrative agencies through the *NY Freedom of Information Law* ("FOIL").

Background and Applicability

FOIA (pronounced "foi-ya") was enacted in 1966 by President *Lyndon B. Johnson* who believed that a democracy works best with *transparency* in the system without harming national security. There is no longer a burden to show that you "need to know" the requested information. Instead, you have a "right to know." The burden is now on the government to show its *need for secrecy*.

However, this *"right to know"* does not come without limitations. A FOIA request can only be made to federal government agencies, which broadly include *government corporations* (e.g., Federal Crop Insurance Corporation), *government controlled organizations*, and independent regulatory agencies (e.g., Library of Congress, Government Accountability Office, Congressional Research Service). FOIA is *not applicable to private companies* or persons who receive federal contracts or grants, or to private organizations.

Additionally, the PA allows U.S. citizens seeking information about themselves to receive *greater information* than what would typically be released to the general public. The primary purpose of the PA is to provide individuals with more control over the gathering, dissemination, and accuracy of information about themselves contained in government files, and to promote greater privacy for citizens. The PA serves to protect agriculture producers and food entrepreneurs from citizens' groups that may wish to obtain private information about their property or farming operation.

Even though FOIA and PA only apply to federal government agencies, every state has enacted its own open public records acts or right-to-know acts that are applicable to state and local governmental agencies. In New York, *Public Officers Law* ("POL") § 84 et seq. establishes the *Freedom of Information Law* ("FOIL"). If you are unsure whether your documents are regulated by the federal or state agency, such as the U.S. Environmental Protection Agency ("EPA") or New York Department of Environmental Conservation ("DEC"), it is best to *make two separate requests*– one request to the federal agency citing FOIA/PA and another to the New York governmental agency citing FOIL.

Making a FOIA/PA or FOIL Request

Decide If It Is Necessary To File a FOIA Request

Not all agency records require a written FOIA request. In 1996, Congress passed the *Electronic Freedom of Information Act* ("E-FOIA"). E-FOIA requires government agencies to have electronic FOIA "reading rooms" available online. The information you seek may be available online such as regulations, agency decisions and statements of policies, staff manuals (e.g., USDA Rural Development Handbooks), forms, and agency publications such as pamphlets, brochures, and books created after November 1, 1996. See 5 U.S.C. § 552(a)(2). For example, the soil composition on your property is available from the Natural Resources Conservation Service ("NRCS") online at http://www.nrcs.usda.gov. All previous records before November 1, 1996 are not required to be in electronic format; however, upon request to the agency, even these can be made available to you in electronic form.

Choose The Government Agency or Agencies To Request Documents

On either the federal or state level, there is not one central office that manages all FOIA or FOIL requests, so you must contact the department or agency itself. Even if you know that you need to obtain records from the USDA, it is helpful if you know the specific sub-agency, such as the Risk Management Agency ("RMA") from which to obtain information on your livestock or crop insurance. Any federal records that are more than twenty-five years old are archived with the *National Archives and Records Administration.*

If you are unclear as to the department or agency to contact, you can call the **Federal Citizen Information Center** toll free at **1-800-FED-INFO** to help you locate the right federal government agency. A list of general FOIA contacts is available with the **Department of Justice** ("DOJ") at www.usdoj.gov/oip/foiacontacts.htm. In New York, the **Committee of Open Government** may be helpful in directing you to the correct New York governmental agency: One Commerce Plaza, 99 Washington Avenue, Suite 650, Albany, NY 12231 or (518) 474-2518.

Draft and Mail Your Written FOIA Request Letter

You cannot make a FOIA request to a federal agency over the telephone. All FOIA requests *must be in writing* (i.e., postal mail, fax, or email). Most federal agencies do not have FOIA forms so you must draft a *written letter.* In New York, a form for emailed FOIL requests is available online from the NYS Department of State at http://www.dos.state.ny.us/coog/emailrequest.html.

To make sure your letter is handled correctly, mark on both the letter and envelope "**Freedom of Information Act Request**" (or "Freedom of Information Law" for New York agencies). The federal government is not required under FOIA to do any research, analyze data, or answer written questions; thus, if you include these types of requests in your FOIA letter, the federal agency is not obligated to answer them. You are encouraged to keep a copy for records and send your letter by certified mail so that you can have proof of the agency's receipt.

Your FOIA request should include the following information:

- *Contact information* including your full name, address, phone number;

- *Description of records requested* (e.g., aerial photographic reproductions from the Farm Service Agency or National Agriculture Library, all records pertaining to a piece of property);

- *Identification of locations* of files are obtained, such as a regional EPA or USDA office (if known);

- The *maximum amount* that you are willing to pay in printing charges for the documents (e.g., $100.00);

- *Written authorization* signed by yourself or an official representative of your agriculture operation or food business; and,

- Request that *non-exempt material* be segregated.

Wait for Government Response

Federal governmental agencies are required to respond to FOIA requests within twenty business days, excluding weekends and holidays, beginning from receipt of the request. However, the government is not required to send you the requested documents within twenty (20) days; instead, the government will likely send you written confirmation of its intent to comply with the request within a reasonable time. In this letter, the government agency might also give you a figure of estimated costs where you are required to agree or cancel the request. If the files are urgent, then you can specifically request that your FOIA request be expedited (include the reasons for the urgency).

In some cases, there is a faster turnaround for requests to New York agencies. *NY Public Officers Law* § 89(3) requires that a state agency either grant or deny access to the FOIL request in whole or in part, or if more time is needed, to minimally acknowledge the receipt of the request in writing *within five (5) business days*. This acknowledgment must include an approximate return date that the agency will either grant or deny the request. This date must be *"reasonable under the circumstances"* but is typically within *twenty (20) business days*.

Pay Fees

There is *no initial fee* to file a FOIA request; however, federal agencies are allowed to request "reasonable standard charges for document search, duplication, and review. . . ." See 5 U.S.C. § 552(a)(4)(A)(ii)(I). Unless no relevant documents were found, the federal agency will send you a letter giving you an estimate of the charges. You will either agree to the costs or cancel the request.

The fees do vary somewhat among agencies; for example, the USDA currently charges $0.20 per page for photocopying and $15 to $40 per hour for search charges, depending on the complexity of the search. If the total fee does not exceed $25.00, the USDA will not charge you a fee at all. There may be additional fees for *aerial photographs* or *negatives of pictures*. Black and white or *color enlargements*, slides, microfilm, scans, and audio/videotape reproductions can also be ordered for an additional fee from most administrative agencies. In New York, there is a $0.25 per page copying fee "or the actual cost of reproducing" the records which may include the hourly salary of the lowest paid employee with the skills necessary to complete the request. See Public Officers Law § 87(1)(b)-(c).

At this time, *you may also request a fee waiver*. Your fees will only be waived if you can persuade the government that it is within the public interest to disclose the document. Waivers are not granted in cases in which an individual livestock producer is not be able to pay the fee–public interest must be argued. If you do not pay your fee, most administrative agencies will begin levying interest charges on an unpaid bill. If affordability is a deterrent for obtaining a FOIA request, as noted above, you should state a maximum fee that you are willing to pay in your original request (e.g., $100.00 or $250.00 maximum).

Review FOIA Request

After the agency has received your fees, it will process your request. The agency may send you a written "initial determination" of documents available. FOIA allows for access to all federal agency records except for documents pertaining to sensitive law enforcement and national security matters. The nine exempted FOIA materials are as follows:

1. Classified *national* defense files;

2. *Internal agency rules* and practices;

3. Information *prohibited* under another federal law;

4. *Trade secrets* and confidential business information;

5. Inter-agency or *intra-agency* communications;

6. Information involving matters of *personal privacy* (but may be obtained under a Privacy Act request);

7. Certain types of information compiled for *law enforcement* (e.g., documents for an ongoing investigation);

8. Information relating to the supervision of *financial institutions*; and

9. *Geological* information on wells.

<u>See</u> <u>also</u> N.Y. Public Officers Law § 87(2) for New York exemptions.

> For example, a company that you are thinking about negotiating a contract with may have pending prosecution with either the U.S. District Attorney or the Attorney General of the State of New York. In such a case, the government is not required to disclose the information that may affect its case.

After receiving your FOIA/FOIL request from the government, make sure that the government did not withhold something that it should not have or inadvertently omitted requested documentation. The government is required to use a *"reasonable effort"* when searching for your records. If you feel that you are missing some records, you can write a letter appealing to either the federal or New York agency. Be sure to check the *maximum time period for preparing an appeal* (which can vary somewhat among government agencies).

Finally, if you find incorrect information in public records about yourself or your farm, you should write back to the agency explaining the changes that you are requesting. Should your request for such changes to be made, the agency is required by law to notify you of its receipt of such an amendment, typically within ten days. The federal agency may request further proof before it will make the correction in the public records on you or your agri-business.

Additional Resources

Environmental Protection Agency, "Freedom of Information Act," at http://www.epa.gov/foia/ (last visited August 13, 2013).

Food and Drug Administration, "Freedom of Information," at http://www.fda.gov/RegulatoryInformation/foi/default.htm (last visited August 13, 2013).

New York State Department of State's, Committee on Open Government, available at http://www.dos.ny.gov/coog/index.html (last visited August 13, 2013).

The FOIA Blog, at http://thefoiablog.typepad.com (last visited August 13, 2013).

U.S. Department of Agriculture, FOIA Service Center, at http://www.dm.usda.gov/foia/ (last visited August 18, 2013).

U.S. Department of Justice, FOIA.gov, at http://www.foia.gov (last visited August 13, 2013).

#FOIAChat (Hashtag) on Twitter.com

CHAPTER 15

FARM TRANSPORTATION LAW

As farms become larger and equipment follows along, farm operations frequently find themselves under the watchful eye of the federal *Department of Transportation* ("DOT"), along with other agencies, such as the *Environmental Protection Agency* ("EPA"), the *NY Department of Environmental Conservation* ("DEC") and *NYSDAM.* Farm operations need to beware of and follow applicable regulations or face stiff penalties that can quickly wipe out any benefits gained from operating large equipment.

Definitions and General Rules

In order to better understand the agriculture transportation regulations, you should keep in mind a few specific definitions:

- **Farmer** – A "farmer" is an individual who operates a farm or is directly involved in cultivating the land, crops, or livestock owned or under the direct control of that individual.

  See *Federal Motor Carrier Safety Regulations* ("FMCSR") § 390.5; see also NY Agric. & Mkts § 301(11) (defining "Farm Operation").

- **Farm vehicle** – A "farm vehicle" has a *gross vehicle weight rating* ("GVWR") of no more than 26,000 lbs. that is:

  1. Operated by a *farmer*;

247

2. Used to *transport agricultural products*, farm machinery, or farm supplies to or from a farm;

3. Not used in the operations of a *common or contract carrier*

Alternatively, a "farm vehicle" is a vehicle with a GVWR greater than 26,000 lbs. that is used within 150 miles of the person's farm. See *NY Vehicle Transportation Law* ("VTL") § 501-a(7).

- **Agricultural truck** – An "agricultural truck" is owned by an individual who does one of the following three activities:

  1. Plants, cultivates and harvests agriculture;

  2. Raises, feeds and cares for livestock, bees and poultry; *or*

  3. Engages in dairy farming.

  Please note that an agriculture truck may only be used to transport a *farmer's products or supplies*, for *personal passenger use*, or for *lumbering operations* incidental to the running of a farm. See NY VTL § 401(7)(E)(2).

- **Farm vehicle driver** – A "farm vehicle driver" is an individual who operates a commercial motor vehicle that is:

  1. Controlled and operated by a farmer;

  2. Used to transport agricultural products, farm machinery, or farm supplies to or from a farm;

  3. *Not* used as a for-hire carrier;

  4. *Not* carrying hazardous materials;

  5. Used within 150 air-miles of the farmer's farm.

See NY VTL § 401(7)(E)(2).

- **Commercial motor vehicle** – A "commercial motor vehicle" is operated on a highway in interstate commerce to transport passengers or property that (one of the following):

  1. Has a single or combined gross vehicle weight rating (GVWR) of 10,001 lbs. or more; or

  2. Is designed or used to carry more than 8 passengers, including the driver, for compensation; or

  3. Is designed or used to carry more than 15 passengers, including the driver, without compensation; or

  4. Is used to transport hazardous material in a quantity requiring a placard.

  See NY VTL § 401(7)(E)(2); see also *New York Codes, Rules & Regulations* ("NYCRR") Tit 17 § 820.1(c).

- **Agricultural equipment** – "Agricultural equipment" is either an agricultural tractor or implement of husbandry. See NY VTL § 100-d.

  o **Tractor** – A "tractor" is a vehicle designed and used as the power unit in combination with a semitrailer or trailer. See NY VTL § 151-a.

  o **Implement of Husbandry** – An "implement of husbandry" is a vehicle designed or adapted exclusively for agricultural, horticultural or livestock raising operations or for lifting or carrying an implement of husbandry. See NY VTL § 100-d.

Registration

Who Should Register?

The following farm vehicles are exempt from New York's registration and drivers' license requirements:

- *Farm type tractors* and *ATVs* used exclusively for agricultural purposes or for personal snow plowing (not for-hire);

- *Self-propelled machines* used exclusively for growing, harvesting or handling farm produce; and,

- *Self-propelled caterpillar* or crawler-type equipment operated on the contract site.

See NY VTL § 125.

All other farm vehicles and agricultural trucks must be registered by filing form MV-82 (*Vehicle Registration/Title Application*) with the *New York Department of Motor Vehicles* and checking the appropriate box designating the vehicle as either a farm vehicle or agricultural truck. If registering a farm vehicle, one must also file form MV-260F, Part 1 (*Certified Farm Vehicle Use*) and attach it to form MV-82. A farm-plated vehicle is a not for-hire vehicle that may only be used within New York state to do one of the following three things:

1. *Travel between points* on a farm or farms;

2. *Transport farm material* to the nearest landfill; or

3. *Transport the vehicle* to a licensed repair shop for repairs or adjustments (with some restrictions).

Travel

A farm-plated vehicle must travel via the most direct route, but no further than twenty-five (25) miles one way from a pre-designated point on the farm. See NYCRR Tit 17 § 820.1(d); see also NY VTL § 401(13).

Exemptions from Federal Farm Safety Regulations

Operation of a *"covered farm vehicle"* is exempt from the following federal safety regulations:

1. CDL requirements;

2. Controlled substances and alcohol use testing;

3. Physical qualifications and examinations;

4. Hours of service; and

5. Inspection, repair, and maintenance.

See MAP-21 § 32934 and FMCSR §§ 382-83, 391, 395-96).

Covered Farm Vehicles and USDOT Numbers

A vehicle must be registered within the state with a license plate or other designation identifying it as a farm vehicle to qualify as a *"covered farm vehicle."* See FMCSR § 390.5

All commercial vehicles *over 10,000 lbs.* are required to obtain a *USDOT number.* Both the USDOT number and the company name must:

1. Appear on both sides of the vehicle;
2. Be in letters that contrast sharply in color with the background on which the letters are placed;
3. Be readily legible during daylight hours from 50 feet; and
4. Be kept and maintained in a manner that retains the legibility.

See FMCSR §§ 390.19 & 390.21 and NYCRR Tit 17 § 820.2.

These regulations apply to both *commercial vehicles* that are operated *across state lines* and those that operate solely within the state of New York. New York farm-plated vehicles weighing less than 18,000 lbs. that are *driven only within New York* are exempt from the USDOT requirement.

License Requirements

One must hold a valid driver's license to operate all farm vehicles not listed above as being exempt. An individual driving a non-exempt farm vehicle within 150 miles of their farm is not required to hold a *commercial driver's license* ("CDL") and may operate the vehicle with a Class D license. <u>See</u> FMCSR § 390.39. The minimum age required to obtain a Class D license in New York is 18; however, a 17 year old may apply if he or she has successfully completed an approved driver's education course. <u>See</u> NY VTL § 502(2)(c).

Although a CDL may not be required to drive a farm vehicle, one will need to obtain a *farm endorsement* in order to operate a farm vehicle or combination of vehicles with a GVWR of more than 26,000 lbs. within 150 miles of the farm. <u>See</u> NY VTL § 501(2)(b)(vi). New York offers 3 types of farm endorsements:

1. **F endorsement** - required on non-CDL to operate farm vehicles and farm vehicle combinations over 26,000 lbs;

2. **G endorsement** - required on non-CDL to operate a single farm vehicles over 26,000 lbs; and,

3. **Z endorsement** - required on non-CDL to transport hazardous materials in a farm vehicle. (NYCRR Tit 15 § 3.2(b)(1)(ii)).

Operation of a commercial vehicle beyond 150 miles of the farm requires a CDL. The minimum age to obtain a CDL that is valid in New York State only is 18. <u>See</u> NY VTL § 502(2)(b). One must be at least 21 to obtain a CDL valid for interstate commerce. <u>See</u> NY VTL § 502(2)(a).

A farmer wishing to operate a commercial vehicle that does not fall under the previously mentioned "covered farm vehicle" exemption must periodically submit a *medical certificate* to the New York DMV demonstrating that he or she is physically qualified to operate a commercial motor vehicle. <u>See</u> NY VTL § 502(1); FMCSA § 391.41(a)(1)(i). The medical certificate must be obtained via *physical exam* performed in accordance with USDOT's Medical Examination Report, available online at Federal Motor Carrier Safety Administration's website located at http://www.fmcsa.dot.gov/documents/safetyprograms/Medical-Report.pdf.

Insurance

The following do not require *motor vehicle insurance*:

1. *Tractors* used exclusively for agricultural purposes or snow plowing (not for-hire);

2. *Farm equipment*, including self-propelled machines used exclusively in growing, harvesting, or handling farm produce; and

3. Self-propelled *caterpillar* or crawler-type equipment while operated at the contract site.

Nonetheless, it is recommended to obtain farm equipment insurance to protect yourself from liability. See NY VTL § 311(2). Make sure to talk to your insurance agent so you understand what is covered.

Sales and Use Tax Exemption

Motor vehicles used more than 50% of the time in either the production phase of farming or in commercial horse boarding operations are exempt from New York sales and use taxes. Review NY VTL § 311(2) for more information.

Hours of Service

The Federal *Motor Carrier Safety Act* sets out specific regulations governing the allowable *working hours* of individuals driving commercial motor vehicles and applicable record keeping requirements. See FMCSA § 395. A commercial vehicle owned by a farmer and operated intrastate by the farmer or employee to haul farm, dairy, or horticultural products is exempt from such hours of service regulations. See NYCRR § 820.6(b)(2).

Slow Moving Vehicles ("SMV")

SMV Emblem

Farm machinery and agricultural equipment designed to operate at 25 mph or less and all animal driven vehicles on public roads must display a slow-moving vehicle emblem as developed by the American Society of Agricultural Engineers. See NY VTL § 375(36)(b), NYCRR

Tit 15 § 68.8 and NY VTL § 375(36(a). If two SMVs are used in combination, such as a tractor and wagon, each must separately display the emblem. See NY VTL § 375(36)(b).

The SMV emblem must:

1. Consist of a *fluorescent yellow-orange triangle* with a dark reflective border;

2. Be entirely *visible* both day and night from distances between 600 and 100 ft. from the rear;

3. Be *maintained and cleaned* to ensure that it is plainly visible; and

4. Be *mounted* 2 to 6 feet above ground level in the center rear of the vehicle with the point up.

See NYCRR Tit 15 § 68.3, 68.5. Please note that the SMV emblem is not a replacement for *other required warning devices* such as tail lamps, reflectors, flashing lights, warning flags, or flares.

Lighting

Self-propelled agricultural equipment used on any public highway or street in New York from 30 minutes after sunset to 30 minutes before sunrise, and when visibility is less than 1,000 ft. in either direction regardless of the time of day, must be equipped with:

1. 2 white front-facing headlamps placed at the same level;

2. 1 rear-facing red tail lamp placed as far left as is practicable;

3. 2 amber hazard lights;

4. Turn signals in the front and rear; and

5. 2 red rear-facing reflectors.

See NYCRR Tit 15 § 43.9; NY VTL § 376(1)(a).

Bulk Agricultural Commodity Implements ("BACI")

BACI is a piece of farm equipment specifically designed for and carrying nonhazardous bulk agricultural commodities. Examples of BACI's are: bulk dry fertilizer spreaders, gravity boxes, hay wagons, and forage wagons. A BACI meeting appropriate size and weight standards may be towed by a registered, inspected, and insured truck if:

1. It is operated from sunrise to sunset;

2. It does not exceed 25 mph;

3. The BACI exhibits a SMV emblem;

4. It is within a 50-mile radius of the address on the truck's registration, or within 50 miles of the dealership leasing the BACI;

5. It uses a properly manufactured hitch pin or safety chains;

6. It is not operated on an interstate or controlled access highway; and

7. It is not driven when visibility is less than 1,000 ft.

See NYCRR Tit 15 § 101.4.

Height, Width, and Weight Restrictions

New York farmers should be cognizant of the following *height, width and weight* restrictions:

*   **Height**: A vehicle shall not exceed 13ft. 6 in. or otherwise posted height restrictions. See NY VTL § 385(2).

*   **Width**: As a general rule, a vehicle, inclusive of load, shall not be more than 96 inches wide plus safety devices except on a qualifying or access highway where the maximum width, including load, is 102 inches plus safety devices.

However, there is a special rule for farm vehicles. A vehicle between 12 and up to 17 feet wide used solely for farm purposes is exempt from the general width limitations above if:

1. It is operated from 30 minutes before sunrise to 30 minutes after sunset;

2. Appropriately sized red or orange florescent flags are properly displayed;

3. Rear-facing amber lights or hazard lights are flashing; and

4. An escort vehicle precedes it when the farm vehicle or load extends beyond the centerline of the highway or is being operated when visibility is less than 1,000 ft.

See NY VTL § 385(1)(c).

- **Weight:** A vehicle may not exceed regulatory weight limitations based on tire ratings, axle weight ratings, wheel loading, or posted limits on roads and bridges. At no time shall the total weight of the vehicle exceed 80,000 lbs. See NY VTL § 385(5)-(14).

Fuel Storage Issues

Farms vehicles use a lot of fuel, and most farms store fuel for rapid access and to control price. *Fuel storage tanks* are subject to a variety of strict rules that must be followed carefully if you want to avoid having legal claims brought against your farm. Following fuel storage tank rules also protects your farm from the possible denial of an insurance claim if disaster strikes. All tanks must be *UL approved*, have an *external gate valve*, *check valves*, and *proper venting*.

Spills, Prevention, and Containment

Farms that began operation after *August 16, 2002* must have *written spill-prevention plans* for all *above-ground oil and fuel storage*, detailing how they will *prevent, handle, and clean up any spills*. Actually, according to the EPA, farms that began operation before August 16, 2002 were required to have the spill prevention plans from 1972, when the *Clean Water Act* ("CWA") was passed, though that has never been enforced.

While plan requirements vary, farms that meet these three requirements have to have a plan in place:

1. The farm stores, transfers, uses, or consumes *oil or oil products*, such as diesel fuel, gasoline, lube oil, hydraulic oil, adjuvant oil, crop oil, vegetable oil or animal fat;

2. The farm can *reasonably expect to discharge oil or fuel into waters of the U.S.*; and,

3. The farm stores *more than 1,320 gallons* in *above-ground* containers

The 1,320 gallon above-ground container count does not include the capacity of tractors, combines, trucks or other mobile equipment or pesticide application containers, or mixing tanks or milk bulk tanks and pipes. It does include the capacity of any containers more than 55 gallons that store diesel fuel, gasoline, lube oil, hydraulic oil, adjuvant oil, crop oil, vegetable oil, or animal fat.

Spill Prevention Plan Requirements

Here are a few pointers to keep in mind in regard to spill prevention:

- If your farm's *combined above-ground oil and fuel storage totals more than 10,000 gallons*, you must have a *professional engineer* prepare a spill prevention plan.

- If you store *between 1,320 and 10,000 gallons* (as long as no single container holds over 5,000 gallons *and* you have no history of major spills), you can use an EPA template to *self-certify your compliance*. You'll have to keep the *plan on file* at the farm and complete *regular updates*.

- Farmers with a *single tank*, storing *between 5,000 and 10,000 gallons*, cannot use the template, but must instead prepare a *more comprehensive plan* themselves or hire a professional engineer to do it.

Secondary Containment Requirements

Secondary containment is required if you have *more than 1,100 gallons of storage* and also requires interaction with the state fire marshal to *register* those tanks. *Dikes, containment curbs and pits* are common *types* of secondary containment used for this purpose. Diked areas must be sufficiently *impervious* to *contain discharges* and prevent escape of any spilled materials.

The *size* of secondary containment should be adequate to contain the entire capacity of the *largest single container*, with sufficient *freeboard* to contain precipitation. The engineering "rule of thumb" for adequate secondary containment is 110 percent of the largest tank's capacity, plus capacity for a 5.5 inch rain in 24 hours.

Labeling Your Fuel

Essentially, if you have *over 119 gallons* in a fuel tank on a farm service-type truck, you will need a placard identifying what *type of fuel* you are carrying. Diesel and farm gas each have a different *number*. It's not the lottery so please do not throw some random numbers up there. The number on the placard is based on the fuel's *flammability*. Remember to label your off-farm fuel as off-farm. Mixing the red with the non-exempt fuel can lead to big fines against your farm.

Additional Resources

Committee on Agriculture Safety and Health Research and Extension, "Agriculture Equipment on Public Roads", USDA-CSREES, Washington, D.C. (2009) available at http://www.csrees.usda.gov/about/white_papers/pdfs/ag_equipmen t.pdf (last visited August 18, 2013).

Environmental Protection Agency, "Oil Spills | Emergency Management", available at http://www.epa.gov/oilspill (last visited July 11, 2013).

Environmental Protection Agency, "Office of Underground Storage Tanks (OUST)", available at http://www.epa.gov/oust (last visited July 11, 2013).

New York City DOT, "Highway and Traffic Rules" at http://www.nyc.gov/html/dot/html/motorist/traffic_rules.shtml (last visited August 18, 2013).

New York Department of Transportation, "New York State Motor Carrier Safety Regulations: NYCRR Part 820", available at https://www.dot.ny.gov/divisions/operating/osss/repository/17%20 NYCRR%20Part%20820.pdf (last visited August 18, 2013).

New York Farm Bureau, "Farmer's Guide to Truck & Farm Implement Laws & Regulations" (3rd Ed) available at http://www.nyfb.org/legal/NYFB_s_Legal_Library_54_pg.htm (last visited July 11, 2013).

New York Safety Council, "New York Defensive Driving" at http://www.newyorksafetycouncil.com/Defensive-Driving-Course.aspx (last visited August 18, 2013).

Northeast Beginning Farmers Project, "#7 Farm Vehicle Regulations" available at http://nebeginningfarmers.org/2012/04/07/7-farm-vehicle-regulations/ (last visited August 18, 2013).

SafeNY, "Slow Moving Vehicles," at http://www.safeny.ny.gov/slowmove.htm (last visited August 18, 2013).

CHAPTER 16

FEDERAL FARM PROGRAMS

It is important for New York agriculture producers to understand the *Farm Bill* and different types of federal farm payments available to them and procedures for appealing an adverse decision. Factors affecting government payments include the *type of crop produced* (i.e., only certain commodities are supported by federal farm programs), the *numbers of acres in production* (i.e., farm size), and *operator's characteristics*, including *production records*.

Farmers should work with an agriculture lawyer to help maximize federal farm benefit. This is sometimes referred to as "*Farm Program Planning*". Although not discussed in this Chapter, farmers should be cognizant of *grants* at the federal and state level applicable to their operation.

The Farm Bill

The "Farm Bill" becomes a topic of debate every four years, the year of presidential elections. The *Food Conservation and Energy Act of 2008* (the 2008 Farm Bill) was extended to September 2013, giving Congress more time to discuss the next Farm Bill. As this book goes to press in September 2013, Congress has not yet passed the 2012 Farm Bill and we may see, for the first time in history, a decoupling of several food and nutrition programs from the Farm Bill.

In way of background, the Farm Bill suspends or repeals the "permanent" farm legislation set forth in the *Agriculture Adjustment Act of 1938* and *Agriculture Act of 1949*. The programs are put in place until the next Farm Bill is revisited in four years.

Farm Bill Titles

The 2008 Farm Bill includes the following 15 titles:

- <u>Title I, Commodities:</u> support for growers of selected commodities (e.g., wheat, feed grains, dairy) through direct payments, counter-cyclical payments and marketing loans.

- <u>Title II, Conservation:</u> federal programs for environmental conservation and farm preservation.

- <u>Title III, Agriculture Trade and Food Aid:</u> exports and food assistance at the international level.

- <u>Title IV, Nutrition:</u> domestic food and nutrition programs including food stamps.

- <u>Title V, Farm Credit:</u> federal direct and guaranteed farm loan programs for agriculture producers along with loan eligibility rules.

- <u>Title VI, Rural Development:</u> various rural community programs at the federal, state and local level for planning and feasibility assessments (e.g., rural broadband).

- <u>Title VII, Research:</u> agriculture research and extension programs (e.g., Cornell University Cooperative Extension).

- <u>Title VIII, Forestry:</u> USDA Forest Service programs.

- <u>Title IX, Energy:</u> programs and grants to assist eligible farmers and rural agri-businesses in purchasing renewable energy systems.

- <u>Title X, Horticulture and Organic Agriculture:</u> covers fruits, vegetables, specialty crops and organic agriculture.

- <u>Title XI, Livestock:</u> covers livestock and poultry production (e.g., mandatory *Country-of-Origin Labeling*).

- <u>Title XII, Crop Insurance and Disaster Assistance:</u> covers crop insurance and supplemental disaster assistance.

- Title XIII, Commodity Futures: covering reauthorization of the *Commodity Futures Trading Commission* ("CFTC").

- Title XIV, Miscellaneous: other federal farm programs for socially disadvantaged farmers and agriculture security.

- Title XV, Trade and Tax Provisions: tax provisions to offset spending initiatives in the Farm Bill.

The *Farm Service Agency* ("FSA") administers most of the government farm programs under the Farm Bill. Some conservation programs are supervised by the *Natural Resources Conservation Service* ("NRCS").

Types of Farm Payments

To remove some of the volatility from farm operations, the government provides *five types of farm payments*:

- **Direct Payments** are a government set amount, paid according to a farm's "base acreage." Base acreage is determined by establishing what percentage of the total acres is devoted to the crop that payments are provided for. Direct payments are unrelated to production or market prices.

- **Counter-Cyclical Payments** ("CCP") are set based on a "target" price, which triggers payment when the commodity price falls below the target and revenue for a commodity falls below a historical guaranteed level.

- Alternatively, the **Average Crop Revenue Election** ("ACRE") program uses revenue guarantees based on a minimum price set by national averages and state yields. Beginning in 2009, farmers could choose between traditional CCP's or ACRE. The ACRE program is available for the same crops as CCP's but are based on planted acres rather than base acres.

- **Loan Deficiency Payments** ("LDP") are based on the difference between commodity loan rates and the payment rate

263

for the loan. This is a streamlined way of handling marketing assistance loans that are offered by the government.

- **Emergency Payment Programs** are triggered in crop failures. Most government program payments are income.

Losing Your Farm Payments

However, you do not have access to farm program payments if you *run afoul of government rules*. You will likely receive a *notice of adverse action or determination* or a *notice of violation*. These are your warning shots that you are not doing what your government thinks you should be doing, regarding federal farm programs. If you receive such a warning, your choices are:

- To continue to do what you want to on your property and no longer participate in the programs (along with potentially having to pay back any benefits you have received);

- To comply with the government's requirements; or

- To appeal the government's decision.

Appealing Adverse Decisions

Appealing a government adverse decision can be accomplished in several different ways. You may appeal to the *county- or state-level committees* that, in theory, govern the government officials assigned to your county. You can ask for reconsideration, go to mediation or file a formal appeal. The appeals are handled through a special administrative procedure that eventually winds up at a special *"National Appeals Division"* ("NAD") of the USDA.

What can you appeal? You may appeal any "adverse decision" made by FSA or any other USDA agency. Examples can include:

- NRCS technical determinations,

- Errors in documentation and calculations necessary to determine program eligibility, or

- Errors in calculations and documentation to determine ability to repay FLP assistance.

These **types of errors** may include the following:

- Either in connection with loan servicing or a request for a new loan;

- All matters relating to correctly applying regulations pertinent to an issue of fact;

- Appraising security, except negotiated appraisals relating to primary loan servicing; or

- Whether a participant is farming in a farmer-like manner.

FSA is required to *notify* participants of "adverse decisions". Those notification letters **must** contain the following:

- **Background** — A brief narrative explaining the *reason* for the letter;

- **General Program Provisions** — A statement about the program for which the participant filed an *application*, executed a *contract*, sought a *determination*, or the *provision* that brought about the need for an administrative determination;

- **FSA's Findings** — A general discussion of the *pertinent facts* based on specific references to either the application, contract, information submitted by the participant, or other relevant information or evidence that can be and is specifically cited and referenced in the decision letter;

- **Discussion** — A narrative explaining the findings together with the general program provisions;

- **Determination** — FSA's decision based on the general program provisions, findings, and discussion; and

- **Mandatory Language** for adverse decision letters.

The FSA has a helpful *handbook* that outlines what mandatory language it must include, yet it *sometimes fails to do so*. For most people, the rules regarding appeals and FSA requirements are complex and truly murky. Finding and using experienced legal representation is highly advisable when telling the government it is wrong – especially if your farm payments are riding on the outcome.

Final NAD determinations are subject to a judicial review in federal district court. A farmer must exhaust administrative remedies through the NAD appeal process before seeking a judicial review.

Additional Resources

Beginning Farmers, "Funding Resources (Loans/Grants)", at http://www.beginningfarmers.org/funding-resources/ (last visited August 18, 2013).

National Agriculture Law Center, Reading Room for "Conservation Programs" available at http://nationalaglawcenter.org/readingrooms/conservation/ (last visited January 9, 2013).

Northeast Beginning Farmers Project, "#31 Grant Opportunities for Farmers," available at http://nebeginningfarmers.org/2012/05/01/31-grant-opportunities-for-farmers/ (last visited August 18, 2013).

SUSAN A. SCHNEIDER, FOOD, FARMING & SUSTAINABILITY (2010) at Chapter 2 ("Economic Support to Agriculture").

USDA Farm Service Agency, available at http://www.fsa.usda.gov/ (last visited January 9, 2013).

U.S. Department of Agriculture's National Appeals Division, available at http://www.nad.usda.gov (last visited January 9, 2013).

CHAPTER 17

AGRICULTURE LIENS

Getting paid for what you do is a business necessity, without which your operations will not continue to function for long. Fortunately, certain legal mechanisms called *agricultural liens* are available to make it easier to ensure that you do, in fact, get paid at the end of the day.

An *agricultural lien* is an *encumbrance*, filed against *farm products or property*, to *secure payment for services and goods* provided to a farm operation or rent on farm property. Liens can operate for you, or those who provide services and goods to your operation can file liens against your property, so it is good to be familiar with the situations that give rise to various liens related to your farm operations.

Background

The scope of the revised *Uniform Commercial Code* ("UCC") Article 9 is newly expanded to cover the perfection, priority, and enforcement of nonpossessory *"Agricultural Liens"* in the farm products of those borrowers involved in farming operations. The definition of "agricultural liens" is different than the broader and more general category of *"secured interest"*. UCC Article 9 does not supersede any existing statutory liens, nor does it create any new lienor interests, but rather integrates with the existing statutory liens. See UCC 9-102(5). Importantly, a financing statement must be filed to perfect all security interest and agricultural liens under the UCC. See UCC 9-310.

Under UCC Section 9-103, an agricultural lien does not enjoy *"purchase money security interest"* prioritization. However, once a

267

security interest on crops is perfected, the security interest has priority over both the owner and other encumbrances. See UCC 9-322(g). In contrast, if there is conflict between an *agricultural lien* on collateral, and a perfected security interest in the same collateral, then the agricultural lien will only get priority if the statute creating the agricultural lien expressly gives this priority.

Clear as mud? Let's look at some specific agriculture liens in New York for the bigger picture.

Landlord's Lien

A landlord's lien used to be superior to other creditors' claims; however, in New York, it *does not arise automatically* because a landlord-tenant relationship is created. Landlords who want to retain title to the products of the land against the tenant's other creditors must *explicitly include a provision* to that effect in the lease.

Both the landlord and tenant should memorialize their intent to create such a *security interest*. The sooner the landlord in this situation files a *UCC-1 statement* with the *NYS Department of State*, the more likely courts are to protect his or her position for payment. Ideally, this filing should be made when the lease is signed.

New York landlords should be cautious about relying on security interests. The *validity of UCC -1 statements* is often the subject of protracted litigation. Accordingly, New York courts have commented that landlords may find more effective protection in the form of insurance. See e.g., Badillo v. Tower Ins. Co. of New York, 686 N.Y.S.2d. 363 (N.Y. Ct. of Appeals 1999).

Liens on Animals and
Other Types of Personal Property

Lien For Service of Stallions or Bulls

Under Section 160 of *NY Lien Law*, the "owner of a *stallion or bull* shall have a lien on each *mare or cow* served together with the *foal or calf* of each mare or cow from such service, for the amount agreed on at the time of service. . ." However, said lien will not be able to be enforced if the owner *falsely states the pedigree* of the stallion or bull. See NY Lien Law § 163 (emphasis added).

The statute requires that a written *Notice of Lien* be properly
268

filed pursuant to the procedures set forth in NY *Uniform Commercial Code* Section 9-501(a). <u>See</u> <u>also</u> <u>Tuttle v. Dennis</u>, 11 N.Y.S.600 (1890) (stating that a lien for the service of a stallion attaches against the mare and her foal at the time of the service so long as the Notice of Lien is properly filed).

The *Notice of Lien* must include the following information:

- specify the *person or legal entity* that the claim is made against,

- the *amount of the claim*, and

- *description of the property* (e.g., mare/cow and foal/calf) upon which the lien is claimed.

Once filed, this lien will terminate in 1.5 years (*18 months*) unless foreclosure procedures were commenced during this period pursuant to Sections 206 thru 210 of NY Lien Law. The lien is *not given* any express statutory priority over other liens.

Lien of Bailee of Animals (a/k/a "Stableman's Lien")

Under Section 183 of NY Lien Law, any *veterinarian* who renders treatment to or boards any dog, cat, or other domestic animal or person keeping a livery stable, *boarding stable* or pasturing animals has a lien over the animal and any equipment kept and stored in conjunction with the animal, such as a "*wagon, truck, cart, carriage, vehicle or harness*". Possession of this property is required for this lien. The bailee may detain the property until the amount due for professional services rendered, care, keeping, boarding or pasturing of the animal or for keeping the wagon, truck, cart, carriage, vehicle or harness, for the amount agreed upon between the parties.

This lien is oftentimes referred to as a "*stableman's lien*." The keeper of a *livery stable or barn* who boards horses at a certain monthly rate per stall but does not feed or care for the horses are still entitled to this lien. <u>See</u> <u>Selner v. Lyons</u>, 110 N.Y.S. 1049 (1908).
This statutory lien does not apply to a livery stable keeper who takes the horse around the country and enters him/her for *horse races*. <u>See</u> <u>Armitage v. Mace</u>, 96 N.Y. 538 (1884). The court must find that there was an express or implied agreement between the owner of the animal

and the bailee. See Cocciolone v. Nastasi, 773 N.Y.S.2d 452 (2nd Dep't 2004). This lien also does not apply to a person who herds or pastures animals as an *employee* of the owner of animals; this lien is only applicable to *independent contractors* who provide animal related services. See Dairy Herd Management Corp. v. Goodwin, 534 N.Y.S.2d 590 (3rd Dep't 1998).

There is no statutory filing requirement for the stableman's lien in New York and it is not given priority over other liens.

Lien on Stray Animals

Under *NY Town Law* § 310, if a person has any strayed horses, cattle, sheep, swine, goats or other livestock animal upon their property which is *not adjoined to the livestock owner's property* (in other words, not your immediate neighbor), then that person may have a lien claim against the stray animals. The livestock must have *caused property damage* and the escape of the livestock must have been caused by the livestock owner's neglect to make or maintain a fence. Upon foreclosure, the lien may be used to satisfy the reasonable fees and costs made to repair the property.

The owner of the stray must be given *written notice* within *thirty (30) days* of the stray coming unto the lienor's land, unless the owner of the stray is not known, in which case a *notice* must run in the *nearest county newspaper for two successive weeks.* See NY Town § 313. If the notice procedures are followed and the owner of the stray does not redeem the animal, then the lienor may foreclose. However, if the notice procedures are not followed, then the lienor's rights are not perfected and the lienor then loses any entitlement to damages and instead becomes liable for costs and expenses incurred by reason of keeping the animals. See NY Town § 316.

Take home point: Maintain your fence and keep good relationships with your neighbors.

Truckman's Lien

Under Section 187 of NY Lien Law, every person or entity engaged in "carting or trucking property shall have a lien upon such property and may retain such portion of the property in his possession" to help ensure payment for the truckman or drayman. See NY Lien Law § 187[1]. Possession of the property is required for this lien. Please note that this lien does not take priority over other liens.

Here are a few important provisions in the statute:

- "If such amount remains *unpaid for thirty [30] days* after demand, such bailee for hire may upon *fifteen [15] days' notice in writing* to the owner, specifying the amount due and informing him that the payment of such amount within fifteen days will entitle him to redeem such property, and if such property is not redeemed, such bailee may *sell such property at public sale to satisfy the account*, including any expense for *storage, insurance*, or otherwise incurred for the protection or preservation of such property." NY Lien Law § 187[2] (emphasis added).

- "The *proceeds of the sale* after paying the expenses thereof shall be applied in liquidation of the indebtedness secured by such lien, and the balance, if any, *shall be paid over to the owner*. Such notice shall be served by *registered mail* directed to the owner's *last known post office address* and by posting in three public places in the town, village or city where the property is located." NY Lien Law § 187[2] (emphasis added).

Please note that there is no filing requirement in New York for this lien.

New York State Milk and Agriculture Products Security Trust Funds

Although most New York statutory liens are under the NY Lien law, NYSDAM has a lien interest under *Section 25-b of NY Agriculture and Markets Law* against *licensed milk dealers*. This interest arises from the Commissioner's role in administering the *Milk Producers Security Fund*. Milk dealers may, however, provide an alternate form of security (such as a letter of credit) in lieu of paying into the Milk Producer's Security Fund. NYSDAM has the same power under a similar program under *Article 20 of the New York Agriculture and Markets Law*, wherein wholesale dealers who do more than *$10,000 annual business* with New York state producers must either both deposit a bond into the agricultural producers security fund and also deposit a fee (based upon annual volume of purchases), or provide a bond or letter of credit. See NY Agric & Mkts. §§ 248, 250-B. In both programs, the purpose of the fund is to provide *prompt payment to producers.*

Under the *Milk Producers Security Fund Program*, the Commissioner must certify the amount of the debt, and the defaulting dealer has both an opportunity to request a hearing from the Commissioner prior to determination of the debt, and another thirty (30) days to *bring a proceeding* under CPLR Article 78 (an action against an administrative agency) to stay and review the Commissioner's final determination.

After service by *first class mail* upon the *defaulting dealer* of the commissioner's certification of payment of a claim from the fund for which the dealer has been found liable "the commissioner may issue a *warrant under seal* of the department directed to the sheriff of any county of the state commanding him or her to *levy upon and sell the real and personal property* of the defaulting" dealer. The commissioner may then file a copy of the warrant with the county clerk to *perfect a lien*, retroactive to the date of the earliest default, against the real and personal property and chattels real of the defaulting dealer. See NY Agric & Mkts. § 258-B[5].

Similarly, under the *Agricultural Producers Security Fund Program*, a producer is paid from the fund if the dealer fails to do so. The defaulting dealer then has 15 days to reimburse the fund, otherwise "the commissioner may issue a warrant under seal of the department directed to the sheriff of any county of the state commanding him or her to levy upon and sell the real and personal property of the defaulting" dealer. The Commissioner of NYSDAM may then file a copy of the warrant with the county clerk to perfect a lien, retroactive to the date of the earliest default, against the real and personal property and chattels real of the defaulting dealer. See NY Agric & Mkts. § 250-B[2].

Other Agriculture Liens in New York

Please take note that New York also has the following agriculture liens:

- **Railway Corporation Lien on Transported Animals** for a railway corporation incurring expenses in caring for transported animals under NY Agric. & Mkts § 359.

- **Artisan's Lien** for a person who makes, repairs or performs work for an article of personal property under NY Lien Law § 180.

- **Carrier's Lien** for the carrier of goods covered by a bill of lading under NY UCC §§ 7-307, 7-308.

- **Warehouseman's Lien** for the warehouseman of goods covered by a warehouse receipt under NY UCC §§ 7-7-209, 7-211.

- **Lien of Silk Processor** for the person who processes silk into yard goods under NY Lien Law § 185.

- **Lien for Damages Caused by Inanimate Property** for the person whose land is damaged by a good or chattel (including timber or drift logs) under NY Town Law § 323.

Foreclosure to Satisfy a Lien

A *lien against animals* may be satisfied by the sale of such property pursuant to Article 9 of NY Lien Law. See N.Y. Lien Law § 200. Before a lien holder can sell personal property, the lien holder *must serve notice* upon the owner with due diligence. See N.Y. Lien Law § 201. "Any notice permitted herein to be served by mail shall be sent by certified mail, return receipt requested, and by first-class mail." N.Y. Lien Law § 201. Similarly, "like notice" shall be served upon persons who have given the lien holder notice of an interest in the property subject to the lien and persons who have perfected a security interest in the property by filing a UCC *financing statement*. See N.Y. Lien Law § 201.

The *Notice of Sale* should include a statement as to the following facts:

1. The *nature of the debt* or the agreement under which the lien arose, with an itemized statement of the claim and the time when due;

273

2.   A *brief description* of the personal property against which the lien exists;

3.   The *estimated value* of such property;

4.   The *amount of such lien* at the date of the notice.

See N.Y. Lien Law § 201. Additionally, it should require the owner to pay the amount of the lien on or before the date demanded which shall not be *less than ten (10) days* from the service of the Notice of Sale. See N.Y. Lien Law § 201. Furthermore, it must state the *date, time and place* the property will be sold if the amount is not paid and the owner's right to bring about a proceeding under section 201-a of Article 9 if he/she disputes the validity of the lien or the amount claimed. See N.Y. Lien Law § 201. The lien holder should also notify the owner if his or her agreement provides for continuous care of the animals accruing additional costs for their care subject to the lien. See N.Y. Lien Law § 201.

Defective service of a Notice of Sale will not invalidate the lien itself but it will render the sale invalid. See McCormack v. Anchor Sav. Bank, F.S.B., 582 N.Y.S.2d 6 (1st Dep't 1992).

Section 201-a of NY Lien Law establishes procedures for a proceeding to determine the *validity of a lien*. Within ten (10) days after service of the Notice of Sale, the owner of *personal property* may commence a special proceeding in any court with jurisdiction to render a judgment for the amount equal to the lien. See NY Lien Law § 201-a.

Section 202 of NY Lien Law requires that the sale of personal property be at a *public auction to the highest bidder* in the city or town where the lien was acquired. The notice of the sale must be *properly advertised* once a week for *two consecutive weeks* in a newspaper published in the town or city where the sale is to be held. See N.Y. Lien Law § 202(1). The sale cannot be *less than fifteen (15) days* from the *first publication*. See NY Lien Law § 202(1). If the town or city does not have a newspaper, then the sale must be advertised in at least six conspicuous places in the town or city. See NY Lien Law § 202(1). Among other requirements set forth in section 202(1), this advertisement of the sale must describe the property to be sold and the name of the person who owns the title of such property.

"Unless the pledge agreement otherwise provides, in all cases where a pledgee may lawfully sell pledged property and the property is sold at public sale, the pledgee, or his assignee or the legal representative of either, may *fairly and in good faith purchase* the pledged property or any part thereof at the sale." NY Lien Law § 202-b (emphasis added). Furthermore, at any time *before the property is sold*, the owner may redeem his or her property by paying the lien holder the *amount due for the lien* in addition to whatever *legitimate expenses have been incurred* at the time of such payment in serving the notice and advertisement of sale. See NY Lien Law § 203.

Under Section 204, after the sale of the personal property, the lien holder may retain the amount sufficient to satisfy the lien including any expenses for the advertisement and sale. However, the balance of such proceeds must be held by the lien holder "subject to the demand of the owner. . . ." See NY Lien Law § 204. The lien holder must notify the owner that he/she is holding proceedings via personal service or by mail. See NY Lien Law § 204. If this balance is unclaimed after thirty (30) days then said balance "shall be deposited with the treasurer or chamberlain of the city or village, or the commissioner of the finance in the city of New York, or the supervisor of the town, where such sale was held" along with the information specified in the statute. NY Lien Law § 204.

The *enforcement of a lien* on personal property does not bar the right to recover the debt that is not paid by the proceeds of the sale of the property. See NY Lien Law § 205. Additionally, a lien holder may also *foreclose upon a chattel* via court action with similar procedures for the foreclosure on real property. See NY Lien Law § 206.

Additional Resources

Cari Rincker, "Overview of New York Livestock Law," Morrisville State College, December 4, 2012, slides available at http://www.slideshare.net/rinckerlaw/overview-of-new-york-livestock-law (last visited July 3, 2013).

Eldon L. McAfee, "Agricultural Liens," 2011 Iowa State Bar Association, Commercial & Bankruptcy Law Seminar (May 15, 2011).

Keith G. Meyer, Steven C. Turner, Terry M. Anderson, Brooke Schuman, Patrick S. Turner, "UCC and Current Agricultural Issues,"

The 2010 Annual Meeting of the American Agricultural Law Association (October 8, 2010).

National Agriculture Law Center, "Updating States' Agricultural Lien Charts," at http://www.nationalaglawcenter.org/assets/agliens/ (last visited August 18, 2013).

New York Department of Agriculture and Markets, "Farm Products Dealer Licensing Program," available at http://www.agriculture.ny.gov/programs/apsf.html (last visited August 18, 2013.

CHAPTER 18

COMMODITY SALES

Commodity sales are a central core component of many farm operations. The operator, of course, can *sell on the market upon delivery*, take a *price-later contract*, sell on a *deferred payment contract*, or *store* the commodity. The old joke is that farmers only sell $5.00 corn instead of $10.00 corn because they are waiting for it to go to $10.50.

The general concept is to use the market to *remove risk* that the production of the product creates. Not all marketers are created equal and if you do not personally enjoy following market trends, such as the weather in South America and Chinese import policy, you can hire professional advisors. Many agriculture companies offer market updates via cell phone text messages sent multiple times a day or offer pay-for-advice text messages to help people follow market trends.

Marketing is hard -- if you let your emotions or your desire to brag at the coffee shop interfere, it can make a *tough job even tougher*. One technique is to figure your cost of production and expected return at a reasonable price per unit sold. Then determine what you would do with that return such as purchasing a new grain bin. Get a picture of that grain bin and the minute you fail to sell at the price that would allow that return, tear the picture up to symbolize what you are giving up.

Grain Storage

When storing grain in a licensed public facility, certain rules and protections exist for the farm operator. In such storage arrangements, a *warehouse receipt* stating the number of bushels deposited is usually issued. The warehouse receipt stands as evidence of ownership of the grain. The warehouse receipt is issued usually at the *close of delivery* of the product.

Whenever the grain is moved in or out, a *scale house ticket* is issued. This is the document issued to the driver who delivers the grain. This is not quite the same as a *warehouse receipt*, as most facilities allow a short time to decide what to do (open time) with the product.

Common Sale Contracts

The following are a few examples of common sale contracts:

- **Cash-forward contracts** are agreements that set a price for *actual delivery* of a commodity at a *future date*. This is a method used by both purchasers and sellers to ensure a set price for set bushels and it is a great tool to cover the costs of production for operators.

- **Price-later contracts** also involve *delivery of a set amount* on a set date, but unlike cash-forward contracts, the *price is set* and *paid later*. Some pricing methods allow for setting a specific future date and time when the price for the product will be determined. Others allow a discount (basis) from a set date, as selected later by the farmer.

- **Deferred payment agreements** envision a current sale, delivery, and price-setting, with payment withheld until a specified later date. This arrangement is commonly used for end-of-year *tax planning*. The farmer must not have the ability to demand the payment earlier if he hopes to convince the IRS that the payment was not available at the time of sale. The *Packers and Stockyard Act* requires settlement of livestock sales within 72 hours of delivery; thus, be cognizant of the risks involved with the deferred payment agreement.

- **Minimum-price contracts** set a *floor for price* but also allow a chance to participate in upswings in the market. Examine these contracts carefully, as they are not offered by the commodity merchant without *built-in pricing protections* in favor of the merchant as well.

- **Futures contracts** are standard agreements set by a

commodity exchange for a predefined quantity of a commodity. A seller and a buyer each promise to fill in the details of when it will be delivered and what price will be paid. A *seller is "going long,"* while a *buyer is "going short."* The futures contract doesn't mean that you have the product at the time when the contract is made, but it indicates you *will* have it to deliver at a later date. Most futures contracts are *reversed* or *liquidated* before the delivery date occurs, though there are some great stories of inattentive traders being delivered 5,000 lbs. of beef or 50,000 lbs. of cotton float through the traders' tales. That is because some buyers, like processors, actually want the product, and the seller runs the risk of not being able to offset the delivery with another purchase.

Hedging

Hedging is a futures-trading method of *managing risk*. To have a true hedge, you take a position opposite to your current position. Grain dealers typically take the hedge risk, but in today's sophisticated market, farm operators are tempted to become directly involved. Detailed study should be undertaken before diving into the hedge market.

A *hedge-to-arrive ("HTA") contract* is a contract used in futures trading in which the futures price is determined when the contract is created, but the basis level is not determined until later, usually just before delivery. A *standard HTA* contract is a *forward contract* in which the farmer promises to deliver a stated quantity of grain for a *price linked to the price of a futures contract that expires in the delivery month.*

- From the *farmer's perspective*, such an HTA contract is a normal forward contract that shifts to the buyer the risk that the market price will fall before delivery (and simultaneously prevents the farmer from taking advantage of rising prices).
- From the *buyer's perspective*, the HTA contract facilitates hedging.

Failure to Deliver

A *failure to deliver* according to the required terms of any of these contracts can be treated by the other party as a *breach of contract,* unless it is *excused.* An event not related to the farmer's control may be an *excuse or justification* for failure to deliver, if the contract is based upon a *specific parcel.* However, events like this will *not* excuse performance on contracts which are merely based on *commodities of a certain type and kind.*

Put another way: One valid excuse for failure to perform any contract is *impossibility* of performance. Impossibility can result from different kinds of unexpected causes, like *natural disasters* (e.g., Hurricanes Sandy and Irene). However, when it comes to delivering commodities, your performance of the obligation to deliver may only be made impossible, if your contract required you to deliver something like commodities from a specific parcel, which cannot be replaced by commodities grown just anywhere.

For example, as a farm operator, if you have a contract to deliver seed beans grown on certain-named farmland, and a tornado comes along and destroys them; therefore, it has become **impossible** to comply with the very clear terms of the contract. Because the beans you agreed to deliver were only those grown on a **specific parcel**, you are likely **not going to be excused** from your obligation to deliver.

On the other hand, even unexpected events will *not* excuse your performance if the product you have agreed to deliver is *replaceable.*

Let's say that you have a contract to deliver 5,000 bushels of beans to the elevator and you planned to fulfill that obligation by delivering beans from your farm. However, the crop protection company sprays your beans with the wrong chemical, killing off the crop. You are **still on the hook** to deliver beans from **wherever you can get them.**

In such a scenario, though, you may be able to recover your damages from the crop protection company (or its insurance company), by filing a claim against it for *negligence.*

There are other legal defenses, such as *mutual mistake* or *incapacity*, which apply to excuse performance of commodities contracts. Consider this example:

> A great story floats around about the farmer who "locked in" corn at $4.00 a bushel. When the price shot up to $7.00 a bushel, the tale goes that he had himself checked into a mental facility and declared incompetent in order to void the contracts. To the casual observer, his sudden motivation for "seeking help" was clearly a ruse to allow him a chance to take advantage of the higher prices. Nevertheless, it worked. But I don't suggest trying this tactic to get yourself out of a bad business move.

Although the story above may seem to be extreme, *incapacity to form a contract*, declared by qualified doctors is a *valid excuse* (i.e., contract defense) not to perform the contract at all. Review Chapter 4 on Contracts in this book for more details about contract defenses.

Additional Resources

Chicago Board of Trade, "Agriculture: Understanding Basis," available at http://www.gofutures.com/pdfs/Understanding-Basis.pdf (last visited August 18, 2013).

Chicago Mercantile Exchange, "CME Commodity Trading Manual," available at http://www.kisfutures.com/CMECommodityTradingManual.pdf (last visited August 18, 2013).

Iowa State University Extension, "Understanding Risk in Basis Contracts," (February 1997) available at http://agmarketing.extension.psu.edu/Commodity/PDFs/UndrstdBasisRisk.pdf (last visited August 18, 2013).

John C. McKissick and George A. Shumaker, "Commodity Options: Price Insurance for the Farmer," available at http://www.ces.uga.edu/Agriculture/agecon/pubs/marketpubs/opti

ons.htm (last visited August 18, 2013).

National Agriculture Law Center, Reading Room on "Farm Commodity Programs," at http://new.nationalaglawcenter.org/research-by-topic/commodity-programs/ (last visited August 18, 2013).

National Agriculture Law Center, Reading Room on "International Agriculture Trade," at http://new.nationalaglawcenter.org/research-by-topic/international-trade (last visited August 18, 2013).

Richard G. Fehrenbacher, "Tax- Planning for Farmers Through the Use of Deferred-Payment Contracts," University of Illinois Law Review (1981) available at http://nationalaglawcenter.org/assets/bibarticles/fehrenbacher_tax.pdf (last visited August 18, 2013).

U.S. Department of Agriculture Economic Research Service, "Farmers' Use of Forward Contracts and Futures Markets," Agriculture Economic Report No. 320 (1976) available at http://www.farmdoc.illinois.edu/irwin/archive/papers/Farmers%20use%20of%20forward%20contracts.pdf (last visited August 18, 2013).

U.S. Department of Agriculture Economic Research Service, "Contracts, Markets and Prices: Organizing the Production and Use of Agriculture Commodities," (November 2004) available at http://www.ers.usda.gov/media/284610/aer837_1_.pdf (last visited August 18, 2013).

CHAPTER 19

BANKS AND FINANCING

Banks and bankers play a big part in most farm operations and agri-businesses because most have to carry long-term, intermediate and short-term debt to operate effectively. Unfortunately, farmers and food entrepreneurs may not invest the preparation time needed to deal with their banks as successfully as they could. The more information you can provide to a bank, the better it can evaluate the risk it could be taking by lending you money. Loan officers do not make loans on a whim based on personal feelings; rather, their decisions are guided by the *bank's internal policies*, availability of *credit* at the lending institution, and the loan review committee's *goals and objectives*.

Loan Applications

Collect Your Records

Providing your banker with the *right records* and other information helps your banker gain a more accurate picture of your operations and your credit-worthiness. These days, farm operations generate a good deal of paperwork and are required to keep a lot of records. While good record-keeping may seem like a burden at times, it can go a long way toward helping you get loans when you need them. Gather your records *before you approach* the bank.

What records should a farm operator or agri-business bring to the bank loan office? If you are operating as a corporation or limited liability company, you should bring both the company financial records and also your own personal financial records. Ideally, you should bring all of the records below, but if you don't have all of them, bring what you do have (and keep in mind that your loan officer may ask for other specific records as well, if your situation calls for it):

283

- Three years' worth of tax returns;
- Three years' worth of financial statements, including a balance sheet, an income statement, cash budget, and a comprehensive cash flow statement;
- Articles of Incorporation (for a corporation) or Articles of Organization (for a limited liability company), if applicable;
- Taxpayer identification proof;
- Legal descriptions of real property owned by you and/or your business;
- Copies of any leases;
- Equipment inventories with serial numbers;
- Proof of insurance for items you are offering for collateral; and
- Information about prior loans, including outstanding balances, payment obligations, contact info for the creditor, and the property used as security or collateral.

Explain Your Records

"Crunching numbers" and collecting a nice package of records is only your first step. Next, help set yourself up for success by making a formal appointment to meet with your commercial banker. You should allow enough time to actually talk with the banker, explain what your records mean, and answer the banker's questions. Swinging by the bank to ask for an operating loan, on your way to run the cattle to the sale barn is not a good way to get that loan. Allow ample time to meet with the banker and treat it as a professional meeting. Follow-up promptly by: (a) providing any additional documents your banker asks for, (b) returning phone calls, or (b) responding to questions.

Make Full Disclosure

Tell the banker the truth —*the good, the bad, and the ugly*. When the banker doesn't understand or you don't understand the banker, keep talking until everyone is clear on the details. This may involve asking questions or restating what you think you heard from the loan officer. Understand that you need to have a plan but be flexible enough to realize that it may need to happen on a different scale than you may have envisioned.

Wait Patiently

Don't harass your loan officer. Some folks like to make their presence felt, but in reality, the squeaky wheel doesn't always get the loan. If you really don't want the loan, then call the loan officer every day badgering him/her for better interest rates over the phone, threaten to leave the bank if your every demand isn't met, spend the money before you even ask for the loan -- or worse, simply ask "how much can I have?" Those tactics seem to radically *increase your chances of being rejected*. All conversations with bankers should be done with respect. *Remember the golden rule* -- he who has the gold makes the rules. If you want a loan, you need to play by the bank's rules and follow their time schedule.

How Does the Bank Decide?

The loan officer is likely going to use a variation of the following factors, known as the *"Five C's,"* to review your loan:

- **Character**. Highly-regarded as the number one issue, if the bank can't trust you, then it will not want to do business with you. The bank will judge your character based on whether you are current on your other obligations, like taxes, credit cards, and student loans.

- **Capacity to Repay**. If you can't make the loan payments based on the revenue you'll have coming in, the expenses you'll have going out, and the historical performance of the enterprise, then your loan application will not appeal to a bank officer. A pre-existing, large line of credit (like a credit card) that could be tapped at any point may make a potential new lender worry that once your loan is granted, you could balloon up debts rapidly.

- **Capital**. How much skin do you already have in the game? Can you meet your current obligations and those of this new project? Will you be back to the bank because you can't afford the feed for the hogs you just borrowed money to buy? If the bank feels that you are stretched too thin with little capital to stand behind you if this enterprise slumps or fails, your loan could be denied.

- **Collateral**. The bank is going to want to know what other assets you have that you can offer as security, in the event that your project goes south and you have to replace the money that you borrowed and could not repay. Do not fall into the trap of over-valuing your 1983 Mustang Convertible, no matter how many dates it got you. Consider the real liquidation value of your assets and *be honest* – with yourself and the bank. Don't pledge household goods (such as your furniture or appliances) as collateral for a business loan -- the bank is unlikely to accept it. Listing it just creates more work for the loan officer who has to *remove that fluff* before an actual evaluation of your assets can be made.

> Different banks want different amounts of skin (or capital), but a good rule of thumb to remember is that the bank will want approximately $150 worth of assets as collateral for every $100 that the bank loans. Banks will also likely want at least $110 available to service $100 of principle and interest, in addition to what you are already spending on expenses.

- **Conditions**. This is a subjective call for both parties to make. Consider the risk of your proposed enterprise, trends, and markets. How might these trends impact your growth or shrinkage of your operation? Bankers think in terms of risk, and they are in business to make money, not fund dreams. Just like in business succession or estate planning, your first rodeo is not likely to be swallowing a farm. Instead, consider building a track record with your bank by first taking out and paying off a small loan to cover operating expenses, followed by an equipment loan, followed by larger loans, and so on. Establishing a good relationship with your bank makes you look like less of a risk.

Types of Loans

Before you approach your bank, you need to know what you're

trying to get, not only in terms of amount, but also in terms of the *type of loan* you're going to ask for and how *the five "C's"* will play into that kind of application. You will need to have a clear vision of the purpose for which you need the money and you will need to decide *what kind* of collateral you may be able to offer the bank.

There are many different types of loans, but they can all be said to fall within *two broad categories*:

- **Secured loans** are those in which the bank lends money and you grant the bank an interest in some asset that you own, called *collateral*. If you fail to repay the loan as agreed, the bank can collect against this asset. A bank that has a security interest in an item of collateral gains certain legal rights of *priority* over those of your general creditors. *Banks like secured loans.*

- **Unsecured loans** are those in which the bank lends you money based on your signature – i.e., your *promise to pay* – with *no collateral* given to secure the loan. If you fail to pay the loan, then your *bank has no special legal rights* (e.g., foreclosure); it just gets lumped in with general collections. For obvious reasons, banks are not so keen on giving unsecured loans these days.

Loans can be further classified into *common specific types of loans*, based on the specific purpose for which you promise to use the funds:

- **Operating Loans**: These loans are intended to provide routine funds to make the operation work. Common examples are seed and chemical expenses, fuel, and equipment repairs that must be made during the year while you're still waiting for the crop to grow and be marketed.

- **Lines of Credit**: Different from an operating loan, a line of credit is more flexible when it comes to what you can permissibly use it for. For example, a line of credit could be used for unscheduled equipment purchases.

- **Chattel Loans**: No, not cattle- *chattel*, which is the legal term for *personal property* (i.e., goods and things that are not real property). To illustrate, these loans maybe be specific to a piece of equipment or horses.

- **Real Estate Loans**: These loans are designed to fund the *acquisitions of real property* (land and the houses or other buildings on it), and a loan like this is oftentimes secured to the real estate by a mortgage. Mortgage loans are time-consuming to prepare and can't be issued on short notice. They usually require (1) a title opinion rendered on an abstract that has been updated within thirty days and (2) an executed promissory note, and (3) a mortgage filed in the appropriate property records to bind the land to the promissory note's promise to pay. Additionally, the lender may require personal lien searches to ensure that no other judgments attach to the property and get "in line" for collection ahead of the bank making the loan.

Secured Loans

Banks want security and they do a number of things to protect their ability to recoup the money they loan out. If something changes with your circumstances after the loan, making you unable to repay as agreed, a bank wants to know that it will have a sure-fire way to collect its money. This is why your bank will likely want *collateral* for your loan, asking you to pledge or impair items you already own, so that the bank will be protected if you decide to take off to Vegas and lose your $20,000 in loan proceeds instead of buying a pot load of cattle.

The process used to make sure collateral is pledged to provide incentive to pay on a loan is called *securing the collateral*. The bank is said to have a *security interest* in the named collateral, and the security interest is said to *attach to the collateral*. At the time of *attachment*, the bank gains the *power to enforce its security interest against you* by taking your collateral if you don't pay.

Attachment happens when *value* is given, and a person with *authority to pledge* the asset signs a *written agreement* (like the loan agreement) that grants the security interest in described property. Generally, the borrower pledges collateral voluntarily; therefore, the process of securing the collateral takes place via a contract.

When you purchase *real estate* with a loan or use real estate you already own as collateral for a loan, the *promissory note* and *mortgage* are the contract documents that together bind the security (the real estate) to the promise to pay (the promissory note). When you pledge *personal property* (i.e., anything that's not real estate) as security for a loan, the promise to pay the loan and the bank's security interest in the collateral are usually set out in a single contract document called a *loan agreement*. In either event, pledging your property as security for a loan means that if you, the loan taker, cannot make the payments, then the bank can take the property and sell it to get its money back.

> Trucks and trailers with titles are a different animal, legally speaking. Due to special rules, the general rule is that if a lien is not noted on the title then the lien does not attach.

Lenders Want Priority

Banks also want to acquire and maintain the highest possible collection *priority* – i.e., the bank's place in line among all of your creditors when it comes to collecting against an item of collateral. A bank may need priority in order to *collect ahead of another secured creditor* where the item has been used as collateral to secure more than one of your debts. An example of this would be a piece of real property, with a "first" mortgage to your bank, and a "second" mortgage owed to a financing company. A bank also needs priority to collect ahead of your *general creditors* (like medical providers or credit card companies) whose claims aren't secured by any specific asset of yours. Put simply, the banks want to come first.

As a general rule, a bank gains collection priority by *perfecting a security interest*, which involves taking certain legal steps. These steps require formal *filings*, designed to give *notice* to the rest of the world that the collateral in question is already subject to the bank's prior lien.

> While the rules on perfection are usually more important to banks than they would be to a debtor, if it happens that you are lending money to someone and taking a security interest in some of his or her property as collateral, then you are in the position of a lender, and you will want to ensure that you take the right steps to perfect your security interest and fix your own place in line.

To perfect a New York *real estate mortgage*, a bank must *record* the mortgage in the county property records office. New York state law then follows the general rule used in most states, that the *first bank to record a mortgage gets priority over a bank recording later* (i.e., "first in time, first in right"). The "race to record" gives the first recorder priority, regardless of the date when the mortgage was signed.

If you've pledged *personal property* (i.e., every good or thing that is not real estate) as collateral for your loan, a bank perfects and gives notice of its security interest in those items by filing a *financing statement* —-a/k/a the *"UCC-1"* in reference to the *Uniform Commercial Code* ("UCC") of New York (available through the NYS Department of State). The financing statement or UCC-1 is a separate document from the loan agreement. It will be *signed by the debtor;* it will show that the debtor has agreed that the bank will have a *security interest* in *property listed* as collateral on the UCC-1. As with the mortgage, UCC-1 filing gives priority to the lender who files first over a lender who files later on the same collateral.

Most often, loan agreements and financing statements with broad, generalized descriptions of collateral that put major assets or groups of assets on the line for minor loans should be considered very carefully before you agree. From your perspective, the more specifically your collateral is described, the better.

When a bank files a UCC-1, it puts the entire *rest of the world on notice*, in theory, about *what assets are already spoken for*, and by whom, in the event of non-payment. Sometimes the UCC-1 includes a *very specific description* of collateral. For example, a UCC-1 might note a security interest in "One (1) Case IH 7120, Serial Number XXXXXXX"); other financing statements might include *broad, generalized descriptions* of collateral (such as "all inventory, equipment, and receivables").

A very *specific description of the collateral* covered by a financing statement offers at least a couple of advantages:

- It leaves your other property free, allowing you the *financial flexibility* to obtain additional credit, collateralizing different specific assets down the line. For example, if you just need money for a tractor purchase, you shouldn't have to cover it by pledging the entire year's crop or "all your farm equipment now owned or acquired after," tying up a major asset or class of assets, over a minor debt.

- You avoid the *risk of losing a major asset* if you are unable to pay a minor debt. To illustrate, if your bank takes an item of collateral and sells it, the bank can only keep what it is owed and must pay you any excess. By the time the bank's share is inflated by various **penalties**, high **default interest rates**, a mixed variety of **bank fees**, the **costs** of sale, and other **expenses**, the small amount you wind up with after the sale is rarely enough to replace the asset you lost.

A bank oftentimes has ample security if it forecloses on the security interest in a specific item of collateral; however, be mindful that the bank may try to pull in as much property as possible. When doing so, some lenders may include language in its loan agreements that try to corral as much as possible.

As a caveat, *bad credit lenders* may even ask for a security interest in "all your assets," leaving the possibility that your personal possessions could be taken to pay a debt for your business. If you decide to knowingly use your personal assets as collateral for a business loan, weigh the risks that you are taking against the possible gains. Please don't let yourself be "tricked" into this situation by failing to *read the small print*. Have an attorney review the loan documents before signing them.

Releases

When a loan is fully repaid, the bank should file a *release* – a document stating that the bank no longer has an interest in the property described in a particular mortgage or UCC-1 filing. Mortgages bind your real estate, or until a release is filed in the property records. Financing statements are only good for a period of five (5) years; then, the financing statement has to be renewed.

> You may find that instead of filing a release, some lenders will keep a UCC-1 financing statement active by renewing it, even if you have little risk or activity on your account. Of course, banks do this to maintain priority – the bank's place in line, when it comes to collecting against an asset.

Place in line is everything to a bank, and a bank may not want to let others cut in line, even when that could benefit you. That said, it behooves you to have the release filed. Having your free assets released in the official records again offers you flexibility to use those assets for other needed financial benefit. If you're entitled to a release, make sure the bank files it. Subsequently, make sure you get a copy of the release for your records.

Defaulting on Payment

In the event that you cannot pay back the loan on time (usually referred to as a *"default"*), the bank can *foreclose* on the collateral you provided to get the loan. The bank will *declare default*, provide *notices*, and take *other actions* required by law or contract to get the property and sell it.

One important right that you may have, by law or contract, is the *right to redeem* your collateral by paying back the loan (which may mean getting a different lender, accelerating your marketing plan, or other steps). This usually has to be done within a *set period of time*, which varies with different kinds of loans.

Loss of Collateral

Destruction

If the collateral is destroyed by an *"Act of God,"* such as flood, accidental fire, drought, pestilence, hurricane or other event that is not your fault, a bank with a security interest *steps into your shoes*. That means that the bank is generally going to be entitled to recover whatever you would be entitled to get in that situation. For example, if an item of equipment was insured, the bank will be entitled to its share of the *insurance proceeds*.

Government disaster payments are considered replacements for a crop that is pledged as security, and they are also captured by security agreements, if:

- The crop has been planted;
- The crop is destroyed; and
- The payment is to be paid to the farmer.

Unauthorized Sale of Collateral

It is important to understand that the bank's perfected security interest in an item of collateral follows that collateral, even if it changes hands. If a bank has perfected a security interest by making the required notice filings in the right places then those filings act as *notice to all the world* that the bank has a security interest in the collateral (even if you never checked and don't actually know about it), and the bank can still seize the collateral even from buyers who are several sales down the line from the loan debtor. Consider the following example:

> Farmer A pledges a **planter as security** for a loan from Bank Z, which perfects its security interest with the proper filings. Farmer A later runs short on cash, and decides to **sell the planter** to Farmer B, who doesn't even know about Bank Z's security interest. Later, once again, Farmer A gets low on money and stops making the loan payments. Bank Z **can seize** the planter from Farmer B even though Farmer B is completely innocent and buys the planter in good faith.

To protect yourself from being Farmer B in the above hypothetical, don't buy anything before you *check for UCC lien filings*. If you do find lien filings, don't pay out the purchase price before you *get proper releases* from the banks or other secured lenders.

Please also note that *trade-ins* are treated the *same as sales* in this situation:

> For example, assume that instead of selling the planter from the above example, Farmer A trades it in to a dealer, and Farmer B purchases it from the dealer. The result will be the same as in the example above – the bank has collection priority and can seize the planter, even from an innocent Farmer B.

What action can Farmer B, the innocent buyer, take to get his money back? Farmer B may have some pretty limited options. He could *sue Farmer A* in both situations and get a court judgment saying that Farmer A owes him the purchase price paid for the planter (plus certain expense for the lawsuit). With such a judgment, if Farmer A has any other property that is collectable (like bank accounts, wages from a job, un-mortgaged real estate, or personal property that isn't exempt from collection under state law), Farmer B could take legal action to *collect against Farmer A's other property*.

Oftentimes, though, Farmer B's judgment against a seller *may not be collectable*. Farmer A may have prior liens against his other property or may just not have enough exempt property to cover what he now owes Farmer B. The bank has seized the planter, so Farmer B can't get it back. Farmer A is just as likely to file for bankruptcy, and if so, then Farmer B will have to make new claims there, and even the bankruptcy court is going to give the planter to the bank that is holding a security interest in it. Farmer B will be lucky to get a portion of what is owed to him, if anything. In the end, Farmer B's judgment may be worth nothing more than the paper it's printed on.

The bank's perfected security interest protects only the bank's interest — not the owner's interest — in the collateral. For example, if you change the facts of the above example a bit, you could get an unexpected result. What if, instead of buying a piece of equipment from your neighbor, you decided to take advantage of a great deal and buy a repaired item from a dealer who normally repairs and sells them? If the dealer sold that item to you, without the owner's permission, can the real owner get it back from you?

However, as you might suspect, the *buyer would still lose the skidloader to a bank with a perfected security interest* in it (except in the rare situation in which the buyer can show that the bank has a habit of letting its debtors sell equipment without requiring a release).

The law surrounding security interests is complex, whether you're creating one, trying to enforce one, or trying to avoid enforcement of one. If you have questions about a secured transaction or the effect that a security interest may have on your plans to buy, sell, or obtain a loan related to an item of property, you should seek professional legal advice.

Disputed Payments

If a *dispute* arises between a debtor and a creditor over the amount still owed on a loan, the debtor may attempt to favorably settle the debt by sending the bank a check with a partial payment and language in the memo stating *"accord and satisfaction"* or *"payment in full."* Many people falsely believe that if the creditor cashes the check, it accepts whatever was written on the check.

It takes more than mere scribbles on a check to settle a debt for less than what is owed. These days, no one with authority to bind a lender even sees your check. It's run through an automatic sorter and scanned. The bank's act in processing a check with "accord and satisfaction" written on it will not relieve your debt. It never hurts to make notation of your purpose on a check, but usually a *bank's action in cashing your check will only settle a debt if you can prove:*

- A *formal dispute* over the amount owed is in the offing (like a pending lawsuit, referral to a collection agency, or demand letters from the bank); and

- The *creditor* has independent *knowledge* (ideally, provable in writing) that the *tendered amount is an offer of settlement* to resolve the disputed amount.

Bounced Checks

It's a *crime* to write a check if you know that you have insufficient funds to cover the check. A *bad check* is considered a *theft*. If you get *notice* that a check has bounced, failure to *make a check "good"* by having sufficient funds *within (ten) 10 days of the check bouncing* can result in *criminal charges* against you. If you are the party *taking a check*, do not take *post-dated* checks! Legally, taking a post-dated check or agreeing to hold a check until a date in the future deprives you of your legal right to get the check writer convicted of theft if the check winds up bouncing.

Additional Resources

National Agriculture Law Center's Reading Room for "Finance and Credit" <u>available</u> <u>http://nationalaglawcenter.org/readingrooms/financeandcredit/</u>.

Monika Roth <u>et al.</u>, "Guide to Farming in New York" at 21 <u>available</u> <u>at</u> <u>http://nebeginningfarmers.org/publications/farming-guide/</u> (last visited December 24, 2012) (Chapter #4 – Financing a Farm Operation).

CHAPTER 20

FARM BANKRUPTCY

Bankruptcy is a federal creation designed to allow people and businesses who meet certain criteria to discharge (or remove) their obligation to pay debts they have incurred. You've probably heard about bankruptcies being filed under one or another of the various *Bankruptcy Code* "chapters," and each chapter has a unique set of requirements, standards, rules and obligations that it imposes on debtors and on creditors who want to file claims. Generally speaking, farm businesses can file under Chapter 7 and 11 (*"Liquidation"*), Chapter 12 (*"Farm Reorganization"*), or Chapter 13 (*"Reorganization"*) of the Bankruptcy Code. Each are briefly discussed in this Chapter.

Bankruptcy Definitions

Before you learn more about the different chapters of the Title 11 of the *United States Code* (commonly referred to as the *"Bankruptcy Code"*), here are a few general definitions you'll need to understand first:

- A *debtor* is a person who owes money to some person or entity.

- A *creditor* is a person or entity to which money is owed by a debtor.

- A *secured creditor* is a creditor that has loaned money to a debtor in exchange for the debtor's agreement that certain property (e.g., house, car, tractor, livestock) belonging to the debtor will stand as collateral to ensure repayment of the loan. To qualify as a secured creditor, a creditor must meet certain formalities. You are only a secured creditor if you have filed a correct *UCC-1 statement* with the New York State Department of State ("NYSDOS"). See N.Y. U.C.C. Law §§ 9-301 - 9-316 (2012)

> For example, if you sell a tractor over time to your neighbor and you file proper forms with NYSDOS, then you are a **secured creditor**. If you just lend money to someone without filing the paperwork, you are an **unsecured creditor**.

- A *bankruptcy trustee* is someone appointed by the bankruptcy court to supervise the action and find assets to sell, so that proceeds can be used to pay creditors.

- The *bankruptcy estate* is all of the debtor's assets and possessions at the time of filing.

Types of Bankruptcy

Chapter 7 Bankruptcy - Liquidation

A *Chapter 7* bankruptcy is a *liquidation* bankruptcy. The ultimate intended result in a Chapter 7 bankruptcy is to do the following: (1) gather all of the debtor's *assets* into a *bankruptcy estate*, (2) determine which assets are *exempt* from liquidation, (3) sell any assets that are *non-exempt*, and (4) use the funds to make payments against the debts owed to *creditors*.

The *debtor* files a *statement of assets and debts* with the court. Notice is given to *creditors*. Then the creditors file *claims* with the court indicating how much is owed to them. The debtor asks the court to identify those debts *non-payable* by the filing debtor.

The debtor gets to retain a list of *"exempt" property* for the debtor's *"fresh start."* On December 22, 2010, Governor Paterson signed a law that made significant changes to the bankruptcy exemptions in New York. See Chapter 568 of the Laws of New York

201). The debtor may elect to take *either the New York or the federal exemptions*; however, the debtor must choose one or the other. The exemptions *cannot be mixed and matched*. This is a new option that was created with the addition of N.Y. Debt. & Cred. Law § 285.

Some of the *New York* exemptions are as follows:

Real Property Exemptions

1. **The "Homestead Exemption"**: Real property including house, co-op, condo, or mobile home used as **principal residence**. See *NY Civil Practice Law and Rules* ("CPLR") § 5206(a). The exemption limits are based on the county in which the property is situated:

   a. $150,000 in Kings, Queens, New York, Bronx, Richmond, Nassau, Suffolk, Rockland, Westchester and, Putnam counties;

   b. $125,000 in Dutchess, Albany, Columbia, Orange, Saratoga, and Ulster counties; and

   c. $75,000 in all other remaining counties in New York.

2. **Burial ground** not exceeding one-quarter (¼) acre and not containing any building or structure other than vaults, monuments, or other places for burial. See CPLR § 5206(f).

$10,000 Personal Property Exemption Limit

1. The *aggregate value* a debtor may exempt for personal property as described below and qualifying annuity contracts shall not exceed $10,000 aggregate limit. See NY Debt. & Cred. Law § 283(1) and CPLR § 5205(a).

   a. *Stoves and home heating equipment* for use in home and fuel for 120 days;

   b. *Religious texts* (e.g., Bibles), family pictures and portraits, and school books;

c. Other *books* not to exceed $500 in value;

d. Seat or pew used for *religious worship*;

e. Domestic animals and necessary food for 120 days, provided total value of animals and food does not exceed $1,000;

f. *Food for debtor and family* for 120 days;

g. *Clothing, household furniture*, crockery, tableware, cooking utensils, and prescribed health aids;

h. One of each of the following: *refrigerator*, radio receiver, *TV set, computer* and associated equipment, and cellphone;

i. A *wedding ring*;

j. A *watch, jewelry, and art* not exceeding $1,000 in value;

k. *Tools of the trade* not to exceed $3,000 and necessary food for the team for 120 days;

l. *One motor vehicle* not to exceed $4,000 in value up to $10,000 in value if equipped for use by disabled debtor; and

m. *If no homestead exemption is claimed*, then $1,000 in personal property, bank accounts, or cash.

2. **If no Homestead and Burial Grounds exemption is taken,** and the *aggregate limit of $10,000 is not reached*, the debtor may exempt cash, savings bonds, and income tax refunds up to the remaining amount or $5,000, whichever is less. See NY Debt. & Cred. Law § 283(2).

Other Personal Property Exemptions

There are also other personal property exemptions for the

following:

1. $600 in shares held in a savings and loan association (NY Banking Law § 407);

2. A *money judgment* and its proceeds resulting from the taking or injuring of exempt personal property for up to 1 year after collection of the proceeds (CPLR Law § 5205(b));

3. Property held in a *spendthrift trust* for the debtor if the trust was created by or has proceeded from a person other than the debtor (CPLR § 5205(c));

4. *IRA*, 401(k), Keogh (HR-10), or other qualified retirement plans (CPLR § 5205(c))

5. *Social Security* (CPLR § 5205(c));

6. *Unemployment compensation* (CPLR § 5205(c) and Labor Law § 595(2));

7. *Local public assistance benefits* (CPLR § 5205(c) and Soc. Serv. Law § 137 & 137-a);

8. *Veterans' benefits* (CPLR § 5205(c));

9. *Workers' compensation* (CPLR § 5205(c) and Work. Comp. Law §§ 33, 218, and 313);

10. *Spousal maintenance and child support* (CPLR § 5205(c));

11. Qualifying payments under a *stock bonus, pension*, profit sharing, or similar plan or contract on account of illness, disability, death, age, or length of service (CPLR § 5205(c));

12. 90% of the income or other payments from a *trust* (CPLR § 5205(d) and 5231);

13. 90% of the debtor's earnings from *services rendered* 60 days before, and at any time after, an income execution is delivered

to the sheriff or a motion is made to secure the application of the judgment debtor's earnings (CPLR § 5205(d) and 5231);

14. Payments made pursuant to award in *matrimonial action* for support (CPLR § 5205(d) and 5231);

15. 100% of pay to a non-commissioned officer, musician, or private in the US or NY state armed forces (CPLR § 5205(e));

16. Land warrant, pension, or other award granted for service in the *armed forces* (N.Y. C.P.L.R. Law § 5205(e));

17. 90% of any money or debt due from *the sale of milk* produced on the debtor's farm (CPLR § 5205(f));

18. *Security deposits* being held for real property rental and utilities associated with the debtor's or debtor's family's residence (CPLR § 5205(g));

19. Necessary *medical & dental items*, guide dog, service dog, hearing dog, or any other similarly trained animal; and

20. Surrender value of *life insurance policy* (CPLR § 5205(i)).

There are also some limited exemptions for a New York State *college choice tuition* savings program trust fund/account, payments for a wrongful death claim, personal injuries, *life insurance proceeds*, disability insurance proceeds, state employee retirement funds, and teacher retirement benefits. CPLR § 5205(j); Debt. & Cred. Law § 282(3); N.Y. Ins. Law § 3212; NY Ret. & Soc. Sec. Law Art. 2 Tit. 12 § 110(2); N.Y. Educ. Law § 524.

Any assets over the **exemption amount** (e.g., campers, ATVs, snowmobiles, livestock, farm equipment) may be taken by the trustee and sold. The proceeds from the sale are then split between the trustee (who takes **25%**) and *all of the creditors* of the debtor.

In a Chapter 7 proceeding, the debtor is then *discharged* from any further obligation to pay most general debts. Certain debts, including back taxes owed and child support obligations owed, are not dischargeable in bankruptcy.

Chapter 13 Bankruptcy – The "Wage Earner's" Plan

Chapter 13 bankruptcy is a *reorganization* of debt and a court-supervised attempt (the plan) to pay debts of the debtor over time. Chapter 13 is also known as the *"wage earner's plan."* The ultimate goal is to *stop collection activity* and give a *working debtor* who has *regular income* an opportunity to *repay debts at an affordable rate.*

In a Chapter 13 bankruptcy case, a debtor develops a detailed repayment plan allowing him to pay creditors' claims, using projected future earnings over *three-to-five years*. During this time, creditors may not undertake collection efforts. Some debts can be reorganized, sometimes against the creditors' wishes, and creditors are placed in different classes, which are paid differently under the plan.

When a Chapter 13 is filed, the *repayment plan* is filed with it. The bankruptcy court must approve your plan, but *payments must start within thirty (30) days of filing*, even if the plan is not yet approved.

There are two main things you should know about Chapter 13 bankruptcy before you decide to file one:

- **Filing a Chapter 13 bankruptcy costs a lot more than a Chapter 7**. Due to its complexity and the time it takes to complete a three-to-five year case, Chapter 13 naturally requires higher legal fees and other expenses.

- **Chapter 13 plans often fail**. It is very common for Chapter 13 plans to fail, because financial ability to make the payments dips when the debtors lose their income or experience other unexpected pitfalls during the three-to-five-year plan period (e.g., divorce, medical issues, family emergencies).

Many people file Chapter 13 because they have too much equity in a home or some other asset with a secured debt. They do not want to liquidate in a Chapter 7, even when they are being smothered by other unsecured debts, like medical bills and credit cards, that could be fully discharged in a Chapter 7. It is true that you can keep more assets in a Chapter 13 if you are successful in fulfilling your plan obligations.

Debtors who are unsuccessful in Chapter 13 cases wind up *converting* their bankruptcies to Chapter 7 after paying out a great deal of money on plan payments and fees. Oftentimes, it is better to be pragmatic from the start, let go of the homestead, and save all that money to use for moving on.

Chapter 12 Bankruptcy – Farm Reorganization

A *Chapter 12 bankruptcy* is a form of Chapter 13 bankruptcy, with *special farm provisions* intended to help farmers reorganize and carry out a *repayment plan* to make installment payments to creditors over *three-to-five years*. A three year payment plan is preferred. Chapter 12 is more streamlined, less complicated, and less expensive than Chapter 11, which is designed for *large corporate reorganizations*. However, Chapter 13 might not be the best fit because it is designed for those who have smaller debts than a farm could be facing.

Unlike Chapter 7, 11 and 13 proceedings, *you cannot be forced to file a Chapter 12 proceeding*. In Chapter 12, *creditors don't have the right to approve your plan* like they do in a Chapter 11. You *must have permission to get rid of assets* if you are in a Chapter 12. If you want to do that, you need to provide the creditor *"adequate protection"* to ensure that the creditor is not left out in the cold.

Farmers eligible for Chapter 12 must be either:

- An *individual* or *individual and spouse*; or
- A *corporation* or *partnership*.

Individuals must meet each of the following *four* Chapter 12 requirements:

1. The individual or husband and wife must be *engaged in a farming operation*;

2. The *total debts* (secured and unsecured) of the operation must be *not over $3,792,650*;

3. At least *half of the total debts* that are fixed in amount (not including debt on the house) must be *related to farming*; and

4. More than *half of the gross income* of the individual or the husband and wife for the preceding tax year or for each of the second and third prior tax years must have been earned *from farming*.

On the other hand, a *corporation or partnership* must meet the following *Chapter 12 eligibility requirements* (as of the date of the *filing* of the petition):

1. *Over one-half of the outstanding stock or equity* in the corporation or partnership must be *owned by one family* or by one family and its relatives;

2. The *family* or the family and its relatives *must conduct the farming*;

3. *Over 80 percent* of the value of the corporate or partnership *assets* must be related to the *farming or fishing operation*;

4. The *total indebtedness* of the corporation or partnership must be *not over $3,792,650*;

5. At least *half* of the corporation's or partnership's *total debts* which are fixed in amount (excluding debt on one home occupied by a shareholder) must be *related to farming*; and

6. If the corporation issues stock, the *stock cannot be publicly-traded*.

Chapter 12 contains a *special automatic stay provision* that protects *co-debtors*. Unless the bankruptcy court orders it, a creditor may not collect a *"consumer debt"* from *any individual who also owes a debt jointly with the debtor*. Consumer debts are those incurred by an individual primarily for a personal, family, or household purpose.

Your Farm as a Creditor

Your operation may find itself in the position of a *creditor*, rather than a *debtor*, when someone who owes you money files bankruptcy. In order to seek repayment in this situation, there are certain things you need to do. Here are answers to a few common questions you might have:

Q. How do I protect my custom farm operation from people filing bankruptcy against it?

A. The simple solution is to get payment at the time you perform the service. If you round bale, collect the payment per bale before the bales leave the field. Not only will you not have a dispute about how many bales are made, but you will not serve as a short-term lender to the person who hired you.

Q. How do I protect my operation once I receive a Notice of Bankruptcy from someone who owes me money?

A. *Stop contacting them at once.* Don't send another statement and don't call them about their debts. The bankruptcy court issues an *"automatic stay,"* – i.e., a court order that halts any attempts to collect a debt, once the debtor files.

However, if you have *secured debt*, you *can* contact the debtor to see if they want to *"reaffirm"* their debt. This means that the debtor indicates that, despite the bankruptcy filing, he or she wants to keep the property. In exchange, the debtor has to continue to pay the debt. If the debtor doesn't want to pay the debt, the debtor can *abandon* the property. If your secured debtor abandons the property, securing the debt owed to you, you can go *retrieve* the property, but you cannot seek any additional funds from the debtor.

Q. What if they come in to pay anyway?

A. If someone files a bankruptcy against a debt they owe you, and then returns to your place of business and attempts to pay you for it anyway, things change. This is called a *reaffirmation* of the debt, and once they pay on it or state they will pay on it despite the bankruptcy, the debt is no longer non-payable and you may take funds from the debtor.

Q. How Do I Deal with Bad Checks?

A. If you are presented a check that is returned for insufficient funds, you have turned into an unplanned creditor. The first step is to call the check issuer and then the bank that the check is issued from. The bank will frequently indicate whether or not the check would be honored, if it were presented again.

If not, you should have the check presented again. After its *second dishonor*, you need to send a written *notice* via certified mail or personal service to the check writer that the check bounced and must be honored within *thirty (30) days*. If the monies are not received, then you should contact your local law enforcement for potential criminal charges.

When you contact someone who owes you money, *never* make *threats*, contact their *relatives*, harass them at *work* or continue to contact them *at all after* he or she indicates that he or she is represented by an *attorney* (contact the attorney instead).

Additional Resources

Robert Moore, "Chapter 12 Bankruptcy: Hope for Financially Stressed Family Farms" available at http://dairy.osu.edu/bdnews/Vol.%2011%20Issue%202%20pdf%20files/Moore-2009_BDN_Chapter_12_Bankruptcy_(2).pdf (May 19, 2013).

Ken D. Duft, "Chapter 12 Bankruptcy in Retrospect; Its Impact on Agribusiness Firms" available at http://www.agribusiness-mgmt.wsu.edu/ExtensionNewsletters/cash-asset/Chap12.pdf (last visited May 19, 2013).

Theodore Feithshans, J.D., "Overcoming Farm Financial Distress: Strategies and Frequently Asked Questions" available at http://www.ag-econ.ncsu.edu/VIRTUAL_LIBRARY/ECONOMIST/econmajn99.pdf (last visited May 19, 2013).

United States Courts, "Bankruptcy Basics," available at http://www.uscourts.gov/FederalCourts/Bankruptcy/BankruptcyBasics.aspx (last visited July 11, 2013).

CHAPTER 21

DIRECT FARM MARKETING

The term *"direct marketing"* refers to a method of marketing when a farmer sells his/her farm-grown food product directly to the consumer instead of a wholesaler or retailer. In other words, the consumer is buying a food product directly from the agricultural producer.

The most typical types of direct marketing methods include roadside stands, farmers' markets, on farm outlets/stands, community gardens, school gardens, and *Community Supported Agriculture* ("CSA's"). Other types of direct marketing sales might include a *farm-to-institution* transactions, such as *farm-to-school, farm-to-restaurant* or *farm-to-hospitals*.

Direct farm marketing has several advantages: (1) it allows farmers to sell the food they raise directly to consumers *eliminating the middle man* (thus, giving the farmer a greater portion of the revenue), (2) it offers consumers a way to buy *fresh local farm* products directly from the producer, (3) it keeps dollars spent on farm products in the *local community*, (4) it helps facilitate *consumer education* in local agriculture industries, and (5) it helps a consumer build a *relationship* directly with the agricultural producer. On the flip side, direct marketing of farm products increases the *potential liability* for the farm and puts the burden on the farmer or food entrepreneur to market his or her product to the consumer.

A Word on Contracts

Traditionally, there are typically no written contracts made in face-to-face marketing sales via direct farm marketing methods. There is greater need for *written contracts* with higher volume sales or non-direct methods such as farm-to-school, farm-to-hospital, farm-to-restaurant or farm-to-grocery store. Additionally, farms that participate in *Community Supported Agriculture* ("CSA") should have a written agreement with their subscribers.

Importantly, Article 2 of the *Uniform Commercial Code* ("UCC") applies to the *Sale of Goods*, which includes food and agriculture products. Section 2-201 of the UCC requires that contracts for the sale of goods over $500 must be in writing *in order to be enforceable*. However, it is always advisable to consider using a written contract even when the sale of goods is less than $500. Some farmers fear that asking for a written agreement conveys mistrust of his/her customer; instead, agriculture producers should view it as a *sound business practice*. Oral agreements lead to confusion and misunderstanding between parties.

Since farming by nature is an *unpredictable business*, it behooves the farmer to have a contract that allows for flexibility in food deliveries due to *weather, pests* and other influences outside his/her control. Clearly written contracts also mitigate the likelihood of payment disputes, especially if the purchaser is a government institution. To encourage timely payment, farmers should memorialize a penalty for *late payments*.

What Can and Cannot Be Sold

In New York, farms are permitted to sell the following products direct to the consumer via farmers' markets, roadside stands, and on-farm retail stores so long as they are *not considered a "retail food store"* under Article 17 of the NY Agric. & Mks Law:

- Unprocessed fruits and vegetables,
- Eggs (if clean and refrigerated at 45° F),
- Grains,
- Legumes,
- Honey, and
- Maple Syrup.

See New York State Department of Agriculture, "Sanitary Regulations for Direct Marketing," available at http://www.agriculture.ny.gov/FS/industry/sanitary.html (last visited August 18, 2013).

NYSDAM permits direct marketing farm businesses to sell some processed foods, including certain highly perishable products like *meat and dairy products* (including hard and soft cheeses), if the products are:

- Processed at an **approved food processing facility**;

- **Prepackaged and properly labeled**; and

- **Kept at required cold temperatures** to prevent spoilage or contamination.

See id.

On the other hand, certain food products *cannot be sold at roadside stands*, on-farm outlets and farmers' markets:

- **Home-canned or jarred fruits and vegetables, pickled products, sauces, relishes and other low-acid foods** (unless manufactured "under an approved processing method at an inspected facility);

- **Cream, custard, pumpkin, meat or other single-crust pies or cream or cheese-filled baked goods** (unless prepared in an approved, inspected baking facility, packaged and properly refrigerated); and

- **Any other prepared foods made with highly perishable ingredients for immediate consumption or reheating** (unless manufactured and vended under proper food processing and vending licenses).

Id.

Sanitation Requirements

Pursuant to Article 17 of the NY Agric. & Mkts Law, NYSDAM regulates food sanitary conditions of retail food establishments including direct marketing businesses like roadside farm markets, on-farm outlets and farmers markets. That said, outlets considered *"retail food stores"* under Article 17 *must comply with stricter sanitary guidelines.*

Even though farmers selling directly to consumers are subject to a food safety inspection from NYSDAM, if the producer is only selling raw fruits/veggies, eggs, grains, legumes, honey and/or maple syrup, then NYSDAM typically will only inspect these products if it receives a consumer complaint. Farmers selling more highly perishable products are inspected more often by NYSDAM.

Roadside stands, on-farm outlets and farmers' markets may not use packaging, cutting, slicing or portioning of fruits and vegetables, meat, dairy products or ready-to-eat food *unless the proper sanitary conditions are met for "retail food stores"* under Circular 962 "Rules and Regulations Relating to Retail Food Stores" available at http://www.agriculture.ny.gov/FS/pdfs/circs/962.pdf. See New York State Department of Agriculture, "Sanitary Regulations for Direct Marketing," available at http://www.agriculture.ny.gov/FS/industry/sanitary.html (last visited August 18, 2013).

Community Supported Agriculture ("CSA")

Farms are encouraged to have a simple *CSA Agreement* signed by the subscribers. Not only does it help secure *payment terms*, but the CSA Agreement should *mitigate potential liability* in the case of a food safety issue arising from the mishandling or misuse of the food product.

The CSA Agreement should specify how long the *"growing season"* will last (e.g., 22 weeks), the type of share (e.g., egg share, vegetable share, fruit share, meat share), products that will be available throughout the growing season (e.g., peaches, apples, cherries, pumpkins, kale, kohlrabi, radishes, mustard greens, swiss chard, basil), and whether the subscribers will receive a guaranteed minimum amount of food for that share (e.g., pounds of meat per week, dozen eggs per week). The following are a few additional issues that should be discussed in the CSA Agreement:

- **Price/Payment Methods**. Not only does a farm need to decide on the price per share, but it needs to determine whether: (1) it will have a sliding scale or reduced price based on limited family income, (2) it will accept a payment plan on a monthly or weekly basis, (3) it will accept payment via credit card, PayPal, and/or Google Checkout, (4) it will offer "half shares", (5) it will charge a fee to deliver to the home directly, (6) it will charge a penalty for *late payments*, and/or (7) it will accept *Electronic Benefit Transfer* ("EBT") (must obtain certification to do so). To offset reduced prices for subscribes of limited means, some CSA's request an additional donation for subscribers that can afford to do so. An explanation of this voluntary request may be memorialized in the CSA Agreement.

- **How a Share is Defined?** What quantity of food product should the subscriber reasonable expect? Is it measured by a box, basket, bag, etc. or by a percentage of the harvest?

- **Subscriber's Risk with Harvest.** The CSA Agreement should note that the subscriber bears the risk of a *partial or total crop failure* due to drought, flood, insects or other conditions that may reasonably impact production. Although the CSA Agreement should state that the farmer will use reasonable efforts to generate a successful harvest, the actual quantity will vary according to the myriad factors that affect a harvest. The CSA agreement should state that the subscriber is sharing these risks.

- **Subscriber's Benefit from Successful Harvest.** On the flip side, the agreement should state that the subscriber will already *reap the benefits* of a better than expected harvest season. From a practical standpoint, some subscribers may not want additional food in this situation. To prevent waste, the CSA Agreement may address procedures for handling a surplus, including an option to donate the food to a local food bank or share with the farm workers and their families. For example, with the Central Park West CSA on the Upper West Side in Manhattan donates the surplus to DOROT, a nearby elderly organization.

- **Delivery/Drop-Off Location.** There may be zoning and/or permit issues depending on where a farm wishes to drop off its food products. Storage and refrigeration of any egg, meat or processed food products may also be a concern at these drop-off locations. If a farm wishes to deliver the product directly to the subscriber, the specifics should be memorialized in the CSA Agreement and procedures for canceling delivery for a week.

- **Forfeited Products**. To prevent a dispute, the CSA Agreement should note that the food products will be forfeited if they are not picked up during the allotted time without alternative arrangements being made. Some CSA Agreements note that forfeited products may be sold or donated (e.g. homeless shelters, food pantries, after-school programs, elder care facilities). In some CSA, subscribers may contact other participants to pick-up his/her products that week. In this case, the CSA Agreement to disclose that names and email addresses may be shared with the other subscribers.

- **Bags/Boxes**. The CSA Agreement should note whether the subscriber must return the box or bag each week for pick-up or bring their own bag. Alternatively, the CSA Agreement could note that bags will be provided.

- **Communication**. There should be a method of communicating with the subscribers in case of an emergency or inclement weather. This mode of communication should be noted in the CSA Agreement (e.g., email). Furthermore, many CSA's have newsletters for its subscribers noting farm news/events, recipes, info about the week's produce selection, and posts from the farm blog to help subscribers feel more informed and connected to the farm and the CSA. Subscription to these newsletters can take place directly in the CSA Agreement and/or the farm's website. Any email newsletter should allow subscribers an option to "opt-out" of the email.

- **Fresh/Frozen Meat**. If applicable, the CSA Agreement should note whether the meat product will be fresh or frozen and what cuts of meat will be available. Any special processing guidelines, such as Kocher or Halal, should be noted.

- **Volunteer Requirements**. Some CSA's require subscribers to volunteer a certain number of hours during the harvest season on the farm ("work shares" or "half work shares") or at the CSA pick-up (e.g., work the sign-in table for one week). Details relating to these requirements should be noted in the CSA Agreement keeping in mind "in kind" compensation and minimum wage requirements under the *Fair Labor Standards Act*, as discussed in Chapter 13 on employment law.

In hopes of building a sense of community, some CSA Agreements use the word "partner". When possible, farms should avoid using the words "partner" or "partnership" in its CSA Agreement and conversations with the subscribers. In fact, the CSA Agreement should clearly note that it is not a partnership. A partnership is a specific kind of legal entity in which the partners go into business together and split profits – each partner is jointly and severally liable for each another's actions. Therefore, it is important to be clear that a CSA is not a general partnership. Along these lines, the words "member" and "shareholder" should be avoided when possible to avoid implying that the consumer has some type of ownership in the farm. The word "subscriber" most accurately describes the relationship.

All of that being said, there has been virtually no litigation thus far with CSA's; however, due to their exponential growth, it is anticipated that legal disputes will arise in the future. It's always prudent to build a written record of a farm's compliance with the CSA Agreement. Records should be kept regarding production, delivery of products, the quality of the delivery, food safety controls (including storage, transportation and refrigeration), etc.

Farmers' Markets

Farmers' markets are a growing trend in New York. For the most current list of farmers' markets available in your community, please visit NYSDAM's online directory available at http://www.agriculture.ny.gov/AP/CommunityFarmersMarkets.asp. According to *Neil Hamilton* in his publication titled "Farmers' Markets Rules, Regulations and Opportunities" (June 2002), "farmers' market" is defined as follows:

(1) Farmers selling produce and food they raise or create,
(2) To individual customers,

(3) At a temporary location, often on public property (e.g., street or parking lot),
(4) On a periodic basis (typically once or twice a week),
(5) For a set period of time (typically 3 to 4 hours),
(6) During the local growing season (usually 5 or 6 months), and
(7) Operated by a government or non-profit organization.

This definition distinguishes farmers' markets from other types of direct market methods such as roadside stands, on-farm stands or CSA's.

Farmers' markets in New York vary greatly: some markets are held once a week with only a few vendors while other markets held multiple times per week with several vendors. Furthermore, there is also great deviation in New York with the type of market, the nature of the farmers' market management (i.e., the Market Manager), its history/purpose, and the organizer's experience.

Market Rules

It's very important for the farmer to clearly understand the rules for each farmers' market ("Market Rules") that he/she participates in. The *Market Rules* (or *"Statement of the Rules"*) vary greatly among farmers' markets. It is important to understand that these Market Rules provide for the contractual terms between the farmer/vendor and the farmers' market sponsoring organization. Farmers are encouraged to have an agriculture lawyer review the Market Rules to make sure there are not any concerns that should be addressed.

A farmer should pay special attention to the definitions section, which will explain key phrases and terms such as Vendor, Allowable Goods, and Categories of Products. The following is a list of common provisions/terms that a farmer may find in the Market Rules:

Provision or Term	General Description (Market Rules may specifically define differently)
Application Process, Fees, and/or Rent	These provisions provide for the *timing of the application*, process for vendor selection, and notification of approval. This clause likely identifies any *fees* associated with the application itself and/or fees associated with security of vendor space including payment method and timing.

	There may be a limitation as to the *number of stalls* that a particular vendor can reserve. Depending on the market, flat fees and/or commissions may be utilized (percentages may vary depending on type of vendor and/or product sold). The market may also require *rent on a weekly, monthly or seasonal basis.*
Approval of Vendors and Products	This provision will identify *who can sell products* at the farmers' markets (e.g., farmer, non-farmer, peddlers) and what type of products may be sold at the markets (e.g., produce, crafts, processed foods).
Carrying Crafts	"Carrying Crafts" are typically non-food items made by vendors (e.g., yarn, quilts); if allowed, said *crafts* usually have to be selected and approved by the Market Manager.
Carrying Rules	This clause may allow vendors to sell products raised *by other farmers.*
Categories of Products	Rules for items such as *raw produce, baked goods, nursery plans, eggs, cheeses, meat, and processed foods,* including but not limited to rules relating to inspections, sanitary conditions and handling are discussed in this provision.
Changes in Ownership and Vendors' Rights	This clause will address issues pertaining to the *transfer/change of business* and seniority for market spaces.
Enforcement Process	These provisions establish procedures for *rule enforcement* (usually from the Market Manager), including reporting violations/grievances, notice, penalties, suspension/removal, and appeals.
Farm Visit (or "Farm Inspection")	In some cases, the Market Manager will *visit the vendor's farm* to make a determination whether the food product was "farm-raised." This prerequisite is

	more typical in farmers' markets that have producer-only standards. The farmer typically must agree to comply with specific inspection procedures which are likely provided for under a document separate from the Market Rules. There may also be a small inspection fee that is required.
Food Safety, Sanitation and Sampling	These provisions will set forth specific rules from the farmers' market pertaining to *sanitation, handling and storing* difference types of food products.
Hold Harmless and Indemnific-ation Clause	Typically, the vendor agrees to *financially protect* the farmers' market and its organizers from any liability.
Length of Market	Usually, the Market Rules will specify the *start and end date* for the farmers' market (typically a 5-6 month span).
Location	The same Sponsor may be running several farmers' markets in *different locations* in a particular community; thus, it may choose to use the same Market Rules for all of its markets. In these cases, the Market Rules may enumerate specific rules *according to different locations*.
Market Manager	The Market Manager is the person designated to run the market on a day-to-day basis. This usually person *enforces* the Market Rules.
Market Operation/ Operational Procedures	This provision will memorialize detailed guidelines/procedures for *set-up, clean-up, selling times*, notification for non-attendance/*tardiness*, parking, vehicles, samples, sanitation, *signage*, hawking, *smoking*/alcohol/drugs, *pet*s (including service animals), display guidelines, shelter requirements from rain/sun, food safety, food handling and food labeling requirements. These

	operational provisions can be very detailed and technical.
Membership and Market Organization	In these cases, an *operational structure* is created for the farmers' market and a separate payment may be required for membership in the sponsoring organization in order to participate as a vendor.
Necessary Documents/ Permits	This section will enumerate the *various documents and licenses* from the NYS Department of Agriculture & Markets. This may include, but is not limited to, *proof of insurance*, tax permits, health certificates, NYSDAM licenses (e.g., Article 28D, Article 5A), farm plan, farm information sheet (describing the size, type and scope of the operation), load lists for products raised, USDA National Organic Program ("NOP") certification, business organizational documents (e.g., Articles of Organization or Incorporation, Certificate of Assumed Name), and federal tax identification number.
Peddlers	Vendors who *buy products at wholesale for reselling* at the market.
Producers-Only	A farmers' market that *only sells items raised by the farmers who sell them* (i.e., no peddlers or reselling of other farm produce).
Proof of Insurance	A form a vendor obtains from the *insurance carrier* (1) as proof of insurance, (2) as a summary of type of coverage obtained, and (3) proof that the farmers' market is a covered party under the insurance policy. Some farmers' markets will require that the vendor has a certain amount of coverage (e.g., $1 million). *Note: Even though a farmers' market may only require X amount of insurance, the farmer or food entrepreneur may have additional insurance needs. Please refer to Chapter 9 in this book on Liability and Insurance.*

Product List	List of food (and non-food) products that the *farmer plans to sell* at the farmers' market which is typically used by the market to help allocate ample space and limit vendors from unapproved products.
Prepared Food	In some farmers' markets, *ready-to-eat* food (e.g., take-away meals and snacks) may be sold.
Processed Food	*Certain processed foods* may be sold at some farmers' markets (e.g., jams, jellies, wine, salsa, canned goods, cider, vinegar, maple syrup, and baked goods) subject to the sanitary guidelines discussed earlier in this Chapter.
Sponsor or Organizer (and its Logo Use)	The Market Rules should note the person or entity legally responsible for creating and operating the farmers' market. This clause generally sets out the philosophy and purpose of the farmers' market. Furthermore, some Market Rules lay out procedures for using the sponsor or farmers' markets logo on advertising materials.
Vendor (and Criteria for Selecting Vendors)	A vendor is a *farmer or other person* designated by the management as having the right to participate in the market. Most Market Rules also state *criteria for selecting vendors* such as any priorities or preferences (e.g., geographic distance) (and the basis for any priority or preference). In some cases, "Categories of Vendors" are described for both seasonal and daily vendors.

See Neil Hamilton, "Farmers' Markets Rules, Regulations and Opportunities" (June 2002) available at http://www.nyfarmersmarket.com/pdf_files/fmruleregs.pdf (last visited August 18, 2013). See also NEIL HAMILTON, THE LEGAL GUIDE FOR DIRECT FARM MARKETING (1999).

In addition to clauses above, there may be other provisions pertaining to product labeling requirements, posting farm names, using legal scales, accepting nutrition checks such as *Supplemental Nutrition Assistance Program* ("SNAP") and the *Women, Infants and Children Program* ("WIC"), pricing guidelines (e.g., prohibition of price-cutting top quality produce), display guidelines, gleaning excess food, tax collection, income reporting, other various prohibitions (e.g., firearms), and miscellaneous legal terms (e.g., *Alternative Dispute Resolution* clause, award for attorneys' fees and court costs to prevailing party, limitation in damages, forum section clause for the local county Supreme Court). Give pause to any indemnification clause –make sure you clearly understand what you are agreeing to if the Market Rules require the farmer to indemnify the farmers' market.

Furthermore, the Market Rules will typically state that the "Choice of Law" is New York and require all vendors to comply with any federal, state or local laws pertaining to the production and sale of food (e.g., food labeling, livestock animal cruelty laws, environmental laws, zoning ordinances). If the Market Rules are silent on a particular issue, the Market Manager will typically determine how to best handle the situation.

There are many questions that a farmer should consider before participating in a farmers' market. A farmer may wish to consider some of the following issues before agreeing to participate in a farmers' market:

(1) Who *sponsors* the farmers' market?

(2) *How long* has the farmers' market been established?

(3) What is the *expected crowd* for the farmers' market (quantity of people and geographic reach)?

(4) What is the *application* fee and/or procedures?

(5) Do vendors *pay seasonally, monthly or weekly* flat fees and/or a percentage of gross sales?

(6) *Who owns/rents* the land on which the farmers' market is located?

(7) Who is *responsible* in case of slip-and-fall accidents or injuries to shoppers?

(8) *Which areas* of the farmers' market get the most traffic?

(9) Who has the authority to decide which farm sets up in which *location*? Is there an *additional fee* for preference?

(10) Is the market a *"producer only"* market or does the market allow for wholesale peddlers or sale of food raised by other farmers?

(11) Can vendors provide *free samples* to consumers?

(12) What is the *penalty* (if any) for violating a market rule?

(13) What is the penalty, if any, for *missing* a market day?

(14) If a vendor is *forced to leave* the market or is unable to continue to participate, is any portion of the fee/rent refundable?

(15) What are the *dispute resolution procedures*, if any? In other words, what are the procedures if there is an alleged violation of the market rules? For example, is there a committee of vendors and customers who decides on whether there is a violation? Are there procedures for non-binding *mediation* or binding arbitration?

(16) Does the market have all the necessary *local business permits* and/or *licenses*? Can the vendor ask for copies of said permit and/or licenses?

(17) Is the farmers' market approved to participate in the *WIC Farmers' Market Nutrition Program* ("FMNP")?

(18) What food products may be sold at the farmers' market (e.g., meat, poultry, eggs, homemade processed foods)?

(19) Does the farmers' market itself carry its *own insurance* in case of accidents?

(20) What type of *insurance* does the farmers' market expect vendors to have (e.g., 1 mil. face value of commercial insurance) and what proof of insurance must be provided to the market?

(21) Do the market rules require the *farmer* to actually attend the market or can vendors send employees/independent contractors to do the selling?

(22) Does the farmers' market require the farmer/vendor to submit a plan before the market season begins listing what produce will be sold and in what approximate volume?

(23) Can the market officials *visit a vendor's farm* to inspect the operation and/or its records?

(24) Are there *special food labeling requirements* other than what is already required under New York and federal law (if applicable)?

(25) How quickly are *Electronic Benefit Transfer* ("EBT") payments received?

(26) What does the farmers' market do to help promote both the farmers' market and its vendors? For example, will the vendors be *listed on its website*?

See Neil Hamilton, "Farmers' Markets Rules, Regulations and Opportunities" (June 2002) and NEIL HAMILTON, THE LEGAL GUIDE FOR DIRECT FARM MARKETING (1999).

Additional Resources

A. Bryan Endres et al., "New York Direct Farm Business: A Legal Guide to Market Access" (2013) available at http://new.nationalaglawcenter.org/wp-content/uploads/assets/articles/NYdirectmarket.pdf (last visited August 23, 2013).

Cari B. Rincker, Dr. Stan Benda, Derrick Braaten, Jason Foscolo, Neil Hamilton, Erin Hawley, Leon Letter, Jesse Richardson, Jr., Rich Schell, Patricia Salkin, "Counseling the Local Food Movement," American Bar Association Continuing Legal Education Webinar (May 10, 2012), available for purchase at http://apps.americanbar.org/abastore/index.cfm?section=main&fm=Product.AddToCart&pid=CET12LFMCDR (last visited July 1 2013).

Cari B. Rincker & Jason Foscolo, "Overview of Local Food Law," Pace Law School Continuing Legal Education (March 13, 2013) (recording available for purchase), presentation available at http://www.slideshare.net/rinckerlaw/local-food-law-pace-law-school-cle (last visited July3, 2013).

Cornell Cooperative Extension of Tompkins County, "Guide to Marketing Channel Selection: How to Sell Through Wholesale & Direct Marketing Channels" (2010) available at http://nebeginningfarmers.org/files/2012/04/Market-Channel-Assessment-132dr2l.pdf (last visited July 17, 2013).

Cornell Small Farms Program, Directory for Articles Relating to "Local Food Markets," at http://smallfarms.cornell.edu/category/local-food-markets/ (last visited August 18, 2013).

Erin Kee and Jason Foscolo, "How to Make a Farmers' Market: The Legal Structure Behind Local Food," Clearing house REVIEW Journal of Poverty Law and Policy (May- June 2013) available at http://www.foodlawfirm.com/wordpress/wp-content/uploads/2013/06/chr_2013_may_june_kee.pdf (last visited July 11, 2013).

Farmers Market Federation of New York, "Farm Business and Marketing" at http://www.nyfarmersmarket.com/resources/resources-for-farmers/farm-business-a-marketing.html and "Guide to Developing Community Farmers Market," available at http://www.nyfarmersmarket.com/publications/BuildingCommunityFM2010.pdf (last visited July 17, 2013).

Harvard Food Law and Policy Clinic, "Good Food, Good Laws: Putting Local Food Policy to Work for Our Communities." (July 2012), available at http://www.law.harvard.edu/academics/clinical/lsc/documents/FINAL_LOCAL_TOOLKIT2.pdf (last visited August 18, 2013).

Jason Foscolo, "Raw Milk, 'Moo-N Shine', and Risk Management" Cornell Small Farms Program available at http://smallfarms.cornell.edu/2012/01/09/raw-milk-"moo-n-shine"-and-risk-management (last visited July 11, 2013).

Jennifer-Claire V. Klotz, "How to Direct Market Farm Products on the Internet," (December 2002), available at http://www.ams.usda.gov/AMSv1.0/getfile?dDocName=STELDEV 3101222 (last visited July 17, 2013).

Jess Anna Speier and Jill E. Krueger, "Understanding Farmers' Market Rules," Farmers' Legal Action Group, Inc. (2006) available at http://www.flaginc.org/wp-content/uploads/2013/03/FarmersMarket.pdf (last visited August 23, 2013).

Martha Goodsell and Tatiana Stanton, "Guide to Direct Marketing Livestock and Poultry" available at http://smallfarms.cornell.edu/resource-guide-to-direct-marketing-livestock-and-poultry/ (last visited May 19, 2013).

Megan L. Bruch and Matthew D. Ernst, "Marketing through Community Supported Agriculture (CSAs)" (December 2010), available at https://utextension.tennessee.edu/publications/Documents/PB1797.pdf (last visited July 17, 2013).

Monika Roth, "Guide to Farming in NY" available at http://nebeginningfarmers.org/publications/farming-guide/ (last visited May 19, 2013) (#26 Direct Marketing Options), also available at http://nebeginningfarmers.org/2012/04/26/26-direct-marketing-options/ (last visited August 18, 2013).

National Agriculture Law Center, "AFRI- Legal Direct Marketing Guides," available at http://new.nationalaglawcenter.org/center-outreach/afri/ (last visited July 17, 2013).

National Agriculture Law Center, Reading Room for "Agritourism," at http://new.nationalaglawcenter.org/research-by-topic/agritourism-2/ (last visited August 18, 2013).

National Agriculture Law Center, Reading Room for "Local Food Systems," at http://new.nationalaglawcenter.org/research-by-topic/local-food-systems/ (last visited August 18, 2013).

National Sustainable Agriculture Coalition, "Guide to Federal Funding for Local and Regional Food Systems," (April 2010) available at http://sustainableagriculture.net/wp-content/uploads/2010/06/6.18-FINAL-Food-System-Funding-Guide2.pdf (last visited August 18, 2013).

NEIL D. HAMILTON, THE LEGAL GUIDE FOR DIRECT FARM MARKETING (JUNE 1999).

New York State Department of Agriculture and Markets "Direct Marketing Survey 2009" (October 2010) available at http://www.nass.usda.gov/Statistics_by_State/New_York/Publicatio ns/Special_Surveys/DirectMkting2009/DirectMarketingPublication20 09.pdf (last visited July 17, 2013).

New York State Department of Agriculture and Markets, "Guidelines for Review of Local Laws Affecting Direct Farm Marketing Activities," (September 1, 2010) available at http://www.agriculture.ny.gov/AP/agservices/guidancedocuments/3 05-aFarmMarket.pdf (last visited July 17, 2013).

Renee Johnson, Randy Alison Aussenberg and Tadlock Cowan, "The Role of Local Food Systems in U.S. Farm Policy," Congressional Research Service Report (7-5700) (R42155) (March 12, 2013), available at http://www.fas.org/sgp/crs/misc/R42155.pdf (last visited August 18, 2013).

Sarah A. Low and Stephen Vogel, "Direct and Intermediated Marketing of Local Foods in the United States," U.S. Department of Agriculture Economic Research Service (November 2011) available at http://www.ers.usda.gov/media/138324/err128_2_.pdf (last visited August 18, 2013).

Steve Martinez et al., "Local Food Systems: Concepts, Impacts, and Issues," U.S. Department of Agriculture Economic Research Service (May 2010), available at http://www.ers.usda.gov/media/122868/err97_1_.pdf.

CHAPTER 22

COTTAGE FOOD OPERATIONS

"Cottage food operations" (or home-based food processing) is one of the fastest growing trends in the local food movement. The majority of states have cottage food operation laws, exempting certain home processers from certain regulations. New York is included on the list of states with cottage food operation law.

Importantly, cottage food laws only apply to home-processed food sold *intrastate* (i.e., within the state of New York); if food is sold *interstate* (i.e., outside the state of New York) then more stringent federal regulations will apply making compliance more difficult for a small scale home processor. If a food entrepreneur does not fit under the cottage food exemption for home-processed food then he/she may need to apply for an Article 20-C License in New York before selling the food product.

Article 20-C Licenses

New York applies an "exemption approach" to cottage food operations by exempting home-processed food from the typical requirements of a commercial kitchen under Article 20-C of the NYS Agric. & Mkts § 251-z-1 et sec. Pursuant to NY Agric. & Mkts Section 251-z-3, "[n]o person shall maintain or operate a food processing establishment unless licensed biennially by [NYSDAM]."

NYSDAM is given broad discretion with administrative sanctions to ensure that foods are properly protected. See R & S Bakery, Inc. v. Barber, 435 N.Y.S.2d 93 (Third Dep't 1980). "Each day's operation of a food processing establishment without a license shall constitute a separate violation. . ." N.Y. Agric. & Mkts § 251-z-10.

Some Definitions

Food entrepreneurs in New York should be cognizant of the following definitions:

1. *"Food"* and *"food products"* under section 251-z-2[3] includes all articles of "food, drink, confectionery or condiment, whether simple, mixed or compound, used or intended for use by man and shall also include all substances or ingredients to be added to food for any purpose."

2. The statute defines a *"food processing establishment"* as "any place which receives *food or food products* for the purpose of processing or otherwise adding to the value of the product for commercial sale" (i.e., making a "value-added" food product). See NY Agric. & Mkts § 251-z-2[1].

The following are exempted from this definition:

   a. Establishments that process/manufacture food (products) that are sold *exclusively at retail* for consumption on the premises;

   b. bottled/bulk water facilities;

   c. Food processing establishments which are covered by Article 4 (*Dairy Products*), Article 4-A (*Frozen Desserts*), Article 5-B (*Sale of Meat*), Article 5-D (*Sale of Poultry and Poultry Products*), Article 17-B (*Licensing of Food Salvagers*) and Article 21 (*Milk Control*);

   d. Service food establishments, including vending machine commissaries, under permit and inspection by the *NYS Department of Health* or local health agency which maintains a program certified and approved by the state commissioner of health;

e. Establishments under federal meat, poultry or egg product inspection; or

f. Establishments engaged solely in the harvesting, storage, or distribution of one or more *raw agricultural commodities* which are ordinarily cleaned, prepared, treated or otherwise processed before being marketed to the consuming public.

3. *"Processing"* under section 251-z-2[3] means "processing foods in any manner, such as by manufacturing, canning, preserving, freezing, drying, dehydrating, juicing, pickling, baking, brining, bottling, packing, repacking, pressing, waxing, heating or cooking, or otherwise treating food in such a way as to create a risk that it may become adulterated if improperly handled."

4. *"Home-Processed Food"* is "any food processed in a private home or residence using only the ordinary kitchen facilities of that home . . . but shall exclude potentially hazardous food. . ." Section 276.3 of the NYS Agric. & Mkts Regulations.

5. *"Value-added"* is generally the process of changing or transforming a product from its original state to a more valuable state. It can also include the production of a product in a manner that enhances its real or perceived value.

Please note that there is no definition under New York for a *"cottage food operation."* It is a colloquial term for home-based food processing.

Exceptions

As noted above, NYSDAM may establish exemptions from the food processing license requirement to "avoid unnecessary regulation and assist in the administration of this article without impairing its purposes." See N.Y. Agric. & Mkts § 251-z-4. However, said "exemptions may be conditioned upon requirements relating to sanitation, record keeping and reporting as the [NYSDAM] commissioner may require." Id. Among other exemptions, *home processed food* is exempt from Article 20-C licensing requirements if certain conditions are satisfied. Even though home processors are exempt under the Article 20-C license requirement, *they are still subject to inspection by the NYSDAM*. From a practical standpoint, NYSDAM will usually only inspect a cottage food operation if there is a consumer complaint.

Applying for an Article 20-C License

If a food entrepreneur does not fit under the cottage food operation exemption in New York and must obtain an Article 20-C license, section 251-z-3 sets forth *application requirements* which include proof of the following:

- That he/she has *good character*;
- That he/she has adequate *experience or competency*;
- That the establishment has *adequate facilities and equipment* for the business conducted; and
- That the establishment can maintain *cleanliness* so that the product will not be adulterated.

You can find the *FSI-202* form online from NYSDAM at http://www.agriculture.ny.gov/FS/license/pdfs/FSI-303.PDF (last visited March 4, 2013). The applicant must also pay $400 every 24 months. The license period varies according to the applicants last name as set forth in the statute.

Suspending or Revoking Licenses

Under Section 251-z-5, NYSDAM may decline to grant a new license or renewal, suspend or revoke an Article 20-C license based on one of the following reasons:

- *False or misleading statement* in the application;

- *Insufficient facilities or equipment* to maintain adequate sanitation for activities;

- Establishment is *not maintained in a clean and sanitary* condition;

- Maintenance of the establishment is such where the food (product) *may be adulterated*;

- Establishment has failed or refused to produce *requisite records* or other information sought;

- The applicant/licensee or any officer, director, partner or owner of 10% or more shares, or any other person in management, has *failed to comply with the statute*;

- The applicant/licensee, officer, director, partners, stockholder, or any other person in management has been convicted of a *felony*.

Requirements of a 20-C Licensee

Some of the requirements for Article 20-C licensees are as follows:

- **Record Keeping**: Under Section 251-z-7, licensees are required to keep such records as required by NYSDAM.

- **Inspections**: Under Section 251-z-8, NYSDAM must have access to inspect the premises during *all reasonable hours* "where food or food products are being manufactured, packaged, processed or stored, or where food or food products are being bought, sold or handled."

- **Education**: Licensees are required to complete an approved food safety education program under Article 20-C.

New York Cottage Food Operation Law

Home-processed food is exempt from Article 20-C licensing requirements if certain conditions are satisfied. However, cottage food operations must be *registered with NYSDAM*, Division of Food Safety and Inspection by completing FSI-989c available at http://www.agriculture.ny.gov/FS/consumer/FSI898c.pdf (last visited March 4, 2013). The cottage food operation must disclose to NYSDAM whether the *water supply is municipal or a private well*.

If the home-based processor is on a private water/well system, then he/she must have a water test analysis performed for Coliform registering with NYSDAM (no more than 3 months old).

Eligibility

Like all states with cottage food operation laws, New York does place limitations on the types of food that can be processed at home and sold for human consumption. New York uses the "non-potentially hazardous" food product limitation. The NYSDAM registration form requires listing the "non potentially hazardous products" that will be processed in a home-based kitchen.

Under NYS Agric. & Mkts Regulations Section 276.3(a)[3], a *"[h]ome processed food"* includes "any food processed in a private home or residence using only the *ordinary kitchen facilities* of that home or residence which are also used to *prepare food for the owner* thereof, his family, nonpaying guests and household and farm employees who reside therein, but shall exclude *potentially hazardous foods* [as defined in the regulation] or thermally processed low-acid foods packaged in hermetically sealed containers [under Part 277] and acidified food packed in closed containers including but not limited to *pickles and relishes* prepared from *low-acid fruits, vegetables, poultry, meat, meat products, fish or seafood."* (Emphasis added).

Commercial equipment is not considered an ordinary kitchen facility. Home processors whose residences contain separate segregated facilities for food processing will need to apply for licensing under Article 20-C.

Conditions for Exemptions

A home-based processor may be exempt from an Article 20-C license so long as the following conditions are satisfied:

1. All finished product containers are *clean, sanitary and labeled properly*;
2. Food may not be either adulterated or misbranded;
3. *Glass containers* for jams, jellies, marmalades, etc. have suitable rigid metal covers; and,
4. Are sold only within the *state of New York.*

See NFSI-898d, "Home Processing" Fact Sheet available at http://www.agriculture.ny.gov/FS/consumer/processor.html (last visited March 4, 2013). Furthermore, the home processed food exemption for Article 20-C licensing is *restricted to the following non-potentially hazardous* home processed foods:

1. *Bakery products* (e.g., bread, rolls, cookies, cakes, brownies, fudge, and double-crust fruit pies) for wholesale marketing or retail agricultural venues such as farms, farm stands, farmers markets, green markets, craft fairs and flea markets;

2. *Traditional jams, jellies,* and marmalades made with high acid/low pH fruits;

3. Repacking/blending dried *spices or herbs*;

4. Snack items such as *popcorn, caramel corn and peanut brittle*; and,

5. *Candy* (excluding chocolate).

See NFSI-898d, "Home Processing" Fact Sheet.

If the product *requires refrigeration* then it is not allowed to be produced under the home processor exemption. New York views food products that may require refrigeration as potentially hazardous. Examples of prohibited items include the following:

1. Fruit/ Vegetable Breads,
2. Pickled or Fermented Foods,
3. Cheesecake, Cream Filled Pastries,
4. Meat, Fish, or Poultry Products,
5. Vegetable Oils, Blended Oils,
6. Garlic and/or Herb in Oil Mixtures,
7. Wine Jellies, Chutneys, Fruit Butters,
8. Cooked or Canned Fruits or Vegetables,
9. Cheese, Yogurt, Fluid Dairy Products, and,
10. Sauces, Salsas, Marinades.

See NFSI-898d, "Home Processing" Fact Sheet.
Please note that the 20-C exemption for home processors does

not apply to direct Internet sales (i.e., commercial on-line transactions or e-commerce). However, it is permissible for farms to use the Internet for communication and marketing (e.g., email, website, social media platforms). See NFSI-898d, "Home Processing" Fact Sheet. Even though some cottage food operations are exempt from Article 20-C licensing requirements, it is still subject to NYSDAM inspection requirements and food labeling regulations.

Labeling

In New York, products made in a home-based kitchen should include the following on the label:

- *name and address* of the home processor;

- *common or usual name* of the food;

- if the food is fabricated from two or more ingredients, the common or usual name of *each ingredient in their order of predominance* (except that spices, flavorings and colorings may be designated as spices, flavorings and colorings without naming each, and spices and flavorings may be designated together as flavorings); and

- the *net weight*, standard measure or numerical count.

Other Legal Considerations

Cottage food operations in a residential area may conflict with *residential leases* or the *local zoning code* that prohibit certain commercial activities in residential zones. *Variances or special use permits* may be required to operate a cottage food operation out of a home. Cottage food operators should consult with an attorney and (if appropriate) local zoning officials for approval before commencing any home based commercial activity, including a home-based kitchen to process foods.

Any food operation has potential liability resulting from the sale of food products (i.e. slip-and-fall from customers, product defects, etc.). Cottage food operations are especially susceptible to liability from the sale of their home-processed food. Due to this, it is paramount that these producers review their insurance policies to determine whether they have ample coverage. When doing so, keep in mind the following:

- A typical *homeowner's insurance policy* usually does not provide coverage for commercial operations such as cottage food operations. Cottage food operators may also lose coverage on the structure/contents as a result of a loss from the business (i.e. fire loss).

- Although a *commercial insurance policy* will cover losses for general commercial liability (e.g., slip-and-fall), most policies do not provide coverage for products produced by cottage food operation labor.

- *Recall insurance coverage* for product recall can be obtained with a special insurance endorsement. Cottage food operators must evaluate their risk and the costs of insurance to determine the efficiency of maintaining the insurance.

Like all business decisions, cottage food operators should make a cost-benefit and risk-benefit analysis to determine the proper insurance formula. Please note that some farmers' markets require a *minimum amount of commercial insurance* (e.g., 1 mil.).

Additional Resources

Bringing Home the Baking, "Cottage Food Laws," at http://www.bringinghomethebaking.com/?page_id=282 (last visited August 18, 2013).

Cari B. Rincker, Dr. Stan Benda, Derrick Braaten, Jason Foscolo, Neil Hamilton, Erin Hawley, Leon Letter, Jesse Richardson, Jr., Rich Schell, Patricia Salkin, "Counseling the Local Food Movement," American Bar Association Continuing Legal Education Webinar (May 10, 2012), available for purchase at http://apps.americanbar.org/abastore/index.cfm?section=main&fm=Product.AddToCart&pid=CET12LFMCDR (last visited July 1 2013).

Cari B. Rincker, "Overview of Local Food Law," Pace Law School Continuing Legal Education (March 13, 2013) (recording available for purchase), presentation available at http://www.slideshare.net/rinckerlaw/local-food-law-pace-law-school-cle (last visited July3, 2013).

Cari B. Rincker, Stan Benda, Jason Foscolo, Alan Fowler, Erin Hawley, Leon Letter, Lindsey Peebles, Amy Salberg, and Jean Terranova, "Counseling Farmers, Food Entrepreneurs, and Restaurants on Food Labeling Laws," available for purchase at http://apps.americanbar.org/cle/programs/t13cff1.html (last visited June 14, 2013).

Cottagefoods.org, "New York- Cottage Food Law," at http://cottagefoods.org/laws/usa/new-york/ (last visited August 18, 2013).

Cornell Cooperative Extension, "Becoming a Small-Scale Food Processor: Guide to Farming in New York State" (December 9, 2009), available at http://nebeginningfarmers.org/2012/04/28/28-becoming-a-small-scale-food-processor/ (last visited August 18, 2013).

Cornell Small Farms Program, "Licenses to Consider" (Including Article 20-C Food Processing Establishments, Article 28 Retail Food Stores, Article 28 Food Warehouses, Article 17-B Food Salvager, Article 19 Refrigerated Warehouse/Locker Plant, Article 5-C Licensing of Rendering Plants), at http://smallfarms.cornell.edu/2012/07/24/licenses-to-consider/ (last visited August 18, 2013).

Harvard Food Law and Policy Clinic, "Cottage Food Laws in the United States" (August 2013) available at http://blogs.law.harvard.edu/foodpolicyinitiative/files/2013/08/FINAL_Cottage-Food-Laws-Report_2013.pdf (last visited August 18, 2013).

HomebasedBaking.com, "Cottage Food Laws," at http://homebasedbaking.com/cottage-food-laws/ (last visited August 18, 2013).

New York Department of Agriculture and Markets, "Food Establishment Licenses," at http://www.agriculture.ny.gov/FS/general/license.html (last visited August 18, 2013).

New York Department of Agriculture and Markets, "Home Based Processors," available at http://www.agriculture.ny.gov/FS/consumer/processor.html (last visited August 18, 2013).

New York Farm Bureau, "Pies, Jams and Cookies: Information for Home Processors of Food," (January 30, 2013) available at http://www.nyfb.org/img/topic_pdfs/file_7v6w18ao0v.pdf (last visited August 18, 2013).

Nicole Civita, "Home Free: Legalizing Home-Produced Foods," Agriculture Law Blog (December 28, 2012), at http://aglaw.blogspot.com/2012/12/home-free-legalizing-home-produced-foods.html (last visited August 18, 2013).

NOLO, "Starting a Home-Based Food Business in New York," at http://www.nolo.com/legal-encyclopedia/starting-home-based-food-business-new-york.html (last visited August 18, 2013).

Jason Foscolo et al., Cottage Food Law Archive, available at http://www.foodlawfirm.com/category/cottage-food-law/ (last visited August 18, 2013).

Roxanne Hill, "Food Safety Laws and Regulations Related to Home-Based Food Businesses: Perceptions of Regulatory Staff, Food Processors, and the Home-Based Food Industry in New York State" International Food Protection Training Institute (2011-2012), available at http://www.afdo.org/Resources/Documents/4-news-and-events/past-presentations/2012/1-Presentation-120605-Food-1600-Hill.pdf (last visited August 18, 2013).

CHAPTER 23

ON-FARM POULTRY SLAUGHTER

Many poultry producers are interested in exploring on-farm poultry slaughter options. The purpose of this chapter is to give a basic overview of the laws applicable to these operations. The law affecting on-farm poultry slaughter is highly technical. This Chapter only gives a general overview. Farmers interested in harvesting birds on their farm should speak to an agriculture lawyer about the options available to them.

1000 Bird Limit Exemption

A New York poultry producer who processes and sells less than 1000 chickens or 250 turkeys (i.e., 1 turkey = 4 chickens) may be subject to the *1000 Bird Limit Exemption* under the *Poultry Product Inspection Act* ("PPIA"), which requires producers to slaughter poultry in a USDA inspected facility. A farmer may harvest and process chickens and turkeys that he/she *raised on farm* and may distribute this poultry without mandatory inspection if the following *five criteria* is met pursuant to under PPIA § 464(c)(4), 9 C.F.R. § 381.10(c) and 9 C.F.R. § 381.175:

1. The poultry producer slaughters *no more than 1,000 birds* of his/her own farm in a calendar year for distribution as human food;

2. The poultry producer *does not engage in buying or selling* poultry products other than those produced from poultry raised on his/her farm;

3. The slaughter and processing are conducted under *sanitary standards*, practices, and procedures that produce poultry products that are sound, clean, not adulterated or misbranded, and fit for human food;

4. The poultry producer keeps the required *records*; and,

5. The poultry product *does not move in interstate commerce* (i.e., exchange or transportation of the poultry product stays intrastate *within the state of New York*).

This 1000 Bird Limit Exemption applies so long as the *slaughtering and processing* are both completed on-site. The slaughter equipment used may be owned, rented or provided in the form of a *Mobile Poultry Processing Unit* ("MPPU"). Please note that this 1000 Bird Limit Exemption applies per farm – not per farmer. If a New York "farm" is harvesting more than 1,000 chickens or 250 turkeys in an on-farm slaughter facility and the product still remains in intrastate commerce, then it is required to have an Article 5-A License; otherwise, it must harvest its birds at a USDA processing facility.

Although sales and transportation of poultry products under this 1000 Bird Limit Exemption are only required to stay in *intrastate* (i.e., within New York), NYSDAM's 2009 guidelines suggest that farms operating under the 1000 bird exemption should *maintain control of its product* through the sale directly to the consumer by limiting sales to on-farm outlets, roadside stands, or farmers' markets.

Record Keeping

Poultry producers are required to keep records relating to the slaughter and sale of poultry products to consumers. USDA Food Safety Inspection Service ("FSIS") or NYSDAM employees review such records to determine compliance with the *1000 Bird Limit Exemption*. Farmers are encouraged to keep thorough records of their activity and archive an electronic copy safe from destruction due to weather or Act of God.

Example record logs including a flock record and slaughter record. Excel spreadsheets work well for these types of logs. To expound, a *flock record log* should note:

- Number of birds,
- Whether the birds were purchased (and where they were purchased) or raised on the farm,
- Health issues,
- Bird losses,
- Bird processing date,
- Product sold, and
- Date product was sold.

Meanwhile, a *slaughter record log* should note the following:

- Date of slaughter,
- Area inspected,
- Any corrective actions needed, and
- Date corrective actions were taken.

Food Packaging & Labeling

Packaging materials for poultry meat must be *safe for their intended use* pursuant to the *Food Drug & Cosmetic Act* ("FDCA"). Poultry products may not be packaged in anything that contains substances that may adulterate its contents or be injurious to human health. Only approved labels from the *Food & Drug Administration* ("FDA") may be used.

New York has adopted the FSIS Mandatory Labeling Requirements. Specifically, the following items are required to be on the principal display panel for all sales of meat or poultry sold in New York:

(1) Product name and description;
(2) Inspection Legend and Establishment Number (for farms processing under this exemption, it should say "Exempted – P.L. 90-492);
(3) Net weight statement (includes "packed on" date, "sell by" date, "net wt lb.", "price per lb", and net weight);
(4) Name and address of the farm; and,
(5) Safe handling statement (if processed under on-farm exemption, then label must say "Exempt P.L. 90-492").

If a poultry farmer makes a nutritional claim, then a Nutrition

Facts Panel must also be included. The Department of Weights and Measures will need to certify the scales used to ensure that the digital scales are suitable for commerce and accurately measure the weight in pounds.

Food labeling rules are *extremely technical*. This Chapter only touches on a few major points. It is *highly suggested* that any poultry labels be reviewed by a food attorney to help ensure compliance.

Article 5-A Licenses

As noted above, if a farmer harvests more than 1000 birds on his/her farm yet the poultry products stay in intrastate commerce, then this farmer must obtain an Article 5-A license. The law governing Article 5-A slaughterhouses is found at New York Agriculture & Markets Law ("N.Y. Agric. & Mkts") § 96-a et seq., 1 New York Code, Rules and Regulations ("NYCRR") § 245.1 et seq. (slaughterhouses), and 1 NYCRR § 246.1 et seq. (refrigerated warehouses and locker plants). Pursuant to Section 96-b, a "person, firm, partnership or corporation *not granted inspection*" under the (a) federal *Meat Inspection Act*, (b) federal *Poultry Products Inspection Act*, (c) Article 5-B of NY Agric. & Mkts [Sale of Meat], or (d) Article 5-D of NY Agric. & Mkts [Sale of Poultry and Poultry Products] may "operate any place or establishment where animals or fowl are slaughtered or butchered for food unless such person, firm, partnership or corporation be licensed by the commissioner [of agriculture]." N.Y. Agric. & Mkts § 96-b(1).

The U.S. Department of Agriculture ("USDA") issues a "grant of inspection" to approved facilities instead of a "license". USDA inspected meat processing facilities that have been issued a "grant of inspect" may butcher and/or process amenable livestock or poultry pursuant to the Federal Meat Inspection Act the relevant regulations.

Exclusions for an Article 5-A license include the following:

(1) "any bona fide farmer who butchers *his own domestic animals or fowl* on his farm exclusively for use by him and members of his *household*[,] non-paying guests and employees";

(2) "any *custom slaughterer*";

> A "custom slaughterer" means "a person, firm, corporation, or association who or which operates a place or establishment where animals are delivered by the owner thereof for slaughter exclusively for use, in the household of such owner, by him, and members of his household and his non-paying guests and employees [provided that] such custom slaughterer does not engage in the business of buying or selling any carcasses, parts of carcasses, meat or meat products of any animal[.]"
> N.Y. Agric. & Mkts § 96-d (emphasis added).

(3) "any person who slaughters not more than [250] turkeys or an equivalent number of birds of all other species raised by him on his own farm during the calendar year for which an exemption is sought . . ." (i.e., the *1000 Bird Exemption*, discussed above); and,

(4) "any person who donates, and any charitable or not-for-profit organization that possesses, prepares or serves game or wild game pursuant to [N.Y. Env. Law § 11-0917 (Possession, transportation and sale of wild game and other wildlife)] (and any person who processes game or wild game on behalf of such donor)."

See N.Y. Agric. & Mkts § 96-d. In such cases, an Article 5-A license is not required.

Application & License Requirements

NYSDAM promulgated license requirements and application procedures for an Article 5-A slaughterhouse. See N.Y. Agric. & Mkts § 96-b(1). In order to obtain a *two-year Article 5-A license*, NYSDAM "must be satisfied that the slaughterhouse complies with *construction, equipment and sanitation* requirements establish by

[Part 245 of the New York Codes, Rules and Regulations]." 1 NYCRR § 245.1(a) (emphasis added); see also N.Y. Agric. & Mkts § 96-b(1).

In deciding whether a slaughterhouse is in regulatory compliance, NYSDAM *may* request an "examination of the premises, equipment and facilities " pursuant to 1 NYCRR § 245.1(a). Under 1 NYCRR § 245.1(a), a "[c]omplete drawing and specifications for new construction, new businesses and alterations of existing premises shall be submitted to the commissioner for approval."

The application form for the two-year license is made available by the NYS Department of Agric. & Mkts on or before May 1st every other year. See N.Y. Agric. & Mkts § 96-b(1). More specifically, the FSI-1200 application form for a *"Poultry-Small Animal Slaughterhouse License"* is available online at http://www.agriculture.ny.gov/FS/license/pdfs/FSI-1200.PDF (last visited March 29, 2012). Along with the $200 application fee, an applicant must furnish evidence of the following:

- his/her *"good character, experience and competency"*;

- "that the establishment has *adequate facilities and equipment* for the business to be conducted";

- "that the establishment is such that the *cleanliness* of the premises can be maintained"; and,

- "that the product produced therein *will not become adulterated.*"

See N.Y. Agric. & Mkts § 96-b(3).

Inspection & Inspection Results

An Article 5-A facility will be inspected and licensees are required to post the results from this inspection at the *public entrance*. See N.Y. Agric. & Mkts § 96-c. "Any room, compartment, equipment or utensil, found by the commissioner to be improper, unclean or unsanitary shall be tagged with a rejection notice. . ." and shall not be used until the condition has been corrected. See 1 NYCRR § 245.9. Please note that these inspection results must "be made available to the public upon request." N.Y. Agric. & Mkts § 96-c.

Sanitation & Cleanliness Requirements

The Article 5-A statute and regulations contain highly technical sanitation and cleanliness requirements. Pursuant to Section 96-e(1)-(4) sets for requirements for cleanliness and sanitation. Voilators of this provision can see violations between $1,000 to $25,000 depending whether it is a first time violation or if there are repetitive issues. Farmers in New York who are conducting on-farm slaughter should be training in Hazard Analysis and Critical Control Points ("HACCP") and be cautious to use generally accepted practices for on-farm poultry harvesting and processing.

Additional Resources

Cari B. Rincker, "Overview of Local Food Law," Pace Law School Continuing Legal Education (March 13, 2013) (recording available for purchase), presentation available at http://www.slideshare.net/rinckerlaw/local-food-law-pace-law-school-cle (last visited July3, 2013).

Cornell Small Farms Program, "Slaughter, Cutting, and Processing," at http://smallfarms.cornell.edu/2012/07/07/slaughtering-cutting-and-processing/ (last visited August 18, 2013).

Lynn Bliven, Tatiana Stanton, and Erica Frenay, "On-Farm Poultry Slaughter Guides," available at http://nebeginningfarmers.org/publications/on-farm-poultry-slaughter-guidelines/ (last visited May 19, 2013).

Martha Goodsell et. al, "A Resource Guide to Direct Marketing Livestock and Poultry", Rev. Ed (January 2011) available at http://smallfarms.cornell.edu/welcome-to-our-temporary-website/rg_livestock_poultry_2011/ (last visited July 3, 2013).

Rachel J. Johnson, Daniel L. Marti, and Lauren Gwin, "Slaughter and Processing Options and Issues for Locally Sourced Meat," USDA Economic Research Service (June 2012) available at http://www.ers.usda.gov/media/820188/ldpm216-01.pdf (last visited August 18, 2013).

CHAPTER 24

EGGS

Poultry producers in New York should be cognizant of the law affecting the sale eggs. This chapter gives a cursory overview of the its regulatory framework at the state and federal level. It also briefly discusses egg grades and labeling.

Federal Agencies

There are two primary agencies that regulate eggs at the federal level: the *U.S. Department of Agriculture* ("USDA") and the *Food & Drug Administration* ("FDA"). The roles of each agency are discussed below.

U.S. Department of Agriculture

The *Egg Products Inspection Act* ("EPIA"), 21 U.S.C. Chapter 15, authorizes the USDA to *inspect eggs* and egg products and *establish* uniform standards. The EPIA applies to eggs shipped both in interstate and intrastate commerce; however, there are exemptions for small producers. Pursuant to EPIA, both the *Agricultural Marketing Service* ("AMS") and *Food Safety Inspection Service* ("FSIS") administer the programs relevant to egg producers.

1. Agriculture Marketing Service ("AMS")

The role of AMS is to prohibit buying, selling, transporting, or offering to buy, sell, or transport *restricted eggs*, unless exemptions apply under 7 C.F.R. § 57.700. "[R]estricted eggs" are eggs that are checks, dirties, incubator rejects, inedible, leakers or loss (i.e., unfit for human food). 7 C.F.R. § 57.1000.

A **"check"** is a quality grade in which there are broken or cracked shells. See 1 NYCRR § 190.6(e).

A **"leaker"** is an "individual egg that has a crack or break in the shell and shell membranes to the extent that the egg contents are exuding or free to exude through the shell." 1 NYCRR § 190.11(c).

"Loss" is defined as "[a]n egg that is inedible, smashed, or broken so that contents are leaking, cooked, frozen, contaminated, or containing bloody whites, large blood spots, large unsightly meat spots, or other foreign material." 1 NYCRR § 190.11(a).

"Loss and inedible eggs" are unfit for human food and cannot be sold. See 1 NYCRR § 191.1.

Restricted eggs must be sent to a *processing facility* (overseen by FSIS), destroyed, or processed into *animal food*. See 7 C.F.R. § 57.720. AMS enforces the prohibition through periodic inspections of facilities, transport vehicles, and records of all persons engaged in the business of *transporting, shipping, or receiving eggs*. See 7 C.F.R. § 57.28. EPIA requires AMS to inspect handlers *packing shell eggs* for sale to the *end-consumer* at least *once per calendar quarter*, unless exempt. See 21 U.S.C. § 1034. AMS also provides voluntary grading services for *class, quality, quantity, or condition* and any combination thereof. See 7 C.F.R. Part 56.

However, AMS exempts egg producers from the restrictions and inspections if they *sell eggs from their own flocks* directly to consumers via a *door-to-door retail route* (e.g., CSA's, delivery to restaurants) or at a place of *business away from the site* of production (e.g., farmers markets) so long as they sell fewer than *thirty (30) dozen eggs* per sale. See 7 C.F.R. § 57.100(c).

Please note that this exemption requires that the producer own and *operate the business* and *personally transport* the eggs. In other words, the person transporting the eggs must be an *employee* of the farm. The eggs must meet the standards for U.S. Consumer Grade B shell eggs. Producers with *fewer than 3,000 hens*, producers selling directly to household consumers, and egg packers selling on site directly to consumers are also exempt from these regulations. See 7 C.F.R. § 57.100(d)-(f).

2. Food Safety Inspection Service ("FSIS")

The EPIA requires USDA to continuously inspect plants processing eggs into egg products. See 21 U.S.C. § 1034. EPIA defines egg products as "any dried, frozen or liquid eggs, with or without added ingredients". 21 U.S.C. § 1052(f). All egg products must undergo *pasteurization*. See 21 U.S.C. § 1036. FSIS oversees the inspection of egg processing plants. See 9 C.F.R. § 590.24. The procedures and standards for inspections are located in 9 C.F.R. Part 590.

Agriculture producers who process their own eggs and sell *directly to consumers* are exempt from *continuous inspection* under the FSIS regulations. See 9 C.F.R. § 590.100(e). However, they must apply for an exemption and their facility and operating procedures must meet all otherwise applicable standards. Although not subject to continuous inspection, exempted facilities must undergo periodic FSIS inspections. See 9 C.F.R. § 590.600-650.

In addition to USDA's regulation under the EIPA, the FDA regulates eggs under the Federal *Food Drug and Cosmetic Act* ("FDCA"). FDA specifies standards of *identity* for egg products, including dried and frozen eggs. See 21 C.F.R. Part 160. If a food does not meet the standard of identity, it is misbranded according to the FDCA. See 21 U.S.C. § 343(g).

Furthermore, some shell egg producers must adhere to FDA's Salmonella testing, handling and treatment standards. Producers with 3,000 or more laying hens at a particular farm that produce shell eggs for the table market, and that do not sell all of their eggs directly to consumers, are subject to the additional Salmonella prevention standards under 21 C.F.R. Part 118.

Regardless of whether eggs are sold interstate or intrastate, the FDA requires all shell eggs for distribution to the consumer to have a safe handling label or be treated to kill Salmonella. See 21 C.F.R. § 101.17(h). The label must read: "SAFE HANDLING INSTRUCTIONS: To prevent illness from bacteria: keep eggs refrigerated, cook eggs until yolks are firm, and cook foods containing eggs thoroughly." The statement must appear on the label *prominently, conspicuously,* and in a type size no smaller than 1/16 of one inch. The statement must appear in a hairline box and the words "safe handling instructions" must appear in bold capital letters. The labeling consultant will be able to assist you with this requirement.

Food & Drug Administration

Pursuant to 21 U.S.C. § 1044(a), the "Secretary may, by regulation and under such conditions and procedures as he may prescribe, exempt specific provisions of this Act" for the following:

(1) the *sale, transportation, possession, or* use of eggs which contain *no more restricted eggs* than are allowed by the tolerance in the official standards of United States consumer grades for shell eggs;

(2) the *processing of egg products* at any plant in which the facilities and operating procedures meet such sanitary standards as may be prescribed by the Secretary, and where the eggs received or used in the manufacture of egg products contain no more restricted eggs than are allowed by the *official standards of United States consumer grades* for shell eggs, and the egg products processed at such plant;

(3) the *sale of eggs* by any poultry producer from *his/her own flocks directly to a household consumer* exclusively for use by such consumer and members of his/her household and his/her nonpaying guests and employees, and the transportation, possession, and use of such eggs in accordance with this paragraph;

(4) the *processing of egg products* by any poultry producer from eggs of his own flocks' production for sale of such products directly to a household consumer *exclusively for use by such consumer and members of his/her household and his/her nonpaying guests and employees,* and the egg products so processed when handled in accordance with this paragraph;

(5) the *sale of eggs* by shell egg packers on his/her own premises directly to household consumers for use by such consumer and members of his/her household and his/her nonpaying guests and employees, and the transportation, possession, and use of such eggs in accordance with this paragraph;

(6) for such period of time (not to exceed *two years*) during the initiation of operations under this Act as the Secretary determines that it is *impracticable to provide inspection*, the processing of egg products at any class of plants and the egg products processed at such plants; and

(7) the sale of eggs by any egg producer with an annual egg production from a flock of *three thousand or less hens*.

21 U.S.C. 1044(a) (emphasis added). Farms will be exempt under 21 CFR § 118.1 if they will be transporting no more than 3,000 or more laying hens.

Egg Grading Requirements

Pursuant to NY Agric. & Mkts § 160-a, "eggs for human consumption shall not be sold or exposed for sale except by the grades or standards so established." See also 1 NYCRR § 191.1(h) ("[a]ll shell eggs when sold or exposed for sale or the consumers for human consumption shall be sold or exposed for sale on the basis of the grades set forth in this Part."). More specifically, 1 NYCRR § 191.3(a) requires any person or business entity selling shell eggs to a consumer *to give notice* of the "exact grade and size of the eggs" by "plainly and conspicuously printing or writing on each carton or container the exact grade and size."

Section 160-b gives NYSDAM the full authority to promulgate egg-grading regulations. The regulations for grading eggs are established in 1 NYCRR § 190.1 et seq. A helpful table is found at 1 NYCRR 190.5, and included in this Chapter, to guide you on egg grading per weight including "jumbo," "extra large" and "large." Factors that affect the grading include:

(1) cleanliness and shape, see 1 NYCRR § 190.7,

(2)   size of air cell, <u>see</u> 1 NYCRR § 190.8,

(2)   color of the egg-white, <u>see</u> 1 NYCRR § 190.9, and

(4)   yolk, <u>see</u> 1 NYCRR § 190.10.

Pursuant to 1 NYCRR 190.3, the grade that goes on the carton is determined by the percentages of eggs in the carton that fall within each of the above categories.

Additionally, keep in mind the following regulations:

- "The mark of grade and size upon any carton, bag or other container in which eggs are exposed for sale shall be in legible printing or writing at least equal in height to all other required markings or not less than three-eighths inch in height." 1 NYCRR § 191.6(b).

- Furthermore, farms *cannot abbreviate the grade or size* statements on the carton or other container. <u>See</u> 1 NYCRR § 191.6(c). Any advertisement for eggs must also "plainly and conspicuously indicate the grade and size." 1 NYCRR § 191.7.

- "No person shall sell, offer for sale, or advertise for sale as fresh eggs, strictly fresh eggs hennery eggs, or new-laid eggs, or under words or descriptions of similar import, any eggs which are not fresh. No egg shall be deemed to be fresh which does not meet the standards of quality of fresh eggs established by the commissioner of agriculture and markets." <u>See</u> N.Y. Agric. & Mkts § 160-c. However, the term "fresh" (e.g., "fresh farm eggs" "fresh cage-free eggs") is not a substitute for a grade designation. <u>See</u> 1 NYCRR § 191.8.

New York Egg Sizes -- 1 NYCRR § 190.5

Size or Weight Class	Minimum Net Weight Per Dozen	Minimum Net Weight Per 30 Dozen	Weight for Individual Eggs at Rate Per Dozen
Jumbo	30	56	29
Extra Large	27	50 ½	26
Large	24	45	23
Medium	21	39 ½	20
Small	18	34	17
Pewee	15	28	————

There is a 3.3% lot tolerance for individual eggs in the next lower weight class so long as no individual case within the lot exceeds 5%.

Weights are listed in grams.

New York Egg Grades-
1 NYCRR §§ 190.3 and 190.4

Consumer Grade	Quality Required	Max % Tolerance	% of Leakers, Dirties or Loss (due to meat or blood spots)
Grade AA (origin)	87% AA	13% not AA; not more than 5% checks (7% if jumbo size)	Not more than 0.5%
Grade AA (destination)	72% AA	28% (at least 10% must be A quality); not more than 7% checks (9% for Jumbo size)	Not more than 1%
Grade A (origin)	87% or better	13% may be B; not more than 5% checks (7% if Jumbo size)	Not more than .5%
Grade A (destination)	82% A or better	18% may be B; not more than 7% checks (9% for Jumbo size)	Not more than 1%
Grade B (origin)	90% B or better	10% may be less than B quality or checks	Not more than .5%
Grade B (destination)	90% B or better	10% may be less than B quality or checks	Not more than 1%

Due to limitation on space, this chart does not delve into the characteristics of B Quality tolerated or the tolerance in lots of two or more egg cases. Readers are encouraged to review the regulations with a licensed food attorney in New York for a complete picture of the regulations affecting egg grades.

Quality Grades For Individual Shell Eggs-
1 NYCRR §§ 190.6, 190.7, 190.8, 190.9, 190.12

Quality Grade	Shell	Air Cell	White
AA	"must be clean, unbroken and practically normal[1]"	"must not exceed 1/8 inch in depth, may show unlimited movement and may be free or bubbly"[2]	"clear and firm so that the yolk is only slightly defined when the egg is twirled before the candling light"
A	"must be clean, unbroken and practically normal"	"must not exceed 3/16 inch in depth, may show unlimited movement, and may be free or bubbly"	"must be clear and at least reasonably firm[3] so that the yolk outline is only fairly well defined when the egg is twirled before the candling light"
Dirty	"an unbroken shell with adhering dirt or foreign material, prominent stains, or moderate stains covering more than 1/32 of the shell surface if localized, or 1/16 of the shell surface if scattered" "moderately stained areas in excess of B quality."		
Check	"has a broken or cracked shell but with its shell membranes in tact and the contents of which do not leak"		

[1] Eggs that are AA or A quality must be "**practically normal.**"
[2] A "**free air cell**" is defined in 1 NYCRR § 190.8(b)-(c).
[3] "**Reasonably Firm**" is defined in 1 NYCRR § 190.9(c).

Egg Yolk –
1 NYCRR § 190.10

Quality Grade	Yolk Description
Grade AA	"A yolk outline that in indistinctly indicated and appears to blend into the surrounding white as the egg is twirled." "A yolk that shows no germ development but may show other very slight defects on its surface."
Grade A	"A yolk outline that is discernible but not clearly outlined as the egg is twirled." "A yolk that shows no germ development but may show other very slight defects on its surface."
Grade B	"A yolk outline that is clearly visible as a dark shadow when the egg is twirled." "A yolk in which the yolk membranes and tissues have weakened and/or moisture has been absorbed from the white to such an extent that the yolk appears definitely enlarged and flat." "A yolk that shows well developed spots or areas and other serious defects, such as olive yolks, which do not render the egg inedible." "A development of the germ spot on the yolk of a fertile egg that has progressed to a point where it is plainly visible as a definite circular area or spot with no blood in evidence."

"Blood caused by development of the germ in a fertile egg to the point where it is visible as definite lines or as a blood ring. Such an egg is classified as inedible."

Additional Resources

New York State Department of Agriculture & Markets, "NYSEQAP" (New York State Egg Quality Assurance Program), available at http://www.agriculture.ny.gov/programs/eggquality.html (last visited July 17, 2013).

CHAPTER 25

FOOD LABELING AND SAFETY

Farmers and food entrepreneurs selling food products direct to the consumer should be cautious of food labeling and safety regulations at the state and federal level. Food labeling law is complex and technical– because of that, only a handful of food labeling issues are briefly noted in this Chapter. Farmers and food entrepreneurs who need food labeling guidance are strongly recommended to work with an experienced food label designer and food law attorney who is knowledgeable about food labeling and food safety.

Food and Beverage Labeling

There are multiple government agencies that regulate the labeling of food and beverages. Due to this fact, it can be difficult to clearly understand each agency's role with regulation.

Under the *Food Drug and Cosmetic Act* ("FDCA") and *Fair Packaging Labeling Act* ("FPLA"), the *Food and Drug Administration* ("FDA") regulates packaged food, fish and beverages with less that 7% alcohol that are sold in *interstate commerce* (i.e., outside the state of New York). On the other hand, the *U.S. Department of Treasury's Alcohol and Tobacco Tax and Trade Bureau* regulates beverages with more than 7% alcohol.

Furthermore, the U.S. Department of Agriculture ("USDA") regulates meat, poultry, and egg products sold in interstate commerce through the *Federal Meat Inspection Act* ("FMIA"), *Poultry Products Inspection Act* ("PPIA"), *Egg Products Inspection Act* ("EPIA"), *Agriculture Marketing Act* ("AMA") and the FDCA. New York government agencies regulates food labeling only sold *intrastate* within the state of New York. That being said, it is important for readers to understand that the line between interstate

357

and intrastate commerce can be blurry. It is important for food entrepreneurs to discuss this issue with a food or agriculture lawyer to ascertain whether it is reasonably foreseeable, in your circumstance, that the food product(s) will enter intrastate commerce.

Front of Package ("FOP") Labels

The *Nutrition Labeling and Education Act* ("NLEA") requires that packaged food display a nutrition facts panel. There are over a hundred FOP food labels with specific requirements including the American Heart Association's "heart check", Whole Grain Council's whole grain stamp, and Smart Choices Program logo.

Food entrepreneurs should be cognizant of whether the FOP label is a *health claim* or *nutrient content claim*. The FDA has established that a *health claim* on a label or ancillary marketing material either by words/statements or symbols suggests a relationship between the food and a disease or health-related condition. See 21 C.F.R. 101.14(a)(1). Health claims may be made if supported by "publically available scientific evidence" and there is a "significant scientific agreement" among qualified experts. See 21 C.F.R. §§ 101.70-101.83. Food entrepreneurs should seek legal advice on the issue of health claims before making an any type of health or wellness assertion on the label.

Allergens

Farmers and food entrepreneurs should be especially careful about the labeling of major food *allergens* including milk, eggs, fish, Crustacean shellfish, tree nuts, wheat, peanuts and soybeans. Additionally, be especially careful about food ingredients that may be derivatives of such allergens.

National Organic Program ("NOP")

Farmers and food entrepreneurs that wish to use the word *"organic"* on the label should understand the USDA's *National Organic Program* ("NOP") promulgated pursuant to the *Organic Food Production Act* ("OFPA") in the 1990 Farm Bill. The *National Organic Standards*, which were amended in 2010, established the rules for producing and handling crops, livestock and processed agricultural products labeled as "organic." Unless otherwise exempted, the National Organic Standards requires agriculture producers who wish to label their product as "organic" obtain certification in the NOP. See 7 C.F.R. Part 205.

Prof. Erin Hawley at the University of Missouri, School of Law discussed NOP in more detail in the ABA webinar "Counseling Farmers, Food Entrepreneurs, and Restaurants on Food Labeling Law" (June 14, 2013). Some notes from her presentation are noted in this section.

Certification procedures with the USDA require the procedure to chose a certifying agent with USDA's *Agriculture Marketing Service* ("AMS"). The farmer must then submit an application to this certifying agent; after a review, the certifying agent will schedule an onsite inspection. The farmer is entitled to a copy of the on-site report and any test results pursuant to 7 C.F.R. § 205.402. If denied certification, farmers are able to reapply, request mediation or file an appeal.

Certified farmers or handling facilities must (1) *pay fees* for the USDA certification, (2) notify the *certification agent* of any prohibited substance, drift or any change that might impact compliance, (3) comply with *organic production and handling* regulations, (4) implement and annually update his/her/its organic production or handling system plan (*"Organic System Plan"*), (5) allow for annual *on-site inspections* on the premises, (6) maintain *5-year records* that are adapted to the particular farming operation or food business that accurately disclose all activities, and that demonstrate compliance with the National Organic Standards. See 7 C.F.R. § 205.103.

> The **Organic System Plan** must include: (1) a description of practices and procedures, and their frequency; (2) a list of each substance to be used as a production or handling input; (3) a description of monitoring practices and procedures and their frequency; (4) a description of the recordkeeping system; (5) a description of management practices and of physical barriers established to prevent commingling and contact with prohibited substances; and (6) any other information deemed necessary by the certifying agent. See 7 C.F.R. § 205.201.

A certified organic farm may seek a *temporary variance* with the USDA for (1) natural disasters declared by the Secretary of Agriculture such as Hurricanes Sandy and Irene, (2) damage caused by drought, wind, flood, excessive moisture, hail, tornado, earthquake, fire, or other *major business interruption*, and (3) organic research/testing. See 7 C.F.R. § 205.290. However, said variance will not allow for certain practices or materials enumerated in 7 C.F.R. § 205.105.

Certified producers are permitted to use *one of three labels* depending on the type of product: (1) "100-percent organic", (2) "Organic" (i.e., with 95% organically produced ingredients), or (3) "Made with organic ingredients" (i.e., multi-ingredient products with 70% organically produced ingredients). The percentages are based on weight or fluid volume, excluding water and salt. See 7 C.F.R. § 205.310. Multi-ingredient agriculture products with less than 70% organically produced ingredients may identify each organically produced ingredient with the word "organic" or with an asterisk to indicate that the ingredient is organically produced (e.g., a candy bar with "organic" peanuts).

FSIS Labels

USDA's *Food Safety Inspection Service* ("FSIS") is the agency responsible for ensuring the truthfulness and accuracy in labeling of meat and poultry products. As a general rule, all livestock harvested at a *USDA-inspected facility* must have FSIS approved labeling. See 9 C.F.R. § 317.4(a). Jason Foscolo discussed this topic in the ABA webinar "Counseling Farmers, Food Entrepreneurs, and Restaurants on Food Labeling Law" (June 14, 2013), some notes from his presentation are below.

FSIS requires pre-approval for meat, poultry and eggs introduced into interstate commerce through its *Label Submission and Approval System* ("LSAS"). FSIS provides helpful information for meat, poultry and egg label submissions online at http://www.fsis.usda.gov/wps/portal/fsis/topics/regulatory-compliance/labeling/Labeling+Procedures/labeling-procedures#.Ubyn7Ss6Vqg. Pursuant to 9 C.F.R. § 303.1(a), meat establishments are exempt from this requirement if the livestock or poultry is slaughtered and/or processed *by the owner* and used by the owner, members of his/her household, guests, and employees or it adheres to the strict regulations for custom slaughter set forth in the regulation.

If a livestock producer wishes to use a *marketing claim* or *animal raising claim* on his/her label such as a management practice (e.g., "Grass-Fed", "Free Range", "Hormone Free", "Humane") or genotype (e.g., DNA marker for tenderness or marbling, livestock breed such as "Angus"), then said livestock farmer is required to seek approval from the USDA for this marketing claim. Each marketing claim has *specific management requirements* to satisfy FSIS. See 9 C.F.R. § 317.4.

Generally speaking, FSIS evaluates labels that contain animal-raising claims by reviewing testimonials, affidavits, animal production protocols, and other relevant documentation provided by animal producers. If an application demonstrates that an animal-raising claim is *truthful* and not misleading, FSIS allows products derived from animals raised according to the protocol to *bear the claim* on their labels. In addition to producer testimonials and affidavits, and operational protocols describing production practices, producers can submit evidence of third-party certification, like USDA's process verification certification to support an application.

An application must include a "*sketch*" or printer's proof of the desired labeling featuring the *size, location, and indication* of final *color*, as specified in 9 C.F.R. § 317.2. Each USDA inspected meat processor has its own *USDA inspector*. A farm should work with the *meat processor directly* or through a food labeling consultant to ensure that the proposed labels meet the requirements for the USDA inspector (including but not limited to *safe handing instructions*, size requirements, ingredients, USDA logo, etc.). The USDA inspector may require documentation for certain claims such as "free range" that should be supplied to the meat processing facility for prior approval. An overview of the FSIS process can be found at FSIS, "Animal Production Claims Outline of Current Process," available at http://www.fsis.usda.gov/OPPDE/larc/Claims/RaisingClaims.pdf.

GMO's

Genetically Modified Organisms ("GMO's") can be controversial--and oftentimes divisive—topic among segments of the food and agriculture industry. Voluntary labels for non-GMO's may be utilized for meat and liquid egg products (i.e., "GM-free"). Said animals with this label may not be fed any genetically modified feed such as corn, soy, and alfalfa. Said label must be pre-approved by the

USDA to ensure it can be verified, such as *Non-GMO Project's* certification procedures.

USDA Process Verified Program

In another effort to assist producers and handlers with the marketing of their agricultural products, the *Agricultural Marketing Service* ("AMS") offers the *Process Verified Program*. This program is designed to provide producers and handlers the opportunity to assure customers of their ability to provide livestock, meat, and other commodities of a *certain quality* or *raised a certain* way.

The program is a collection of voluntary, audit-based, user-fee funded programs that allow producers and handlers to have third-party verification for various practices. Livestock producers with approved USDA Process Verified Programs are able to make *marketing claims* associated with their process verified points – these include age, source, feeding practices, or other raising and processing claims. They may market products as "USDA Process Verified" and use the *"USDA Process Verified"* shield.

To illustrate, the *"naturally-raised"* marketing claim standard states that livestock used for the production of meat and meat products have been raised entirely without *growth promotants*, antibiotics (except for *ionophores* for parasite control) and have never been fed animal by-products. The voluntary standard will establish the minimum requirements for those producers who choose to operate a USDA-verified program involving a naturally-raised claim. See 74 Fed. Reg. 3544. The naturally-raised marketing claim standard is independent of the FSIS label approval policies governing use of such claims with regard to post-harvest processing. The naturally-raised claim pertains only to *pre-harvest livestock production practices*. See 74 Fed. Reg. 3544.

Alternatively, the *"grass-fed"* standard states that grass and/or forage shall be the feed source consumed for the lifetime of the ruminant animal, with the exception of milk consumed prior to weaning. The diet shall be derived *solely* from forage and animals cannot be fed grain or grain by-products and must have continuous access to pasture during the growing season. The grass-fed label does not limit the use of *antibiotics, hormones, or pesticides*. See 72 Fed. Reg. 58631.

Some additional process verified points include but are not limited to (1) *source verified* beef cattle, (2) age verified beef cattle, (3)

Non-Hormone treated Verified Beef Cattle ("NHTC"), (4) *Anti-Biotic Free* Verified Beef Cattle, (5) Raised *Cage Free*, (6) *Humanely Raised*, and (7) *Free Range*. In summary, there are numerous process-verified marketing claims through AMS that a New York livestock operation may already meet with current production practices. With a third-party audit and ample record-keeping, said operations may qualify for a USDA process-verified claim for their label.

Food Labeling Requirements for Farm Products Sold Direct to Consumers

Any packaged food sold at a roadside stand, on a farm outlet, or farmers' market must be properly labeled. For example, one may not represent that a store-bought baked good is "**homemade**" or "**home-baked**" or a market-bought produce as "**home-grown**." See New York State Department of Agriculture, "Sanitary Regulations for Direct Marketing," available at http://www.agriculture.ny.gov/FS/industry/sanitary.html (last visited August 18, 2013).

NYSDAM has a helpful pamphlet summarizing its food labeling regulations (FSI-514) available on its website located at http://www.agriculture.ny.gov/FS/pdfs/FSI514.pdf. It recommends that labels be submitted to NYSDAM for review prior to printing. Please review this pamphlet and current regulations for the most accurate information on the food labeling requirements.

There are five basic label requirements: (1) identity of food in package form, (2) name of manufacturer, packer or distributor, (3) place of business, (4) ingredient declaration, and (5) net quantity of contents. The label must also contain other general information.

On a final note, it is recommended that farmers consult an attorney and label designer to help ensure that the label meets the statutory requirements. Food labeling requirements are highly technical and will differ depending on whether the food product is being sold in interstate commerce.

Food Safety Modernization Act ("FSMA")

FSMA was signed into law by President Obama on January 4, 2011. Under FSMA, the food regulatory system is still managed by two government agencies – FDA and USDA (e.g., meat and poultry). FSMA simply gave FDA additional authorizes under the FDCA. Its goal was to increase the record-keeping, inspection and safety of our food through a preventative approach.

There are *several* applicable exemptions to small farms under FSMA. For example, Section 102 of the FDCA requires the *registration* of any facility that manufactures, processes, packs or holds food for consumption. Farms, restaurants and certain retail food establishments selling direct-to-consumer (e.g., roadside stands, farmers' markets, CSA's) are exempt from this registration requirement. Interestingly, a "consumer" is an individual only and not a business under FSMA.

> 7 CFR 249.2 defines community supported agriculture as "a program under which a farmer or group of farmers grows food for a group of shareholders (or subscribers) who pledge to buy a portion of the farmer's crop(s) for that season."

In 2013, the FDA published two proposed rules of special concern to New York farmers: (1) the *Produce Rule*, and (2) the *Preventative Controls Rule*. Each briefly discussed below. Lauren Handel, Esq. wrote a nice blog on this issue; the citation is listed in the reference section in this Chapter.

Produce Rule

The *Produce Rule* requires certain food safety procedures (*HACCP-like* regulations) for produce farmers with an average of $25,000 of sales, per year (taking into consideration the farm's gross sales over the previous three years). However, a New York farmer would have a "qualified exemption" under the Produce Rule if:

- More than 50% (one-half) of its gross sales are sold *direct to consumers* (e.g., farmers' markets, CSA's, roadside stands) or to restaurants or food retailers located within the state of New York <u>or</u> within 275 miles; and,

- Its total food sales are *less than $500,000 a year* (on average).

A farm with a qualified exemption must still comply with labeling requirements and *point of purchase identification* (including the name and address of the farm who grew the produce). Additionally, if a farm has a food safety issue, the FDA can withdraw the exemption. The Produce Rule does not apply if the produce is rarely consumed raw (e.g., beets, potatoes), raised for on-farm consumption, or intended for commercial processing (e.g., canning).

Preventative Controls Rule

On the other hand, the *Preventative Controls Rule* updated existing *Good Manufacturing Practice* ("GMP") regulations to help protect against cross-contamination. It also established new hazard analysis and risk-based preventative controls (e.g., food safety plan). This rule applies to farms if it is a registerable "facility" under the FDCA that manufactures, processes, packs, or holds food for consumption. Farms that are exempt from this "facility" registration are also exempt under the Preventative Controls Rule. However, farms with a registerable "facility" are exempted from the following on-farm activities:

- Animal production and *aquaculture*;
- Crop production and harvesting (e.g., gathering, washing, shelling);
- Packing or holding food that is grown, raised or consumed on the farm *under the same farm ownership*; and,
- Manufacturing or processing food for consumption on the farm *under the same farm ownership* (e.g., cutting, chopping, canning).

New York farms are also exempt from this rule if (1) it is a *small business* (i.e., has less than 500 employees or less than $500K in food sales) and conducts low-risk on-farm manufacturing, processing, packing or holding activities, (2) produces products *covered by other regulations* (e.g., juice), (3) is involved solely in storing *raw agricultural commodities* intended for further distribution or processing, or (4) is solely involved in storing unexposed packaged food. There are also other exemptions to this *Preventative Controls*

Rule. Farmers are encouraged to speak to a food lawyer to determined whether this regulation applies to their farm.

Additional Resources

Animal Welfare Institute, "Food Labeling for Dummies: A Definitive Guide to Common Food Label Terms and Claims" available at http://www.animalwelfareapproved.org/wp-content/uploads/2013/04/Food-Labelling-for-Dummies-screen-v9-041013.pdf (last visited July 28, 2013).

ATTRA - National Sustainable Agriculture Information Service, "Preparing for an Organic Inspection: Steps and Checklists" (January 2005) available for purchase at https://attra.ncat.org/publication.html (last visited July 28, 2013).

ATTRA- National Sustainable Agriculture Information Service, "National Organic Program Compliance Checklist for Producers" (June 2003) available at http://cses.uark.edu/ATTRA_compliance.pdf (last visited August 23, 2013).

Cari B. Rincker, Stan Benda, Jason Foscolo, Alan Fowler, Erin Hawley, Leon Letter, Lindsey Peebles, Amy Salberg, and Jean Terranova, "Counseling Farmers, Food Entrepreneurs, and Restaurants on Food Labeling Laws," American Bar Association Continuing Legal Education Webinar available for purchase at http://apps.americanbar.org/cle/programs/t13cff1.html (last visited June 14, 2013).

Cari B. Rincker, Dr. Stan Benda, Derrick Braaten, Jason Foscolo, Neil Hamilton, Erin Hawley, Leon Letter, Jesse Richardson, Jr., Rich Schell, Patricia Salkin, "Counseling the Local Food Movement," American Bar Association Continuing Legal Education Webinar (May 10, 2012), available for purchase at http://apps.americanbar.org/abastore/index.cfm?section=main&fm=Product.AddToCart&pid=CET12LFMCDR (last visited July 1, 2013).

Cornell Cooperative Extension of Jefferson County, "Food Safety Recommendations for Farmers Markets," available at http://www.nyfarmersmarket.com/NYFMFoodSafety/Handouts/Farmers-Market-Recomms.pdf (last visited August 18, 2013).

Cornell Cooperative Extension, "#30 Organic Certification," available at http://nebeginningfarmers.org/2012/04/30/30-organic-certification/ (last visited August 18, 2013).

Elizabeth Rumley and Rusty Rumley, "Non-GMO Labeling" available at http://nationalaglawcenter.org/assets/articles/rumleys_nongmo.pdf (last visited May 16, 2013).

Elizabeth Rumley, "Food Labeling for Specialty Crop Producers" available at http://nationalaglawcenter.org/assets/articles/erumley_foodlabeling.pdf (last visited May 16, 2013).

Farmers' Legal Action Group, Inc., "Understanding How the Country of Origin Labeling Program Affects Farmers" (2009) available at http://www.flaginc.org/wp-content/uploads/2013/03/COOL_FactSheet_long.pdf (last visited August 23, 2013).

Food and Drug Administration, "Food Labeling Guide" (October 2009) available at http://www.fda.gov/Food/GuidanceRegulation/GuidanceDocumentsRegulatoryInformation/LabelingNutrition/ucm2006828.htm (last visited August 18, 2013).

Food and Drug Administration, "Food Safety Modernization Act (FSMA) Fact Sheets" at http://www.fda.gov/Food/GuidanceRegulation/FSMA/ucm247546.htm (last visited August 18, 2013).

Food and Drug Administration, "Dietary Supplement Labeling Guide" (April 2005) available at http://www.fda.gov/Food/GuidanceRegulation/GuidanceDocumentsRegulatoryInformation/DietarySupplements/ucm2006823.htm (last visited August 18, 2013).

Harrison M. Pittman et al., "A Legal Guide to the National Organic Program," National Agriculture Law Center (January 2011) available at http://new.nationalaglawcenter.org/wp-content/uploads/assets/articles/pittman_organicprogram.pdf (last visited August 23, 2013).

Lauren Handel, "The Food Safety Modernization Act for Farmers," (May 29, 2013) available at http://www.foodlawfirm.com/2013/05/the-food-safety-modernization-act-for-farmers/ (last visited July 3, 2013).

LORA ARDUSER AND DOUGLAS R. BROWN, HACCP & SANITATION IN RESTAURANTS AND FOOD SERVICE OPERATIONS: A PRACTICAL GUIDE BASED ON THE USDA FOOD CODE (2005).

Jill E. Krueger, "If Your Farm Is Organic, Must It Be GMO-Free?" Farmers' Legal Action Group, Inc. (September 2007), available at http://www.flaginc.org/wp-content/uploads/2013/03/OrganicsAndGMOs2007.pdf (last visited August 23, 2013).

Jason Foscolo, "New Proposed Food Safety Laws," Cornell Small Farms Program available at http://smallfarms.cornell.edu/2013/03/27/new-proposed-food-safety-laws/ (last visited July 11, 2013).

JAMES SUMMERS, FOOD LABELING COMPLIANCE REVIEW (2007) and DIETARY SUPPLEMENT LABELING COMPLIANCE REVIEW (2004).

National Agriculture Law Center, Reading Room on "Food Labeling," at http://new.nationalaglawcenter.org/research-by-topic/food-labeling/ (last visited August 18, 2013).

National Agriculture Law Center, Reading Room on "Food Safety," at http://new.nationalaglawcenter.org/research-by-topic/food-safety/ (last visited August 18, 2013).

National Agriculture Law Center, Reading Room on the "National Organic Program," at http://new.nationalaglawcenter.org/research-by-topic/national-organic-program/ (last visited August 18, 2013).

NEIL D. FORTIN, FOOD REGULATION (2007).

Northeast Organic Farming Association, "Understanding Food Safety Regulations for Farm-Direct Sales: A Study of Connecticut, Massachusetts, New York and Vermont) (March 2009), <u>available</u> at <u>http://www.nofa.org/policy/regulations.php</u> (last visited August 18, 2013).

PATRICIA CURTIS, GUIDE TO FOOD LAWS AND REGULATIONS (2005).

CHAPTER 26

MILK PRICES

According to the USDA, New York State is the fourth largest milk-producing state in the country. In 2011, dairy farmers in New York produced nearly 13 million pounds of milk representing over $2.7 billion in gross farm income. This impressive output has occurred notwithstanding a decrease of over 60 thousand cows from 25% of dairy producers within a decade. State and federal programs can provide means to mitigate risk in a complex environment of potentially high fluctuation in milk price.

Milk Producers' Security Program

Through its power of auditing and financial oversight, and through its *Milk Producers' Security Program*, NYSDAM's division of milk control audits licensed milk dealers and milk cooperatives, and enforces the prompt payment of milk. Chapter 17 on *agricultural liens* further describes how payment to milk producers is a secured transaction.

Milk Marketing Orders ("MMO")

The minimum price of all milk produced by New York farmers is enforced under a *Federal Northeast Market Area Milk Marketing Order* or the *Western New York State Milk Market Order*. In both, the NY Agriculture and Markets law empowers NYSDAM to achieve uniformity of laws and regulations involving the terms of both federal and state milk marketing orders. The essence of milk price regulation is to distribute the benefits and burdens of the milk market in a way that both avoids driving down the price of premium-priced fluid milk and makes the 'blended' minimum price payable to all producers irrespective of the use of their milk.

Although the *state and federal programs* somewhat differ, both involve a *similar process*. Milk producers, normally through their cooperative, petition for a *public hearing* to discuss a change in market conditions which are "affecting the orderly marketing of milk in such area that public interest requires regulation of prices of milk . . . and equalization of the burden of surplus milk and expense of handling it, and sharing the benefits. . . ."

The hearings themselves are a combination of evidentiary briefs, letters, and public testimony that cover pricing, and terms of the market order. The market order then determines a minimum price payable to producers. The *minimum price calculation* is based on classification of milk by how it will be used:

- **Class I** milk is a *fluid milk* product in packaged form, while **Class II** through **Class IV** relate to milk used to manufacture other dairy products (**Class II** are cultured *soft dairy* products, **Class III** are *cheeses*, **Class IV** are *butter and dry* milk products);

- How the **components** of the milk (fluids and solids) are accounted for; and

- The **difference in value** between the Class I (fluid for consumption) and Class III (cheese grade) milk, called the producer price differential.

For example, under the most recent consolidated Northeast order, the minimum price payable to producers is the **sum of the butterfat, protein, and other solids values plus the total volume multiplied by the applicable producer price differential at the location of the plant where the milk is first received.** Generally speaking, most handling plants must pool all milk received and pay individual farmers based on a weighted average price, which in turn is based upon the components of the milk received and the use of the milk by the handler.

If that sounds complicated, frankly, it is. The hearing process for adjusting the market order can be frustratingly slow, even taking years in some cases. As a result, the MMO system has come under increased criticism for being unresponsive to market demand.

Dairy Forward Pricing

The *USDA Dairy Forward Pricing Program* has been extended through September 30, 2013. The program is a market-driven price mitigation mechanism. Under the program, farmers may voluntarily enter into a contract to lock in a price of milk for some period of time: the amount of milk, and the calculation of the price and all of the associated terms and conditions are governed by the contract rather than the MMO, subject to the rules of the program. Although the handler is subject to accounting rules under the MMO, enforcement of the program itself (which includes rules about how to contract and additional rules of accounting) and enforcement of the MMO for any non-contract milk is subject to the MMO. Enforcement of the contract is a civil lawsuit and not an agency enforcement action.

Milk Income Loss Contract Program ("MILC")

The federal **Milk Income Loss Contract Program** ("MILC") can provide some price protection to an **eligible dairy operation.** The price protection comes in the form of a contract offered by USDA to make certain *payments* for quantities of milk when the *Class I milk price per hundredweight in Boston* (as set by the Northeast Federal milk marketing order) falls below an index price set by USDA. Eligibility to participate in the program requires the participant to:

- be a single dairy operation involved in domestic commercial production and marketing of milk,
- provide evidence of the amount of milk produced,
- provide evidence that the entity's adjusted gross nonfarm income does not exceed caps,
- obtain certification of compliance with environmental regulations, and
- file all documents timely and in the correct format.

Additional Resources

National Agriculture Law Center, Reading Room on "Marketing Orders," at http://new.nationalaglawcenter.org/research-by-topic/marketing-orders/ (last visited August 18, 2013).

New York Agriculture and Markets, Division of Milk Control and Dairy Services, at http://www.agriculture.ny.gov/DI/DIStats.html (last visited August 18, 2013).

ABOUT THE AUTHORS

Cari Rincker is the principal attorney at **Rincker Law, PLLC**, a national law firm concentrating in food and agriculture law. Cari is licensed to practice law in the State of New York, State of New Jersey, State of Connecticut and the District of Columbia. Cari grew up on a Simmental farm in Shelbyville, Illinois showing cattle through 4-H and FFA and is still involved in her family's beef cattle operation. Cari enjoys judging county and state fair livestock shows in her free time. She is also an adjunct professor at teaching food law at *New York University*, Steinhardt School of Education, Department of Nutrition, Food Studies and Public Health.

Cari is a Distinguished Alumni from *Lake Land College* in Mattoon, Illinois where she obtained her Associate in Science in Agriculture. She went on to receive her Bachelors in Science in Animal Science from *Texas A & M University* where she also become a member of the All-American Livestock Judging Team. In 2012, Cari received an Outstanding Early Career Award from Texas A & M University, College of Agriculture and Life Sciences. Under the supervision of Dr. Larry Berger, Cari received her Masters of Science in Ruminant Nutrition from the *University of Illinois* where her thesis research was focused in the area of beef feedlot nutrition and genetics. Cari obtained her *Juris Doctor* with Certificates in Environmental Law and International Law from *Pace University, School of Law* in White Plains, New York.

Before starting Rincker Law, PLLC, Cari was an associate with Budd-Falen Law Offices, LLC in Cheyenne, Wyoming, a consultant with the Food & Agriculture Organization ("FAO") of the United Nations ("UN") in Rome, Italy, and a junior delegate with the Permanent Mission of the Marshall Islands to the UN in New York, New York. Cari is currently the Chair of the American Bar Association ("ABA") General Practice, Solo & Small Firm Division's *Agriculture Law Committee* and is a member of the New York State Bar Association's Agriculture & Rural Issues Committee. She was elected as the "Best Agriculture Lawyer" in the 2011 and 2012 Best of Barns Competition and is the Founding Member of New York Agri-Women.

You can contact Cari at cari@rinckerlaw.com or (212) 427-2049. You can subscribe to her Food, Farm & Family Law Blog at www.rinckerlaw.com/blog or follow her on Twitter @RinckerLaw or @CariRincker.

Pat Dillon is an Iowa farmer, who happens also to be an Iowa lawyer, frequently known to admit that he "became a lawyer to support his farming habit." Pat was born in Oelwein, Iowa, and grew up as part of a diversified family farm operation, graduating from Sumner Community Schools. Together with his brothers and his father, Pat operates a farm in northeast Iowa, with operations that include corn and soybean production, beef cattle, and timber management. Pat resides with his wife, Shelly, and three children, in a refurbished 1880's farm house near Sumner, and he practices law in the Sumner, Iowa, offices of **Dillon Law, PC**.

All protests aside, Pat Dillon also loves the law, and he takes genuine pleasure in catching problems early and in finding solutions to the legal issues, large and small, faced by his clients. Pat routinely represents clients in agricultural, real estate, estate planning, bankruptcy, and business issues.

Pat attended Iowa State University, earning a Bachelor of Science (with Distinction) in Agricultural Studies (Farm Operation), in 1997. Following four years of active duty service as a United States Army Transportation Officer, during which he Commanded the 513th Transportation Company and the 22d Transportation Detachment, Pat obtained his *Juris Doctor* (with High Honors) in 2003, from the Drake University Law School in Des Moines, Iowa.

Pat can be contacted at (563) 578-1850 or patdillon@50674law.com. You can also visit him through his website at www.50674law.com.

SPEAKING ENGAGEMENTS

Have Cari Speak At Your Next
New York Food or Agriculture Event!

Cari Rincker is a prolific writer and recognized speaker on a myriad of food and agriculture law topics. She is available to speak on food and agriculture law topics at your next event in New York. Her speaking engagements include: Animal Agriculture Alliance Annual Stakeholders Summit, New York Farm Bureau Animal Welfare Conference, New York Farm Bureau Young Farmers' and Ranchers' Conference, Texas Bar CLE, Ohio Agriculture Law Symposium, North Carolina Agriculture Law Conference, American Agriculture Law Association's Annual Meeting, American Bar Association, New York Agri-Women Annual Meeting, Bar Association for the City of New York, American Cattlewomen National Beef Speakers Bureau, Pace Law School, Lawline, New York 4-H, Cornell Cooperative Extension, and the National Agriculture Law Center.

To book Cari for your next New York event, either call (212) 427-2049 or write Cari via email at cari@rinckerlaw.com, facsimile (212) 202-6077, or via U.S. mail at 535 Fifth Avenue, 4th Floor, New York, NY 10017, with the following information:

- Name of the event,
- Date, time, and location of the engagement,
- Suggested food and agriculture law topics,
- Anticipated audience,
- Technology available for the event,
- Deadline for materials, and
- Transportation costs and honorarium.

INDEX

66481669R00225

Made in the USA
Lexington, KY
15 August 2017